Digital Objects, Digital Subjects:
Interdisciplinary Perspectives on Capitalism, Labour and Politics in the Age of Big Data

Edited by
David Chandler and Christian Fuchs

UNIVERSITY OF
WESTMINSTER
PRESS

University of Westminster
www.uwestminsterpress.c(

D1354547

Published by
University of Westminster Press
101 Cavendish Street
London W1W 6UW
www.uwestminsterpress.co.uk

Printed in the UK by Lightning Source Ltd.
Print and digital versions typeset by Siliconchips Services Ltd.

ISBN (Hardback): 978-1-912656-08-0
ISBN (PDF): 978-1-912656-09-7
ISBN (EPUB): 978-1-912656-10-3
ISBN (Kindle): 978-1-912656-11-0
ISBN (Paperback): 978-1-912656-20-2
DOI: https://doi.org/10.16997/book29

The full text of this book has been peer-reviewed to ensure high academic standards. For full review policies, see: http://www.uwestminsterpress.co.uk/site/publish. Competing Interests: the editors and contributors declare that they have no competing interests in publishing this book

To read the free, open access version of this book online, visit http: https://www.uwestminsterpress.co.uk/site/books/10.16997/book29 or scan this QR code with your mobile device:

Contents

CHAPTER I

Introduction

Christian Fuchs and David Chandler

1. Introduction

In May 2017, *The Economist*'s front cover headlined a feature on Big Data titled 'The World's Most Valuable Resource'. The feature argued that data is the world's new oil. Data would drive development in the twenty-first century in the same way as oil transformed the world's economy and society in the early twentieth century. Such popular discourses claim that Big Data enables new ways of generating knowledge that will lead to innovative and creative possibilities.

In the same month as *The Economist* ran this feature on Big Data, we organised the interdisciplinary symposium 'Digital Objects, Digital Subjects: Activism, Research & Critique in the Age of Big Data Capitalism' at the University of Westminster (May 20-21, 2017)[1]. The symposium was hosted by the Westminster Institute for Advanced Studies and the Department of Politics and International Relations. It featured ten presentations by leading international experts on the study of the digital in politics, the economy and society. This edited collection is a product of the conference, and provides further reflections on the presentations given.

We especially thank Denise Rose Hansen from the Westminster Institute for Advanced Studies, who brilliantly managed the organisation of the conference and supported us in bringing this book to publication. We also thank Andrew Lockett from University of Westminster Press for his interest in publishing this

How to cite this book chapter:
Fuchs, C. and Chandler, D. 2019. Introduction Big Data Capitalism - Politics, Activism, and Theory. In: Chandler, D. and Fuchs, C. (eds.) *Digital Objects, Digital Subjects: Interdisciplinary Perspectives on Capitalism, Labour and Politics in the Age of Big Data.* Pp. 1–20. London: University of Westminster Press. DOI: https://doi.org/10.16997/book29.a. License: CC-BY-NC-ND 4.0

2 Digital Objects, Digital Subjects

book and his editorial help. We are also grateful to our colleagues from the Communication and Media Research Institute and the Centre for the Study of Democracy who have acted as chairs and respondents, as well as to the speakers, contributors, volunteers, interpreters, technicians and administrators whose work helped to make the conference a big success.

Many claims have been made about the emergence of a 'digital turn' that is said to have radically transformed the possibilities for politics by undermining traditional modernist binaries of subject/object, state/society, politics/economics, public/ private, consumption/production, time/space, mind/body, labour/leisure, culture/ nature, human/posthuman. This turn has run through several phases, including cybernetics, automation technologies, mainframe computers, databases, artificial intelligence, personal computers, the World Wide Web, smart phones, geographical information systems, social media, targeted digital advertising, self-quantification, Big Data analytics, Cloud computing and the Internet of Things.

This collected volume presents interdisciplinary assessments of the digital's impact on society. The contributions interrogate the claims of both digital optimism and digital pessimism. Digital optimists assert that digital technologies have radically transformed the world, promising new forms of community, alternative ways of knowing and sensing, creative innovation, participatory culture, networked activism and distributed democracy. Digital pessimists argue that digital technologies have not brought about positive change, but have rather deepened and extended domination through new forms of control. The pessimists speak of networked authoritarianism, digital dehumanisation, alienation 2.0, networked exploitation and the rise of the surveillance society.

The chapters engage with questions of the digital in respect to activism, research and critique. They engage with the possibilities, potentials, pitfalls, limits and ideologies of digital activism. They reflect on whether computational social science, the digital humanities and ubiquitous datafication enable new research approaches or result in a digital positivism that threatens the independence of critical research and is likely to bring about about the death of the social sciences and humanities. The volume explores the futures, places and possibilities of critique in the age of digital subjects and digital objects.

The main question this book asks is: what are the key implications of the digital for subjects, objects and society? This question is examined through three lenses: digital capitalism/Big Data capitalism, digital labour, and digital politics. These three perspectives form three sections in the book. Each section consists of six chapters: three presentations each followed by a comment or response. The first section focuses on society in its totality as digital capitalism. Digital capitalism exists wherever capitalist society is shaped by computer technologies. In recent years, Big Data has become an important aspect of digital capitalism, leading to the emergence of a new dimension of Big Data capitalism. The three contributions by David Chandler, Christian Fuchs and Paul Rekret, as well as the three comments (Christian Fuchs' comments on David Chandler, Chandler's on Fuchs, Robert Cowley's on Paul Rekret) focus on digital capitalism in general, as well as aspects of Big Data. Chandler discusses how Big Data capitalism brings about a new form of digital governmentality focused on correlation. Fuchs argues that Karl Marx helps us to critically understand digital capitalism and Big Data capitalism. Paul Rekret criticises the posthumanist approaches of Donna Haraway and Bruno Latour in the context of digital capitalism.

When analysing capitalism critically, we are dealing – as the subtitle of Marx's opus magnum *Capital* indicates – with the critique of political economy. Political economy has an economic side and a political dimension, and these interact. Sections II and III approach digital political economy. Section II focuses on digital labour and Section III gives attention to digital politics.

The three chapters in Section II – by Kylie Jarrett, Phoebe Moore and Jack L. Qiu – focus on a range of issues concerning labour and class in the digital age: the digital houseworker (Jarrett), the digital worker's quantified self (Moore), and slavery in the digital age (Qiu). Joanna Boehnert comments on Kylie Jarrett, Elisabetta Brighi on Phoebe Moore, and Peter Goodwin on Jack L. Qiu.

The three chapters in Section III – by Jodi Dean, Paolo Gerbaudo and Toni Negri – discuss aspects of digital politics, namely social movements in the context of communicative capitalism (Dean), political parties in the digital age (Gerbaudo), and the question of how social struggles can advance digital alternatives (Negri). Paulina Tambakaki comments on Jodi Dean, Anastasia Kavada on Paolo Gerbaudo, and Christian Fuchs on Toni Negri.

Taken together, the three sections, with their nine presentations and accompanying comments show that we face a contradiction of subjects and objects in contemporary digital capitalism, and that structures of domination and exploitation threaten social cohesion and democracy. Digital domination and the exploitation of digital labour are the hegemonic structural forces shaping digital capitalism. But the situation is not hopeless, because there are potentials for struggles that can establish alternatives. For example, potentials for establishing a society of the digital commons are emerging within digital capitalism. Toni Negri, in his contribution, therefore asks how we can politically appropriate digital machines. The interest in advancing the digital commons and establishing a society of the commons is a political perspective that holds together many of the contributions to this book.

In the remainder of this introduction to the collected volume, we will discuss the relationship of digital subjects and digital objects (Section 2) and the notion of Big Data capitalism (Section 3), which form the background and context of the nine presentations and responses in this book.

2. Digital Subjects/Digital Objects

This volume engages with the changes that objects and subjects are undergoing in digital society. It asks what are the key implications of Big Data and the digital for subjects, objects and society.

Computing and digitality are not exclusively phenomena of the twentieth and twenty-first centuries. Digital logic has a much longer history. Already in 1703, Gottfried Wilhelm Leibniz suggested basing mathematics, not on the decimal system, but on binary logic: 'But instead of the progression of tens, I have for many years used the simplest progression of all, which proceeds by twos, having found that it is useful for the perfection of the science of numbers. Thus I use no other characters in it bar 0 and 1, and when reaching two, I start again' (Leibniz 1703, np). In the history of computing, pioneering work was done by Charles Babbage and Ada Lovelace in the nineteenth century. Babbage and Lovelace were ahead of their time because the technological standards of the nineteenth century were focused on what Marx (1867/1976) termed large-scale industry, rather than building a computer. Computing devices as we know them today go back to Alan Turing's concept of the Turing Machine that he invented in 1936. The digital logic of zeros and ones is a key feature of the way a Turing Machine operates. During the Second World War, Turing built computers for the British military in order to decipher the Nazis' encoded messages. In this light, the Second World War was not merely a war of military might, but also the first computational and digital war.

The example of the Turing Machine indicates that computing and the digital always stand in a broader social, political, economic and ideological context. Today, digital computing is ubiquitous and shapes all aspects of contemporary life, including capitalism, governance, everyday life, culture, education, welfare and science.

Technologies have always impacted human capacities. We cannot, therefore, easily separate technological objects from human subjects. The computer, the digital machine, has from its beginning changed the way subjects act and interact in the world. In the history of warfare, we have gone from hand-to-hand combat to killing at a distance through computerised technologies that enable smart bombs, killer robots, drone assassinations and pre-emptive warfare. These technologies do not only make warfare more distanced in space and time, but they also distance it morally. The example of digital warfare shows us that digital machines change the way subjects and objects relate to each other and are constituted.

This edited collection focuses on the latest stage of digital life and the digital transformation of society. We call this latest stage 'Big Data capitalism'. Algorithms that generate Big Data have today become central to political and ethical concerns, but there is no clear consensus on the distinctiveness of algorithmic knowledge.

The United Nations argues that Big Data analytics are central to solving the world's most pressing problems, from food shortages to conflicts and environmental crises. For example, the UN Global Pulse project developed a model of real-time food price changes by collecting and analysing more than 40,000 tweets about food prices in Jakarta, Indonesia. Less altruistically, Big Data is also crucial for Facebook and its users who share over 5 billion posts and upload more than 300 million images per day. More than 500,000 comments are posted per minute. Facebook's 2016 advertising profits of US$ 10.2 billion were generated by targeting users based on the analysis of Big Data generated through users' activities and content.

'Smart cities' like London and Barcelona deploy Big Data analytics to more efficiently administer these urban complexes. Transport for London (TfL) captures and analyses 20 million Oyster travel card taps per day in order to manage traffic flows and innovate transportation. In Barcelona, more than 20,000 smart meters are installed on bins, streetlights and other pieces of infrastructure, collecting socio-environmental Big Data. At Walmart, the world's largest company with a turnover of almost half a trillion US dollars per year, an analytics team analyses hundreds of data streams in real time, including customer data, sales data, meteorological data, social media data and event and location data, all with a view to responding rapidly to emerging trends and thereby increasing sales and catering to its customers' perceived needs.

These examples, in the areas of disaster risk (UN Global Pulse), media and communication (Facebook), smart cities (Transport for London) and business (Walmart), demonstrate the vast amount, variety and speed of data collection and analysis. Big Data has transformed our ways of knowing in different fields, and algorithmic knowledge is impacting on everyday practices and processes. This book aims to clarify what is at stake when knowledge, subjects, objects and society become digital and algorithmic. Algorithmic detection of correlations across time and space enables Big Data approaches to operate in 'real-time' scenarios, as in the examples of food prices in Jakarta, TfL's data management of traffic, Facebook's advertising practices, and Walmart's retailing strategies.

Although there is no agreed definition of what Big Data means, it tends to be understood as being related to volume, variety and velocity (Kitchin 2014, 68). Big Data's *volume* refers to datasets so large that they cannot be processed and analysed by humans but only by machine-driven algorithms. There is a wide *variety* of sources and types of Big Data. Big Data has a high *velocity*: it is produced, circulated and acted upon in real time, and at very high speeds.

Connected digital devices such as CCTV, drone cameras, Internet of Things sensors, Twitter, Google, Facebook, smartphones, UN Global Pulse technologies, smart city technologies, news feeds, weather report stations, demographic and population data collectors, price and economic data tools, or Walmart's data collection methods, create constant streams of data. Algorithmic knowledge enables Big Data analytics that are produced by correlating these data streams to identify and analyse patterns of occurrences that enable new understandings and ways of seeing the world.

In philosophy, the rationalist tradition saw knowledge as existing in fixed causal relations and in fixed properties or essences of entities that were independent of and prior to experience, while empiricism argued that knowledge was experiential, contextual and obtained through the human sense organs. It was Immanuel Kant who advanced an epistemology that stressed the importance of the distinction between rational knowledge and sensual knowledge. 'To the extent to which knowledge is subject to the laws of sensuousness it is sensuous; to the extent to which it is subject to the laws of intelligence it is *intellectual* or rational' (Kant 1770, 50). Algorithmic knowledge undermines this distinction.

The algorithm is a notion found in mathematics and computing that has long been associated with the pursuit of rational forms of knowledge. 'An algorithm is a reliable, definable procedure for solving a problem. The idea of the algorithm goes back to the beginnings of mathematics' (Henderson 2009, 7). Today, algorithms not only calculate existing data but also develop new forms of 'sensual' or 'empirical' knowledge by finding correlations. Algorithmic knowledge seeks to find patterns and relationships, enabling new ways of seeing, sensing, responding and adapting to life in its complex emergence.

In this process, the Kantian distinction between rational knowledge obtained through the brain's reflective capacity, and experiential knowledge obtained through the sense organs, breaks down. Digital machines generate Big Data through sensors, and thereby simulate and automate human experience. At the same time, ethical rationality is increasingly perceived as residing in machines, which results in automated decision-making. Knowing and sensing seem to become a unified algorithmic procedure that resides across the human/machinic divide. This volume takes a deeper look at digital transformations and asks what their consequences are for our understanding of what subjects and objects are, and how they operate in society.

Big Data studies is a rapidly expanding research field (see Mayer-Schönberger and Cukier 2013, Kitchin 2014, Mosco 2014) that deals with how Big Data and algorithmic knowledge transform the economy, politics, culture and the environment. This growing volume of research is matched by publications about Big Data. In the summer of 2017, Web of Science listed approximately 5,800 articles published in the years 2014, 2015, 2016 that have 'Big Data' in their titles. Important fields where Big Data research has had an impact include disaster research, media/communication studies, smart cities, and management and organisation studies.

In disaster research, Big Data is increasingly deployed to predict and prevent disasters and minimise their impacts on humans and nature. Big Data is also used in disaster response, where Unmanned Aerial Vehicles (also called drones) gather data about disaster sites, while machine-learning algorithms identify patterns in disaster-related data. Digital humanitarianism is increasingly deployed before and after disasters. Digital humanitarianism 'examines how new uses of technology and vast quantities of digital data are transforming the way societies prepare for, respond to, cope with, and ultimately understand humanitarian disasters' (Meier 2015, xi). In disaster and political research, Big Data analytics and new information technologies are increasingly perceived as essential when it comes to dealing with a wide range of international issues, such as development (Coyle and Meier 2009), conflict (Karlsrud 2014, USIP 2013, Himelfarb 2014) and natural disasters (Meier 2015). Big Data analytics are key to the implementation of the UN's 2030 Agenda for Sustainable Development Goals: 'More diverse, integrated, timely and trustworthy information can lead to better decision-making and real-time citizen feedback. This in turn enables individuals, public and private institutions, and companies to make choices that are good for them and for the world they live in (UN 2014)'. The United Nations has called for 'a data revolution for sustainable development', arguing that 'improving data is a development agenda in its own right', and that the divides between rich and poor can be mitigated through the provision of more data that will enable more efficient adaptation to the emergence of problems at all levels of society (UN 2014). Indeed, the 'data gap' is increasingly held to be the cause of growing inequalities (Stuart et al. 2015).

In media and communication studies, Big Data is used for generating new understandings of political, economic and everyday life through communication on Twitter, Facebook and other social media platforms. Big Data has changed human communication's actors, structures, systems, contents, effects, contexts, and power structures. boyd and Crawford (2012) argue that Big Data creates challenges and opportunities for communication research, knowledge, research ethics and power structures. Communication research about Big Data has, for example, focused on online agenda-setting and online attention (Neuman et al. 2014), Big Data analytics in targeted online advertising (Couldry & Turow 2014), Big Data's aspects of communication power (Andrejevic 2014), data journalism (Fink & Anderson 2015), automated text extraction and classification as tools for measuring culture (Bail 2014), the analysis of political communication during election campaigns (Larsson & Moe 2012), and the prediction of users' attitudes and behaviours (such as their political affiliation, see Colleoni et al. 2014). In 2014, the journal *Big Data & Society* was founded. Between 2014 and 2016 it published more than 130 articles, demonstrating that Big Data communication research is a booming sub-field of media/communication studies.

The study of smart cities and citizen sensors analyses how Big Data is transforming urban life (Greenfield 2013, Kitchin 2014, Krivy 2016, Thrift 2014, Townsend 2013). The development and application of Big Data is driving a transformation in the understanding of city governance and planning. This transformation is taking place with the aid of ubiquitous sensing technology, often termed the Internet of Things, whereby digital devices connected to everyday objects, such as roads, litterbins and street lights, enable new forms of city management. Much of the research into these applications of Big Data argues that new digital technologies can enable citizens and governments to connect in more meaningful ways, empower communities, distribute knowledge, and allow better control over public goods and services. Already the majority of the world's population live in cities, and by 2050 it is projected that 75% of the global population will be urban. Many cities around the world are seeking to become 'smart' by using networked, digital technologies and urban Big Data to tackle a range of issues, such as improving governance and service delivery, creating more resilient critical infrastructure, growing the local economy, becoming more sustainable, improving mobility, offering greater transparency and accountability for collective activities, enhancing the quality of life, and increasing safety and security. In short, the desire is to use digital technology to improve the lives of citizens, advance city management and foster economic development.

In the field of management and organisation studies, Big Data is deployed for understanding consumers and users' individual preferences, tastes, lifestyles, behavioural choices, attitudes, interests, and so on. This application of Big Data to the individual enables differentiated pricing and targeted and personalised advertising. Big Data also transforms every aspect of the production process, including the surveillance of employees and the monitoring and datafication of products, transport and logistics. Big Data is also used for understanding and predicting the development of financial markets. George et al. (2014) argue that Big Data enables organisations to identity new markets and products, gather new management knowledge, and track members of workgroups. Other research focuses on how to use Big Data for managing a product's lifecycle (Li et al. 2015) as well as managing the supply chain (Hazen et al. 2014). Google's chief economist Hal R. Varian (2014) argues that Big Data analytics should be used as a standard research method in economics (see also Einav & Levin 2014). Another strand of research has been termed consumer analytics (Erevelles et al. 2016). This focuses on the analysis of consumer interests and satisfaction, and on identifying brand strategies (Tirunillai & Tellis 2014).

Even this brief summary shows that Big Data research is a rapidly growing research field. At the same time, however, it is highly fragmented. Big Data researchers are often preoccupied with their complex data collection and analysis processes. They rarely find the time or opportunity to reflect on the broad changes that theory, methodologies, knowledge and society are undergoing in the age of algorithmic knowledge. This collection seeks to rectify this gap through surveying the application of Big Data and new forms of algorithmic governance through the lenses of digital capitalism, labour, and politics.

The former editor of *Wired* magazine, Chris Anderson, famously claimed that Big Data and the development of algorithmic knowledge puts an end to the need for theory, causal modelling and hypothesising: 'With enough data, the numbers speak for themselves [...] [When] faced with massive data, this [traditional] approach to science – hypothesize, model, test – is becoming obsolete' (Anderson, 2008). Big Data promises an epistemological revolution. It is claimed that Big Data will make existing methodological approaches in the social and natural sciences obsolete, and will mean the death of theory. At any rate Big Data, with its focus on context and revealing unseen relations, is increasingly breaking down disciplinary boundaries.

Savage and Burrows (2007) discuss how research methods, theories and epistemologies have changed in the age of Big Data. They argue that 'the repertoires' of research methods 'need to be rethought' so that there is 'greater reflection on

[...] the proliferation of social data gathered by others [...] [and] a radical mixture of methods coupled with renewed critical reflection' (Savage and Burrows 2007, 895–896). Evgeny Morozov (2014) points out that Big Data also poses fundamental challenges to ethics and political regulation: 'Why rely on laws when one has sensors and feedback mechanisms? If policy interventions are to be – to use the buzzwords of the day – 'evidence-based' and 'results-oriented,' technology is here to help.' Savage and Burrows stress the importance of Big Data methodologies, whereas Morozov (2014) reminds us of the political and ethical implications of algorithmic knowledge.

The diverse processes that constitute digital transformations and Big Data capitalism have not been adequately engaged with in terms of their epistemological, ontological and ethical implications. This volume seeks to address this deficiency through nine presentations and responses, which collectively use and develop conceptual tools from the fields of critical political economy, governmentality studies, political theory and communication theory. Political economy is 'a distinct way of understanding how economies work and how they interact with the larger societies around them' (Wolff and Resnick 2012, 1). Governmentality studies is a field of inquiry that analyses 'any method of government' (Foucault 2008, 13), 'the development of real governmental practice' and its rationalisation in 'the exercise of sovereignty' (22).

This volume provides an overview of the difference that digital and Big Data capitalism has made to politics, activism and theory. It engages with key epistemological, ontological and ethical questions arising from the transformations of digital subjects and objects. These questions include the following:

- How does the digital impact the logic of governance and power?
- How does the digital change the nature of knowledge and the understanding of causation?
- How does the digital deal with new problems of uncertainty, risk, complexity and unpredictability?
- How does the digital impact critique, activism and political organisation?
- How does the digital interact with changes within capitalism and labour?
- How can critical theories explain the role of the digital in society?
- How does the digital impact reproduction and gender relations?
- How does the digital change the relationship between culture and nature, as well as between humans and their environment? How does the digital shape the Anthropocene?

3. Big Data Capitalism [2]

Although most observers of society will agree that capitalism concerns the accumulation of capital, there is no general agreement on how to define capital or who produces it. Marx (1867) and Marxists tend to argue that capital is money that is increased through exploitation of labour and the sale of commodities. Followers of Bourdieu (1986) argue that capital is more general, extending to the realms of politics and culture. Bourdieu distinguishes between economic, political/social and cultural capital, and also uses the notion of symbolic capital, which he claims interacts with all other forms of capital.

No matter how one defines capital and capitalism, many scholars and observers agree that capitalism is a societal formation that is based on the logic of the accumulation of money and power. It tries to instrumentalise everything for this purpose, and therefore produces a highly instrumental society based on what Horkheimer (2004) terms instrumental reason.

If capitalism is a societal formation, then digital capitalism may be a stage and phase of its development and/or a dimension and mode of the production of life and society. In turn, Big Data capitalism is a way of signifying the latest development of the digital within the broader context of the economy, politics, culture, ideology, domination and exploitation.

The basic sociological question concerning the digital asks at what level of capitalism and society we should situate digital transformations. We can speak of four main positions. The first argues that the digital constitutes a radical transformation of society, such that we no longer live in a capitalist or modern society, but in a radically new type of society. So for example Nico Stehr (1994) argues that the knowledge society means that 'the age of labor and property is at an end' (iix), and that the 'emergence of knowledge societies signals first and foremost a radical transformation in the *structure of the economy*' (10) and, as a result, the 'emergence of a new structure and organization of economic activity' (122). For Manuel Castells, writing at the turn of the millennium, the rise of the 'network society' means that a 'new world is taking shape' (Castells 2000, 367). Castells also argues that the 'information technology revolution induced the emergence of informationalism, as the material foundation of a new society' (Castells 2000, 367).

The second, more critical, position argues that information society discourse is a neoliberal ideology that presents information technology as constituting a radically new society, one which promotes techno-optimism and techno-determinism. Garnham (1998/2004, 165), for example says that information society theory is 'the favoured legitimating ideology for the dominant economic and political powerholders'. Walter Runciman (1993, 65) argues that 'it cannot be claimed that any new sub-type of the capitalist mode of production has emerged [...] 'Terms such as 'managerial' capitalism, or 'late' capitalism, or 'finance' capitalism, or 'corporatist' capitalism have all generated more confusion than illumination' (Runciman 1993, 54; see also Freedman 2002).

This sceptical line of thought, while recognising that society has undergone profound changes, questions the assumption that we live in a radically new society. There is, however, also a variety within this approach. So, third, we find positions that argue that digital capitalism is the dominant dimension or type of contemporary capitalism. And fourth, there are positions that argue that digital society/capitalism is a form or development that is subsumed under other modes of capitalist development.

The third type of argument argues that digital capitalism is the dominant dimension or type of contemporary capitalism. This assumption can be found in approaches that speak of cognitive capitalism. Cognitive capitalism theory has been advanced in particular by autonomist Marxist approaches. Yann Moulier-Boutang (2011) argues that cognitive capitalism is 'founded on the accumulation of immaterial capital, the dissemination of knowledge and the driving role of the knowledge economy' (50). 'We can distinguish three principal configurations in the history of capitalism: first, mercantile capitalism, which was based on the hegemony of mechanisms of merchant and finance accumulation and developed between the start of the sixteenth century and the end of the seventeenth. Next came industrial capitalism, which was based on the accumulation of physical capital and the driving role of the large Manchester-style factory in mass-producing standardised goods. Then came cognitive capitalism' (50) as the 'third type of capitalism' (56).

Jean-Marie Monnier and Carlo Vercellone (2010) argue that cognitive capitalism is 'a new historical system of accumulation', in which 'the cognitive and intellectual dimensions of labour take on an increasingly important role and displace the previous centrality of fixed capital and material labour' (76). '[I]ndustrial capitalism succeeded mercantile capitalism, and then gave rise to a new historical system of accumulation called cognitive capitalism' (76). 'Cognitive capitalism is the result of a restructuring process through which capital attempts to control collective conditions of knowledge production and tends to absorb and redirect its energy toward a new logic of capital accumulation' (83).

Toni Negri (2008) speaks of 'the era of *cognitive capitalism*' that followed 'the phase of manufacturing and the subsequent phase of heavy industry. In this cognitive era the production of value depends increasingly on creative intellectual activity' (64). '[I]mmaterial labor power (involved in communication, cooperation, and the production and reproduction of affects) occupies an increasingly central position in both the schema of capitalist production and the composition of the proletariat' (Hardt and Negri 2000, 53). Immaterial labour constitutes 'a third and current paradigm in which providing services and manipulating information are at the heart of economic production' (Hardt and Negri 2000, 280). The 'dominant figures of property in the contemporary era – including code, images, cultural products, patents, knowledge, and the like – are largely immaterial and, more important, indefinitely reproducible' (Hardt and Negri 2017, 187). Toni Negri characterises the digital aspects of immaterial production as a digital assemblage (see his contribution to this book).

For Franco 'Bifo' Berardi, the move to digital capitalism 'marks a shift from the cognitive model of conjunctive concatenation to a model of connective concatenation' (2015, 11), by which he means a negation of embodied experience. Thus 'with the digital, we have reached the end-point of this process of increasing abstraction, and an apex in the increasing dissociation of under-standing from empathy' (17). This is of fundamental importance in under-standing algorithmic governance through the reduction of the world to code and the digitalisation of the sign. For Beradi, the contemporary stage of capital-ism is 'semiocapitalism', where language and economy combine. This is because any kind of production (whether material and immaterial) is a process of 'com-bination and recombination of information (algorithms, figures, digital differ-ences)' (113). Therefore, in this new stage, 'digital abstraction adds a second layer to capitalist abstraction" (161). In this process of abstraction (following Baudrillard), signs proliferate and interact, losing any links to their original referents or meanings.

Berardi makes the important point that Big Data capitalism has implica-tions for governance, in that the 'abstract concatenation of technical functions replaces conscious elaboration, social negotiation, and democratic decision' (Berardi 2015, 217). In other words, 'the automatic connection of a-signifying segments replaces the dialogic elaboration of an order, and adaptation replaces consensus' (Berardi 2015, 217). Algorithmic governance responds or adapts to perturbations and changes through pattern recognition rather than the crea-tion of knowledge or an act of interpretation.

This separation or alienation from embodied processes of creativity and judgement is also taken up in Maurizio Lazzarato's (2014) *Signs and Machines*. Lazzarato argues that Big Data capitalism can be understood as the production of subjectivity through machinic enslavement, a concept he takes from Deleuze and Guattari: an assemblage, which 'no longer distinguishes between human and non-human, subject and object, or words and things' (Lazzarato 2014, 13). By 'enslavement', Lazzarato means the cybernetic conception of automated governance, control and regulation, 'ensuring the cohesion and equilibrium of the functioning whole' (25). In this process, the human does not stand separate to or above the machine, but is contiguous with machines and inside machinic processes, as one more molecular component to be combined and recombined with others.

For Lazzarato, the rise of digital capitalism means that 'one always acts within an assemblage, a collective, where machines, objects and signs are at the same time "agents"' (30). Capitalism is thus a 'semiotic operator' managing the flow of asignifying signs (without a subject as referent) which act directly on mate-rial flows: 'The sign machines of money, economics, science, technology, art, and so on, function in parallel or independently because they produce or con-vey meaning and in this way bypass language, significations, and representa-tion' (60). Lazzarato also identifies transformative effects that produce Being and go beyond the Anthropocene. In this context he draws on the work of Bruno Latour:

> Through asignifying semiotics machines 'speak', 'express themselves', and 'communicate' with man, other machines, and 'real' phenomena.

Through 'power signs' they interact with the expression and content of the atomic and chemical strata of matter, the biological strata of living being [...] Machines and asignifying semiotics are able to 'see' these strata, 'hear' them, 'smell' them, record them, order them, and transcribe them, something that is impossible for human senses and language. (87–88)

In the new forms of being and thought instantiated by digital capitalism, the subject is no longer interpolated as *homo oeconomicus* – a rational reflective subject. For Lazzarato, 'we have moved beyond "'cognitive capitalism'"' (100) and its privileging of dualistic linguistic and representational constructions of digital objects and digital subjects. Instead, we must take into full account the shift from 'work' to 'process' and from 'subjection' to 'enslavement' (119).

David Harvey is a representative of the fourth type of argument in relation to the question at what level of capitalism and society digital transformations should be situated. He has characterised contemporary capitalism as a regime of flexible accumulation (Harvey 1989), a new imperialism (Harvey 2003) and a form of neoliberal capitalism (Harvey 2005) that are based on the processes of accumulation by dispossession and financialisation. These constitute potentials for actual crisis because real accumulation diverges from the accumulation of fictitious capital. Digital technologies within this overall transformation of capitalism play, for Harvey, a mediating role. They are tools of time-space compression. 'I use the word 'compression' because a strong case can be made that the history of capitalism has been characterized by speed-up in the pace of life, while so overcoming spatial barriers that the world sometimes seems to collapse inwards upon us' (Harvey 1989, 240). For Harvey, these transformed conditions of capitalism require and call forth the development of digital technologies: 'Computerization and electronic communications have pressed home the significance of instantaneous international coordination of financial flows' (Harvey 1989, 161). 'The production of space examines how new systems (actual or imagined) of land use, transport and communications, territorial organization, etc. are produced, and how new modes of representation (e.g. information technology, computerized mapping, or design) arise' (Harvey 1989, 222).

In his most recent work *Marx, Capital and the Madness of Economic Reason*, Harvey (2017) elaborates on the role of the digital in contemporary capitalism. 'What was initially conceived as a liberatory regime of collaborative production of an open access commons has been transformed into a regime of hyper-exploitation upon which capital freely feeds. The unrestrained pillage by big capital (like Amazon and Google) of the free goods produced by a self-skilled labour force has become a major feature of our times. This carries over into the so-called cultural industries' (Harvey 2017, 96). 'It is also interesting that some of the most vigorous sectors of development in our times – like Google and Facebook and the rest of the digital labour sector – have grown very fast on the back of free labour' (Harvey 2017, 102). 'Factory labour still dominates in some parts of the world (e.g. East Asia) but in North America and Europe it is much diminished and replaced by various other labour systems (digital labour and the like)' (Harvey 2017, 57).

Harvey acknowledges the relevance of digital labour and digital capital today, but at the same time cautions against assuming that they constitute a new stage of development. He stresses the continued relevance of physical labour and the old inequality between capital and labour within the digital industries, as well as within capitalism as a whole. 'In the case of digital labour, for example, labour practices have emerged that are uncannily similar to the putting out system of early textile manufacturing in Britain in the late eighteenth century' (Harvey 2017, 104). This adds up to a redefinition of capital:

> as money in motion rather than value in motion. Such a redefinition facilitates concentration on the churning speculative market in property rights to culture, knowledge and entrepreneurial endeavours as well as to the widespread practices of speculation in asset markets as the distinctive form of contemporary capitalism. Hence the claim that we are entering a new phase of capitalism in which knowledge is pre-eminent, and that a brilliant techno-utopia based on that knowledge and all its labour-saving innovations (such as automation and artificial intelligence) is just around the corner or, as someone like Paul Mason maintains, already here. Such a redefinition may look about right from the perspective of Silicon Valley, but it falls flat on its face in the collapsing factories of Bangladesh and the suicide-ridden employment zones of both industrial Shenzhen and rural India where microfinance has spread its net to foster the mother of all sub-prime lending crises. (Harvey 2017, 105).

Harvey also stresses that Big Data has turned into an ideological fetish: 'The idea, for example, that the construction of smart cities managed through the mining of vast data sets can be the answer to all urban ills such that poverty, inequalities, class and racial discriminations and the extraction of wealth through evictions and other forms of accumulation by dispossession will all disappear is plainly ludicrous. It is counter-productive if not counter-revolutionary. It creates a fetish fog – a vast distraction – between political activism and the urban realities, pleasures and travails of daily life that need to be addressed' (Harvey 2017, 126).

These, then, are the main positions taken by authors in relation to the effect of Big Data capitalism upon society. There is ample evidence, however, to contest the first two positions (Fuchs 2008, 2014). The first one underestimates the continuities of power and capital. If we lived in a new type of society that was non-capitalist, then the crises of capitalism that usher in unemployment, precarity, nationalism and international conflicts would necessarily need to have been abolished. But today we are experiencing an ongoing economic crisis of capitalism, accompanied by a crisis of the state and political crises that have together constituted a legitimation crisis of political formations such as the European Union. The second position overestimates continuity and ends up with a static model of economic, political and societal development. It was one of Marx's main insights that capitalism is a dynamic, complex, evolutionary system that lives and develops through the exploitation of labour, social struggles and crises. Capitalism remains the same by changing itself. It develops the productive forces and differentiates the relations of economic and social production in order to reproduce what Marx called 'the whole old shit'[3] (Marx and Engels 1845/1846a/1959, 35) of alienation and exploitation.

The emergence and differentiation of digital technologies is the consequence of the development of the productive forces that increase the organic composition of capital. Developing the productive forces requires an increasing role knowledge (the general intellect) and education in society and the economy so that quantitative increases at a certain point turn into new qualities (Fuchs 2016b, 2014, 2008). The third and fourth positions do not agree at which level of capitalist organisation this shift takes place, but they do agree that capitalism is a dynamic system and that the emergence of digital machines, digital capital and digital labour is an expression of capitalist differentiation that today constitutes a significant dimension of the capitalist economy and society.

The computer is a universal machine because it can turn many aspects of the world into digital patterns. This characteristic explains the ubiquity of computing in everyday life. The apps on your smartphone have something to tell you about almost every situation you may find yourself in, from telling you what to do when you get lost in the streets to playing games on the Tube as a pastime. But the computer's universality is not universal enough. It reduces life to calculability: zeros, ones and quantities. Computer algorithms cannot understand love, ethics, morals, solidarity, care, affects, and other distinct human qualities. The reduction of the human to computing and instrumental reason therefore also brings with it certain dangers, such as the application of digital machines for exploitation and domination. At the same time, the human use of computing also advances new potentials for cooperation, community, solidarity, resistance and sociality that, even from within capitalism, point *beyond* it. The computer within capitalism is therefore the antagonistic digital machine. Digital and Big Data capitalism is an antagonistic societal formation that deepens alienation and exploitation while at the same time advancing potentials for liberation (Fuchs 2017).

Contemporary capitalism is a complex unity of diverse interacting and mutually encroaching capitalisms, including finance capitalism, neoliberal capitalism, imperialism, digital/communicative capitalism, hyper-industrial capitalism, mobility capitalism, authoritarian capitalism and Big Data capitalism. (Fuchs 2014, Chapter 5). The relation of these dimensions is variable. Empirical studies of concrete capitalist phenomena in specific regimes of space-time show which dimension is dominant for this specific phenomenon. For example, in 2014, 33.5% of the world's largest 2,000 corporations' profits were situated in the FIRE sector (finance, insurance and real estate), 19.0% in the mobility industries, 18.6% in the assemblage and manufacturing industry, and 17.3% in the communication and information industry (see Fuchs 2016a, Table 1). The data indicates that transnational corporations' structures are to varying degrees characterised by finance capitalism, mobility capitalism, hyper-industrial capitalism and informational/communicative/digital capitalism. And these dimensions interpenetrate: digital media corporations in Silicon Valley and elsewhere are based on large injections of venture capital (a specific type of finance capital). Their goal is to make an initial public offering on the stock market. They are prone to creating financial bubbles. Digital communication is both cause and effect of mobility and time-space compression (Harvey 1989). As a consequence, the transportation of people and commodities has been growing and accelerating. Digital commodities and digital commons are not weightless goods. They require not just information labour, but also capital's exploitation of the physical labour of miners and assemblers in Africa and China, who are situated in an international division of digital labour (Fuchs 2014).

Finance capitalism, mobility capitalism, hyper-industrial capitalism, digital capitalism and further capitalisms constitute a dialectical capitalist unity that consists of interrelated, contradictory moments. Capitalism is a unity of many capitalisms that develops dynamically and historically. A dimension that makes the picture even more complex is authoritarian capitalism. Authoritarian capitalism is a form of capitalism that in recent times, in the context of the economic and political crisis of capitalism, has become strengthened, which poses the question of how neoliberal capitalism and authoritarian capitalism are related (Fuchs 2018).

Notes

[1] See: https://icts-and-society.net/events/digital-objects-digital-subjects-a-symposium-on-activism-research-critique-in-the-age-of-big-data-capitalism-the-6th-icts-society-conference/

[2] This section was authored solely by Christian Fuchs.

[3] Translation from German to English [CF]. The English translation of this passage from *The German Ideology* in the Marx and Engels-*Collected Works* is, as in many other cases, imprecise, as it translates 'die ganze alte Scheiße' (Marx and Engels 1845/1846a/1957, 35) as 'old filthy business' (Marx and Engels 1845/1846b/1976, 49). There are different types of filth, including dust, mould, rubble, rust, cigarette butts, food particles and shit. So shit is just one type of filth, although certainly a particularly unpleasant one that you do not want to find mixed into your food, which

of course happens under unsanitary industrial conditions that aim at the maximisation of profit at the expense of human health, which is why the Richard Linklater movie *Fast Food Nation* asks how the shit comes into the burgers that school children and others eat. There are indications that fast food sold in major chains is indeed poo fast food (MacDougall 2017). To just say that capitalism produces and reproduces filth is therefore an underestimation. Marx's original formulation got it right by stressing the connection of capitalism and shit. Capitalism is not just shit, but makes us get treated like shit, produce shit, consume and eat shit.

References

Anderson, Chris. 2008. 'The End of Theory: The Data Deluge Makes the Scientific Method Obsolete.' *Wired Magazine* 16 (7), 23 June. Available at: https://www.wired.com/2008/06/pb-theory/ (accessed 14 May 2018)

Andrejevic, Mark. 2014. 'The Big Data Divide.' *International Journal of Communication* 8: 1673–89.

Bail, Christopher. 2014. 'The Cultural Environment: Measuring Culture with Big Data.' *Theory and Society* 43 (3–4): 465–82.

Berardi, Franco 'Bifo'. 2015. *And: Phenomenology of the End*. South Pasadena, CA: Semiotext(e).

Bourdieu, Pierre. 1986. *Distinction. A Social Critique of the Judgement of Taste.* London: Routledge.

boyd, danah and Kate Crawford. 2012. 'Critical Questions for Big Data.' *Information, Communication & Society* 15 (5): 662–79.

Castells. Manuel. 2000a. *End of Millennium. The Information Age: Economy, Society and Culture. Volume 3.* Malden, MA: Blackwell. Second Edition.

Colleoni, Elanor, Alessandro Rozza and Adam Arvidsson. 2014. 'Echo Chamber or Public Sphere? Predicting Political Orientation and Measuring Political Homophily in Twitter Using Big Data.' *Journal of Communication* 64 (2): 317–32.

Couldry, Nick and Joseph Turow. 2014. 'Advertising, Big Data, and the Clearance of the Public Realm: Marketers' New Approaches to the Content Subsidy.' *International Journal of Communication* 8: 1710–26.

Coyle, Diane and Patrick Meier. 2009. *New Technologies in Emergencies and Conflicts: The Role of Information and Social Networks.* Washington, DC: United Nations Foundation and Vodafone Foundation.

Einav, Liran and Jonathan Levin. 2014. 'Economics in the Age of Big Data.' *Science* 346: 715–21.

Erevelles, Sunil et al. 2016. 'Big Data Consumer Analytics and the Transformation of Marketing.' *Journal of Business Research* 69 (2): 897–904.

Fink, Katherine and C. W. Anderson. 2015. 'Data Journalism in the United States Beyond the "Usual Suspects".' *Journalism Studies* 16 (4): 467–81.

Foucault, Michel. 2008. *The Birth of Biopolitics*. Basingstoke: Palgrave Macmillan.

Friedman, Jonathan. 2002. 'Modernity and Other Traditions.' In *Critically Modern*, ed. Bruce M. Knauft, 287–313. Bloomington, IN: Indiana University Press.

Fuchs, Christian. 2018. *Digital Demagogue: Authoritarian Capitalism in the Age of Trump and Twitter*. London: Pluto.

Fuchs, Christian. 2017. *Social Media: A Critical Introduction*. London: Sage. Second edition.

Fuchs, Christian. 2016a. Digital Labor and Imperialism. *Monthly Review* 67 (8): 14–24.

Fuchs, Christian. 2016b. *Reading Marx in the Information Age. A Media and Communication Studies Perspective on 'Capital Volume I'*. New York: Routledge.

Fuchs, Christian. 2014. *Digital Labour and Karl Marx*. New York: Routledge.

Fuchs, Christian. 2008. *Internet and Society: Social Theory in the Information Age*. New York: Routledge.

Garnham, Nicholas. 1998/2004. 'Information Society Theory as Ideology.' In *The Information Society Reader*, ed. Frank Webster, 165–83. New York: Routledge.

George, Gerard, Martine R. Haas, and Alex Pentland. 2014. Big Data and Management. *Academy of Management Journal* 57 (2): 321–26.

Greenfield, Adam. 2013. *Against the Smart City*. New York: Do Projects.

Hardt, Michael and Antonio Negri. 2017. *Assembly*. Oxford: Oxford University Press.

Hardt, Michael and Antonio Negri. 2000. *Empire*. Cambridge, MA: Harvard University Press.

Harvey, David. 2017. *Marx, Capital and the Madness of Economic Reason*. London: Profile Books.

Harvey, David. 2005. *A Brief History of Neoliberalism*. Oxford: Oxford University Press.

Harvey, David. 2003. *The New Imperialism*. Oxford: Oxford University Press.

Harvey, David. 1989. *The Condition of Postmodernity. An Enquiry into the Origins of Cultural Change*. Oxford: Blackwell.

Hazen, Benjamin et al. 2014. 'Data Quality for Data Science, Predictive Analytics, and Big Data in Supply Chain Management.' *International Journal of Production Economics* 154: 72–80.

Henderson, Harry. 2009. *Encyclopedia of Computer Science and Technology*. New York: Facts on File.

Himelfarb, Sheldon. 2014. 'Can Big Data Stop Wars Before They Happen?' *Foreign Policy*, 25 April.

Horkheimer, Max. 2004. *Eclipse of Reason*. London: Continuum.

Kant, Immanuel. 1770. *Kant's Inaugural Dissertation of 1770*. Translated into English by William J. Eckoff. New York: Columbia College.

Karlsrud, John. 2014. 'Peacekeeping 4.0: Harnessing the Potential of Big Data, Social Media, and Cyber Technologies.' In *Cyberspace and International Relations: Theory, Prospects and Challenges*, eds. Jan-Frederik Kremer and Benedikt Müller. 141–60. London: Springer.

Kitchin, Rob. 2014. *The Data Revolution: Big Data, Open Data, Data Infrastructures and their Consequences*. London: Sage.

Krivý, Maroš. 2016. 'Towards a Critique of Cybernetic Urbanism: The Smart City and the Society of Control.' *Planning Theory*, Online First, DOI: https://doi.org/10.1177/1473095216645631.

Larsson, Anders and Hallvard Moe. 2012. 'Studying Political Microblogging: Twitter Users in the 2010 Swedish Election Campaign.' *New Media & Society* 14 (5): 729–47.

Lazzarato, Maurizio. 2014. *Signs and Machines: Capitalism and the Production of Subjectivity*. South Pasadena, CA: Semiotext(e).

Leibniz. 1703. 'Explanation of Binary Arithmetic'. Available at: http://www.leibniz-translations.com/binary.htm

Li, Jingran et al. 2015. 'Big Data in Product Lifecycle Management.' *International Journal of Advanced Manufacturing Technology* 81 (1–4): 667–84.

MacDougall, Lauren. 2017. 'A BBC Watchdog Test Found Levels of 'Poo Bacteria' in Drinks at KFC, McDonald's and Burger King.' *KentLive*, 28 June 2017.

Marx, Karl. 1867/1976. *Capital Volume I*. London: Penguin.

Marx, Karl. 1845/1846a/1959. 'Die deutsche Ideologie.' In *Marx-Engels-Werke (MEW), Band 3*, 5–530. Berlin: Dietz.

Marx, Karl. 1845/1846b/1976 'The German Ideology.' In *Marx and Engels Collected Works (MECW) Volume 5*, 19–539. London: Lawrence & Wishart

Mayer-Schönberger, Viktor and Kenneth Cukier. 2013. *Big Data: A Revolution that will Transform How We Live, Work and Think*. London: Murray.

Meier, Patrick. 2015. *Digital Humanitarians: How Big Data Is Changing the Face of Humanitarian Response*. Boca Raton, FL: CRC Press.

Monnier, Jean-Marie and Carlo Vercellone. 2010. 'Labour and Welfare State in the Transition to Cognitive Capitalism.' In *Cognitive Capitalism and its Reflections in South-Eastern Europe*, ed. Vladimir Cvijanović, Andrea Fumagalli and Carlo Vercellone, 71–85. Frankfurt am Main: Peter Lang.

Morozov, Evgeny. 2014. 'The Rise of Data and the Death of Politics'. *The Observer Online*, 20 July.

Mosco, Vincent. 2014. *To the Cloud: Big Data in a Turbulent World*. Boulder, CO: Paradigm.

Moulier-Boutang, Yann. 2011. *Cognitive Capitalism*. Cambridge: Polity.

Negri, Antonio. 2008. *Reflections on Empire*. Cambridge: Polity.

Neuman, W. Russell et al. 2014. 'The Dynamics of Public Attention: Agenda-Setting Theory Meets Big Data.' *Journal of Communication* 64 (2): 193–214.

Runciman, Walter G. 1993. Has British Capitalism Changed Since the First World War?' *British Journal of Sociology* 44 (1): 53–67.

Savage, Mike and Roger Burrows. 2007. 'The Coming Crisis of Empirical Sociology.' *Sociology* 41 (5): 885–99.

Stehr, Nico. 1994. *Knowledge Societies*. London: Sage.

Stuart, Elizabeth et al. 2015. *The Data Revolution: Finding the Missing Millions*. London: Overseas Development Institute.

Thrift, Nigel. 2014. 'The 'Sentient' City and What it May Portend.' *Big Data & Society* 1 (1): 1–21.

Tirunillai, Seshadri and Gerard J Tellis. 2014. 'Mining Marketing Meaning From Online Chatter: Strategic Brand Analysis of Big Data Using Latent Dirichlet Allocation.' *Journal of Marketing Research* 51 (4): 463–79.

Townsend, Anthony M. 2013. *Smart Cities: Big Data, Civic Hackers, and the Quest for a New Utopia*. New York: W.W. Norton & Co.

United Nations (2014) *A World That Counts: Mobilising the Data Revolution for Sustainable Development: Report Prepared at the Request of the United Nations Secretary-General*. Geneva: UN.

United States Institute for Peace (USIP). 2013. *Sensing and Shaping Emerging Conflicts*. Washington, DC: National Academies Press.

Varian, Hal R. 2014. 'Big Data: New Tricks for Econometrics.' *The Journal of Economic Perspectives* 28 (2): 3–27.

Wolff, Richard D. and Stephen A. Resnick. 2012. *Contending Economic Theories*. Cambridge, MA: MIT Press.

SECTION I

Digital Capitalism and Big Data Capitalism

CHAPTER 2

Digital Governance in the Anthropocene: The Rise of the Correlational Machine

David Chandler

1. Introduction

Digital governance is a new mode of governance that is highly dependent on the application of new technologies for data analysis. These have been developed across contemporary society, from the technologies of the quantified self to the application of data analysis in schools and businesses, to the development of new sensing capacities through international collaborative initiatives. The latter include the United Nations' Global Pulse, established by the UN Secretary-General to research and coordinate the use of Big Data for development;[1] the World Bank's Open Data for Resilience initiative (OpenDRI), designed to see the emergence of natural hazards and the impacts of climate change in real time;[2] and the PopTech and Rockefeller Foundation initiatives on Big Data and community resilience.[3] Big Data approaches, as will be introduced this chapter, can be usefully understood on the basis of governance through 'correlational machines'. Digital governance is increasingly developing through non-modern ontologies which construct the world through processes

How to cite this book chapter:
Chandler, D. 2019. Digital Governance in the Anthropocene: The Rise of the Correlational Machine. In: Chandler, D. and Fuchs, C. (eds.) *Digital Objects, Digital Subjects: Interdisciplinary Perspectives on Capitalism, Labour and Politics in the Age of Big Data.* Pp. 23–42. London: University of Westminster Press. DOI: https://doi.org/10.16997/book29.b. License: CC-BY-NC-ND 4.0

of emergence and highlight the development of new post-epistemological approaches that view correlation as a more reliable and more objective 'empirical' method than the extrapolations and predictions of causal analysis.

This chapter argues that digital governance works on the surface, on the 'actualist' notion that 'only the actual is real' (Harman 2010, 180; see also Harman 2009, 127). As Roy Bhaskar, the originator of the philosophy of critical realism, has argued, 'actualism' can be seen to be problematic in that hierarchies of structures and assemblages disappear and the scientific search for 'essences' under the appearance of things loses its value (Bhaskar 1998, 7–8). It is for pragmatic reasons, though, that a new mode of governance through 'the digital' appears to be emerging. Digital governance accepts that little can be done to prevent problems (understood as emergent or interactive effects) or to learn from problems, and that aspirations to transformation are much more likely to exacerbate these problems than solve them. Rather than attempt to 'solve' a problem, or adapt societies, entities or ecosystems in the hope that they will be better able to cope with problems and shocks, digital governance seeks to establish how relational understandings can help in the present by sensing and responding to the process of emergence.

This chapter is organised in four further sections. The first introduces digital governance as the governance of effects rather than causation, focusing on the work of Ulrich Beck and Bruno Latour in establishing the problematic of contingent interaction, rather than causal depth, as key to emergent effects, which can be unexpected and catastrophic. The second section considers in more depth how digital governance puts greater emphasis on relations of interaction than on ontologies of being, and links this methodological approach closely to actor network assumptions that disavow structures of causation. The final two sections analyse how correlation works to reveal new agencies and processes of emergence, and how new technologies have been deployed in this area, providing some examples of how the shift from causal relations to sensing effects has begun to alter governmental approaches.

2. The Digital Governance of Effects

Digital governance understands problems in terms of their effects rather than their causation. Today, analysts are much more likely to highlight that the complexity of global interactions and processes militate against ambitious schemas for intervention that aim at finding the root causes of problems or developing solutions through ambitious projects of social and political engineering from the ground up (see, for example, Ramalingam et al. 2008; Ramalingam 2013). In a more complex world, linear or causal ontologies can appear to be reductionist, and are easily discredited by the growing awareness that any forms of governance intervention will have unintended side effects. It is in the attempt to minimise these unintended consequences that the focus of policy-makers has shifted to 'digital governance', which focuses on the responsive governance of effects rather than the attempt to address ostensible root causes. For example, rather than seeking to solve conflict or to end it (which might result in possibly problematic unintended consequences), international policy intervention is increasingly articulated as 'managing' conflict, developing societal strategies to cope with it better and thereby limit its effects (Department for International Development, Foreign and Commonwealth Office and Ministry of Defence 2011). This focus on managing effects rather than engaging with causative chains makes the forms and practices of policy intervention quite different to addressing the causes of problems directly.

The link between conceptual discussions of governance and epistemic questions of knowledge is usefully highlighted by developing Giorgio Agamben's framing of a shift of concern from causation to effects, which he understands as a depoliticising move (Agamben 2014). Debates about addressing causation involve socio-political analysis and policy choices, putting decision-making and the question of sovereign power and political accountability at the forefront. Causal relations assume that power operates in a hierarchy, with policy outcomes understood to be products of conscious choices, powers and capacities. But Agamben argues that, whilst the governance of causes is the essence of politics, the governance of effects reverses the political process:

> We should not neglect the philosophical implications of this reversal. It means an epoch-making transformation in the very idea of government, which overturns the traditional hierarchical relation between causes and effects. Since governing the causes is difficult and expensive, it is more safe and useful to try to govern the effects. (Agamben 2014)

The governance of effects can therefore be seen as a retreat from modernist or causal assumptions of governance. However, the shift from causation to effects involves a corresponding shift in the conceptualisation of governance itself. Digital governance — governing by attempting to enhance system and community responsivity to effects — shifts the focus away from the formal public, legal and political sphere to the capacities and abilities of systems or societies for responsiveness to changes in their environmental context. The management of effects involves redistributing agency, understood as responsive capacity, and thereby evades the question of the responsibility or accountability for problems or the need to intervene on the basis of government as a form of political decision-making (see further, Chandler 2014b; 2014c).

Policy interventions have shifted to digital modes of governance as governing agencies have sought to respond to the effects of indeterminacy and risk as inherent in the complex and interdependent world, rather than understanding problems in a modernist telos of solutionism and progress. Problems in their emergence are the ontological product of complex feedback loops and systemic interactions that often cannot be predicted or foreseen. Surprising and catastrophic effects therefore call for new ways of thinking and governing, ways that go beyond modernist linear cause-and-effect assumptions and that can potentially cope with unexpected shocks and unseen threats.

As 'effects' become more central than causes, 'solutions-thinking' becomes less useful. It even has the potential to act as a a barrier to responsiveness, because 'problem-solving' tends to affirm current practices and approaches rather than emphasising the need to be alert to emergent effects.[4] The promise of 'solutions' seems to deny our entangled responsibilities and commitments, while greater sensitivity to effects enables us to become increasingly aware of them. Initially, the leading theorist to problematise 'problem-solving' approaches was perhaps Ulrich Beck, who argued that the risk of unintended effects could no longer be bracketed off, compartmentalised or excluded in what he called the 'Second Modernity' (Beck 1992). Beck argued that unexpected feedback effects from policy-making were an inevitable result of globalisation and interconnectivity, suggesting that the boundaries of liberal modernity – between the state and society and between culture and nature – were increasingly blurring. Surprises and shock events could no longer be treated as exceptions to the norm, to be quantified and insured against.[5]

The radical awareness of interconnectivity and feedback effects articulated by Beck was initially presented as purely negative, as a factor to be addressed, and potentially minimised, through governing under the 'precautionary principle'.[6] The awareness of entanglements that might lead to unintentional effects thus began to integrate concerns of contingency into the practices of governance. Beck's precautionary principle still had a modernist legacy in the positing of a potentially knowing and controlling subject able to manage unintended effects, but as the assumptions of modernity began to ebb away and discourses of globalisation morphed into those of the Anthropocene, this subject increasingly had to act more humbly and cautiously, testing and experimenting rather than assuming cause and effect modalities.[7] Unfortunately, Beck focused on the regulation of effects through ways of predicting or imagining the consequences of human actions, which seemed logically impossible to foresee. For example, even if scientists reached a consensus on the safety of a new procedure or initiative before its application, scientific experimentation in the laboratory cannot reproduce the same conditions as those of real, differentiated and complex life. This vulnerability led critics like Bruno Latour to convincingly argue that, once included, effects could not be prevented or minimised through precautions, but instead had to be followed through 'all the way' (Latour 2011, 27; Latour's thesis will be considered in greater detail below).

Towards the end of his life, Beck – in line with the times – shifted the presentation of his approach, stating that the appreciation of effects enables governance rather than merely constraining it (Beck 2015, 79). There were also positive feedback effects of the entanglements of culture and nature, indicating the need to adequately understand the new anthropogenic manufacture of risks such as global climate change. Thus, the awareness of the catastrophic effects of climate change and other risks could be seen to be potentially positive (Beck 2015, 76). For Beck,

> Anthropological shocks provide a new way of being in the world, seeing the world and doing politics. The anthropological shock of Hurricane Katrina is a useful example [...] Until Hurricane Katrina, flooding had not been positioned as an issue of environmental justice – despite the existence of a substantial body of research documenting inequalities and vulnerability to flooding. It took the reflection both in the publics and in academia on the devastating but highly uneven 'racial floods' of Hurricane Katrina to bring back the strong 'Anthropocene' of slavery, institutionalized racism, and connect it to vulnerability and floods. This kind of connecting the disconnected is the way the cosmopolitan side effects of bads are real, e.g. the invisibility of side effects is made visible. (Beck 2015, 80)

The flooding of New Orleans illustrated how devastating emergent effects could be, but it also had the consequence of enabling governing authorities to recognise the connection between risks that were thought to be natural or external, and racial, social and economic inequalities which were thought to be purely social. This necessitated bringing together governance expertise on the basis that the natural and the social were intermingled, and that the politics of race was not disconnected from the politics of ecology.[8] In the same way, the natural and the social sciences needed to be brought together in rethinking how to engage with the world beyond this posited culture/nature divide (see also Beck 2016). For Beck, this 'Metamorphosis is not social change [...]. [It] is a mode of changing the mode of change. It signifies the age of side effects. It challenges the way of being in the world, thinking about the world and imagining and doing politics.' (Beck 2015, 78)

A new form of governance thus emerges from the inclusion of effects: the understanding of crises and disasters no longer sees them as purely natural or purely social, but as contingent and emergent processes beyond governing control:

> Metamorphosis is deeply connected with the idea of unawareness, which embeds a deep and enduring paradox. On the one hand, it emphasizes the inherent limitations in knowledge [...]. [N]ano-technology, bio-engineering, and other types of emergent technology contain not only knowable risks but also risks we cannot yet know, providing a window of fundamental limitations to society's ability to perceive and govern risks. (Beck 2016, 104)

Beck's understanding of the Anthropocene as 'the age of side effects' (Beck 2015, 78) nicely encapsulates how the contingent and unforeseeable emergence of effects has been captured and incorporated into governance under discourses of the digital. Beck had not much more to offer than that the 'imagination of a threatening future' would focus attention on the ways in which contingent processes interacted.

Bruno Latour has sought to go beyond the limits of Beck's work in this area by seeking to trace the effects of human actions in real time feedback loops, a method requiring less of the imagination and more of digital science and technology. Latour has deployed to great effect the radical discourse of understanding problems in their emergence, having long waged war on modernist binary understandings, particularly that of the separation of culture and nature. For Latour, just as humanity has become more entangled with nature than ever before, ecologists have sought to emphasise the need for separation to protect 'nature', and modernist science aspires to know the world of 'nature' as a somehow separate and fixed reality (see, for example, Latour 1993a; 2004). Therefore, along similar lines to Beck's later work, Latour sees global warming, not so much as a sign of the failure of modernity, but an enabler of new forms of digital governance in the Anthropocene. The awareness of emergent effects such as climate change reveals the entanglements of humanity and the environment, and is a critical stimulus to radically reorganise the governance of the planet on the basis of a more inclusive understanding that 'nature' cannot just be left alone, but must be 'even more managed, taken up, cared for, stewarded, in brief, integrated and internalized into the very fabric of policy' (Latour 2011, 25).

Digital governance is crucial for Latour's project of enfolding the unintended effects of planetary interaction into the everyday governance of the Anthropocene. The effects of interaction are understood to be concrete and contingent, and thus depend on an ability to trace the surface of interactive relations through seeing effects, to follow the unintended and unforeseen consequences of human actions 'all the way'. Latour enthuses,

> [T]he principle of precaution, properly understood, is exactly the change of *zeitgeist* needed: not a principle of abstention – as many have come to see it – but a change in the way *any action* is considered, a deep tidal change in the linkage modernism established between science and politics. From now on, thanks to this principle, unexpected consequences are *attached* to their initiators and have to be followed through all the way. (Latour 2011, 27)

Latour's subject is the initiator of actions, and is thereby responsible for the interactive consequences of this initiation.[9] For Latour, the consequences of human actions can be traced by seeing or being sensitive to the network formed through their effects.[10] Thus digital governance seeks to trace these links on the surface. The need to be responsive to effects also drives debates that seek to determine the networks of entanglement of the Anthropocene, calling for greater sensitivity to the everyday feedbacks that bring these relations and interactions to light.[11] For some authors, extreme weather events or outbreaks of new viruses, for example, indicate networked interactions spanning the globe, revealing contingent linkages, interconnections and feedback loops (see, for example, Haraway 2015; Tsing 2015, 37–43; Gillings 2015).

The ability to see or sense the actual effects of relational interactions becomes more enabling the more connections can be established or imagined across greater distances and across more varied forms of interactive life. These complex and intricate feedback loops also call for greater technological capacities. Thus, these tasks can be accomplished, according to Latour,

> [B]y crisscrossing their [the loops'] potential paths with as many instruments as possible to have a chance of detecting in what ways they are connected [...] laying down the networks of equipment that render the consequences of action visible to all the various agencies that do the acting [...]. '[S]ensitivity' is a term that applies to all the agencies able to spread their loops further and to feel the consequences of what they do come back to haunt them [...] but only as long and as far that it [humanity] is fully equipped with enough sensors to feel the feedbacks. (Latour 2013, 96)

Latour's framework sees the ability to sense effects as crucial to revealing the unseen and unknown interconnections of the Anthropocene, involving the technology and regulatory mechanisms necessary to 'trace and ceaselessly retrace again the lines made by all those loops' with a 'strong injunction: keep the loop traceable and publically visible' so that 'whatever is reacting to your actions, loop after loop [...] weighs on you as a force to be taken into account' (Latour 2013, 135).

New sensorial forms of digital governance are given a material political form as a new set of political competencies and responsibilities are established: 'Such an accumulation of *responses* requires a responsible agency to which you, yourself, have to become in turn *responsible*.' (Latour 2013, 96) Unlike earlier modes of governance, digital governance does not seek to make causal claims;[12] the emergence of effects can be traced to reveal new relations of interaction and new agencies or actants to be taken into account, but there is no assumption that effects can be understood and manipulated or governed through transcendental policy goals.[13] Real time responsive forms of management through digital sensing increasingly focus on the 'what is' (Latour 2013, 126) of the world in its complex and plural emergence.

The fact that the 'what is-ness' of the world is not a concern within a modernist ontology of being and causation is often neglected in considerations of the digital as a mode of governance, so it will be considered here and in more detail in the following section. Latour, in the 'Facing Gaia' lectures, argues that nature has to be understood in 'post-epistemological' terms (Latour 2013, 26). By this he means that modernist forms of representation, reduction, abstraction and exclusion cannot know a world that is plural, lively and interactive. This is post-epistemological because knowledge can no longer be extracted from its concrete context of interaction in time and space. In this framing, knowledge, to be 'objective' – to be real – has to be plural, fluid and concrete (Latour 2013, 49). This is very similar to Donna Haraway's understanding of 'situated epistemology', which rejects modernist drives to extract knowledge, i.e. to turn knowing into abstractions from real emergent processes through methods of scaling up, generalising and universalising, and to fix knowledge apart from its plural, changing and overlapping context of meaning (Haraway 1988). In this way of rethinking knowledge, the modernist divisions between subjective and objective, and qualitative and quantitative, are dissolved (see further, Venturini and Latour 2010).

Latour's is a flat ontology, where speed, size and scale are momentary and contingent products of interaction, unable to construct and shape path-dependencies. As Latour repeats, in a world of unknowable contingencies 'it is the *what is* that obstinately requests *its due*' (Latour 2013, 126). This 'empirical' displacement of causal understandings can also be intimated from Beck's later work. Beck imagined the development of real-time empirics as able to evade both the dangers of critical immanent approaches – which tended to reproduce the knowledge scepticism of postmodernism – and the hubristic knowledge claims of transcendental frameworks of cause-and-effect. Thus, the world could be governed in its complex emergence by focusing on effects as the starting point for governance:

> Seen this way, climate change risk is far more than a problem of measures of carbon dioxide and the production of pollution. It does not even only signal a crisis of human self-understanding. More than that, global climate risk creates new ways of being, looking, hearing and acting in the world – highly conflictual and ambivalent, open-ended, without any foreseeable outcome. As a result, a compass for the 21st century arises. This compass is different from the postmodern 'everything goes' and different from false universalism. This is a new variant of critical theory, which does not set the normative horizon itself but takes it from empirical analyses. Hence, it is an empirical analysis of the normative horizon of the self-critical world risk society. (Beck 2015, 83)

In the digital governance mode of sensing, the focus on empirical analysis to facilitate real-time responsiveness enables emergent effects to discursively frame governance without an external subject 'setting the normative horizon'. This new 'normative horizon' would now be set by the world itself, and accessed through the development of new mechanisms and techniques sensitised and responsive to the world in its emergence. The post-epistemological implications of frameworks of digital governance seem to underlie the fascination with Big Data approaches as a way of generating increasingly sensitive real-time responses to emergent effects (see, for example, Mayer-Schönberger and Cukier 2013; Kitchin 2014).

3. Big Data, Objects and Relations

As already intimated in the consideration of Latour's work in the previous section, digital governance can be usefully engaged with as a mode of governance that necessarily shares the ontopolitical assumptions of Actor-Network Theory (ANT) and can be informed by a consideration of the long-running engagement between Bruno Latour (the leading proponent of ANT) and Graham Harman (a leading speculative realist) over the conceptualisation of this approach (see Latour et al. 2011). Harman takes Latour to task precisely for the 'actualism' at the heart of the ANT approach, stating that, for Latour, momentary relations are more important than the substance of entities (or 'actants'):

> For Latour an actant is always an event, and events are always completely specific: 'everything happens only once, and at one place.' An actant [...] is always completely deployed in the world, fully implicated in the sum of its dealings at any given moment. Unlike a substance, an actant is not distinct from its qualities, since for Latour this would imply an indefensible featureless lump lying beneath its tangible properties... And unlike a substance, actants are not different from their relations. Indeed, Latour's central thesis is that an actor is its relations. All features of an object belong to it; everything happens only once, at one time, in one place. (Harman 2009, 17)

This focus on relations in the present and actual, and not on the possibilities that may lie latent or virtual in entities, ecosystems or assemblages, is crucial to the distinction with a causal ontology:

> Since Latour is committed to a model of actants fully deployed in alliances with nothing held in reserve, he cannot concede any slumbering potency lying in the things that is currently unexpressed. To view a thing in terms of potential is to grant it something beyond its current status as a fully specific event. (Harman 2009, 28)

As Harman argues, 'Latour is the ultimate philosopher of relations', and in this his philosophy inverts the assemblage theory of DeLanda (Harman 2010, 176), which understands assemblages as never fully actualised and thus enabling the possibility for causal interactions to bring forward alternative paths of emergence. For Harman and object-oriented ontologists, ANT falls down because of its failure to distinguish between objects and their relations. Harman argues that ANT makes the mistake of 'flattening everything out too much, so that everything is just on the level of its manifestation'. As a consequence, this approach 'can't explain the change of the things' or the hidden potential of alternative outcomes (Latour et al. 2011, 95). For actor network theory, the emergence of new aspects of reality is not a matter of causal depth but of seeing what actually exists, but is consigned to the background. As Latour argues,

> I call this background *plasma*, namely that which is not yet formatted, not yet measured, not yet socialized, not yet engaged in metrological chains, and not yet covered, surveyed, mobilized, or subjectified. How big is it? Take a map of London and imagine that the social world visited so far occupies no more room than the subway. The plasma would be the rest of London, all its buildings, inhabitants, climates, plants, cats, palaces, horse guards [...]. [Sociologists] were right to look for 'something hidden behind', but It is neither behind nor especially hidden. It is *in between* and not made of social stuff. It is not hidden, simply *unknown*. It resembles a vast hinterland providing the resources for every single course of action to be fulfilled, much like the countryside for the urban dweller, much like the missing masses for a cosmologist trying to balance out the weight of the universe. (Latour 2005, 244, emphasis in original).

For ANT, as an alternative science of relationality, what is missing in terms of governmental understanding is not relational depth but relationality on the surface, the presence of actual relations which give entities and systems their coherence or weight in the present moment. Thus, for ANT, modernist understandings of the world, whether those of natural or of social science, give too much credence to entities, as if these entities had fixed essences (allowing causal relations) rather than shifting relations to other actants:

> The world is not a solid continent of facts sprinkled by a few lakes of uncertainties, but a vast ocean of uncertainties speckled by a few islands of calibrated and stabilized forms... Do we really know that little? We know even less. Paradoxically, this 'astronomical' ignorance explains a lot of things. Why do fierce armies disappear in a week? Why do whole empires like the Soviet one vanish in a few months? Why do companies who cover the world go bankrupt after their quarterly report? (Latour 2005, 245)

In February 2008, Latour and Harman participated in a public seminar at the LSE, in which the differences between what are heuristically described here as the ontopolitical assumptions behind digital governance were brought to the surface. At the seminar Noortje Marres made some useful interventions regarding the importance of ANT for the discovery of new ways of seeing agency in the world on the pragmatic basis of 'effect' rather than a concern for emergent causation: 'because pragmatists are not contemplative metaphysicians, because they say "we will not decide in advance what the world is made up of", this is why they go with this weak signal of the effect. Because that is the only way to get to a new object, an object that is not yet met nor defined' (Latour et al. 2011, 62). Marres argued that taking 'as our starting point stuff that is happening' was a way of 'suspending' or of 'undoing' ontology, in order to study change (Latour et al. 2011, 89). This aspect is vital to digital sensing as a mode of governance, as it enables a focus upon the surface appearances of change, which are not considered so important in an ontology of causality:

> It is about saying that we have a world where continuously new entities are added to the range of existing entities, everything continually changes and yet in this modern technological world everything stays the same. We have stabilized regimes [...]. But if we engage in studying specific objects, we do not find this singularized thing that is well put-together, as an object. We do not find it at the foundation but we find it as an emergent effect (Latour et al. 2011, 90–91).

The appearances of things are continually changing as their relationships do, not through an ontology of depth but in plain sight through networks and interactions on the surface, As Latour states, regarding the 'plasma' or the 'missing masses' of ANT: 'It is not the unformatted that's the difficulty here. It is what is in between the formatting. Maybe this is not a very good metaphor. But it's a very, very different landscape, once the background and foreground have been reversed.' (Latour et al. 2011, 84)

My argument here is that the ontopolitical assumptions of digital governance can be usefully grasped in terms of actor network theory in that the focus is not upon on the nature of systems or substances, but on the ways in which change can be detected through seeing processes of emergence as relational. Relational processes without a conception of depth are co-relational rather than causal, as the processes of relation may be contingent and separate conjunctions. The fact that all forms of being are co-relational means that new opportunities arise to see with and through these relations and co-dependencies: whether it is the co-relation of pines and matsutake mushrooms (mobilised by Anna Tsing 2015, 176) or the co-relation between sunny weather and purchases of barbecue equipment, or the co-relation between Google search terms and flu outbreaks (Madrigal 2014). These are relations of 'effects' rather than of causation: when some entities or processes have an effect on others, they can be seen as 'networked' or 'assembled' but they have no relation of immanent or linear causation which can be mapped and reproduced or intervened in.

The co-relational rather than causal aspect of actor network theory distinguishes it from assemblage theory or the neo-institutional or ecosystem approaches with their ontology of causal depth. Actor network approaches therefore lack the temporal and spatial boundedness of assemblages or of nested adaptive systems, and make no assumptions of iterative interactions producing state changes to higher levels of complex ordering.[14] They say nothing of 'ontology' or of the essences of things, merely focusing on the transmission of effects at particular moments; thus they can draw together 'litanies' of actors and actants – the plasma, or 'missing masses' – crucial for describing or understanding how change occurs in systems or states. Suspending or 'undoing' ontology, opens ANT approaches to the world of interaction in the actual, or brings the open-ended processual understanding of the virtual into the actual. New actors or agencies are those brought into being or into relation to explain 'effects' and to see processes of emergence through 'co-relation'. In this respect, new technological advances, driving algorithmic machine learning, Big Data capabilities and the Internet of Things, seem perfectly timed to enable the digital as a mode of governance.

4. The Rise of the Correlational Machine

Human–non-human assemblages of sensors enable new forms of responsivity, but this advance is not concerned with causal knowledge but with the capacities to see through the breaking down of processes via the development of 'correlational machines'. I use the term 'correlational machines' to distinguish the mode of digital governance as a very distinct paradigm in contrast to causal ontologies of depth and immanence. The development of correlational machines is not new to the Anthropocene, but is part-and-parcel of the extension of human agency through the use of artificial prostheses to enable sensing the environment. Perhaps the classic example, provided by Merleau-Ponty's work on the phenomenology of perception, would be the walking stick, which enables the blind to sense the obstacles around them, through the resistance to touch and the sounds made (Merleau-Ponty 1989). Another example would be the deployment of canaries as sensors for carbon monoxide in mineshafts.

Human, non-human and technological aids thus have long histories in enabling the extension of human responsivity to effects, through the power of co-relation or correlation. It is important to illustrate why this is correlation and not causation, as this is key to digital modes of governance. Digital governance relies on causal laws or regularities, but the key aspect is that they are secondary to correlation rather than primary. As Latour would argue, the key concerns are not ontological but relational: the causal becomes background to the relational foreground. Take the example of the canary in the mineshaft. The precondition for the canary signalling the existence of carbon monoxide is the causal regularity of poisonous gas killing the canary before mine workers are aware of its existence and prone to its effects. However, the problem of carbon monoxide is not addressed at the level of causation (predicting it or preventing it from appearing or solving the problem afterwards) but through developing a method of signalling the existence of poisonous fumes and of increasing human sense-ability through the power of correlation. The canary is a non-human correlational machine for signalling the existence of carbon monoxide. The canary enables the unseen to be seen: it brings the 'missing masses', which exist in the mineshaft, into perception. The addition of the canary into the situational context reveals the existence of other actants, the poisonous gases, which were there but which previously operated unseen.

Two everyday examples that draw out more clearly the 'machinic' nature of artificial prosthetics for digital governance are the development of the thermometer and the compass. Both the thermometer and the compass enable the extension of human sensitivity and agency. The prosthetic support they provide is correlational, although based upon causal laws or regularities. The compass, based originally on the magnetic qualities of the naturally occurring mineral magnetite or lodestone, can enable a magnetised needle to point a course in relation to the geomagnetic north pole. Thus mariners could see or sense their direction through the power of the compass as a 'correlational machine', enabling new 'actants' (magnetic fields of attraction) to be enrolled in navigation through their correlational effects (Dill 2003).

The story of the thermometer is similar: it relies on a causal relation between an increase in temperature and the thermal expansion of solids or liquids, such as water, alcohol and mercury. These thermal properties of expansion were known to the ancient Greeks and applied or 'machinised' in the eighteenth century with the development of the Fahrenheit scale (Radford 2003). A thermometer is an artificially constructed correlational machine that enables the seeing or sensing of atmospheric changes that would otherwise be unseen. New 'correlational machines' are being developed all the time, enabled by a variety of new technologies. For example, more accurate quantum thermometers can now measure thermal changes at the quantum level. This example shows how new actants – in this case, intrinsic quantum motions – can be enrolled to create new machinic prostheses for seeing changes in temperature at ever more precise levels (NIST 2016).

Correlational machines have proliferated under digital governance, enabling new high-tech assemblages involving the extensive use of new sensing technologies, often termed 'the Internet of Things', where sensors can be connected to the Internet and provide real time detection of changes in air and water quality, earth tremors or parking capacity, and so forth. The potential use of sensing technologies is extensive. At the MIT Senseable City Lab, for example, researchers informed me of work being carried out using robotic sensors in sewers to track minute quantities of bio-chemical material. Potentially, local authorities could receive real time information on localised health profiles and illegal drug use.[15] If sewers can be turned into key information generators for bio-sensing and drug and health profiling, it is clear that new digital modes of governing can provide a whole range of new avenues for monitoring and regulatory policing.[16] Thus new assemblages are being artificially constructed that enable new actants to be enrolled in governance, including non-human and non-living actants, and in doing so, changes can be seen or sensed and therefore responded to, often revealing new threats or dangers or expanding human sensitivity to existing ones.

While these 'more-than-human' machinic assemblages are constructed on the basis of causal laws and regularities, their purpose is a correlational one: seeing what exists in the present, in the actual, but is unknown or unseen. To take one contemporary example of new forms of digital governance, Elizabeth Johnson has done insightful work on more-than-human forms of governance in her analysis of the work of commercial biosensing and the use of organic life to monitor fresh and marine water sources for pollution (Johnson 2017). Here an array of animal species, including small fish, worms, molluscs, crustaceans and micro-organisms are monitored intensively to discover their norms of functionality and to develop ways of measuring changes in these indicators. They are then ready for use as 'correlational machines':

> [The company] monitors a suite of 'behavioral fingerprints' as these organisms are exposed to different systems. Locomotor activity, reproductive rates, and embryonic developments are measured together to indicate the severity of hazardous anthropogenic chemicals as well as biologically produced toxins, such as blue-green algae. In this way the company boasts, it can make 'pollution measurable.' (Johnson 2017, 284)

As Johnson notes, the mode of digital governance is less about causation than seeing the unseen: 'making imperceptible harms perceptible' (Johnson 2017). This approach sees through correlation, which enables new problems and possibilities to be detected. For example, changes in the bodily indicators of the animal organs can alert human agents to potential problems, even if the sources of those problems are unknown. Thus the company concerned argues that problems can be detected 'in due time before pollution irreversibly spreads in the environment or even harms human health' (Johnson 2017). In a technological extension of the non-human prosthesis of the canary down a coalmine, 'biosensing enables a way of seeing with non-human life' (Johnson 2017, 286).

Just as the properties of mercury needed to be understood for the thermometer to work as a correlational machine for biosensing technologies, green florescent protein (GFP) has been a widely used tool to enable organic life to be modified into correlational machines, potentially signalling a wide range of changes in acidity and alkalinity, as well as the presence of pathogens, toxins and cancer-causing agents (Johnson 2017, 285). Digital governance, on the basis of developing new forms of correlational sight, enables a fundamental shift from governance on the basis of 'problem-solving' and analysis of 'root causes' to the governance of effects. In this mode of governance, distinctions between scientific disciplines and individual entities, which historically depended upon organic conceptions of causation, tend to disappear. In contrast, the ontopolitics informing digital governance is not concerned with entities or with causation, enabling 'more-than-human' assemblages of responsivity to become the new governmental norm.[17]

5. Conclusion

Digital governance is less concerned with adaptive change (preventing problems before they occur or with their resolution afterwards) than with responsiveness to problems understood as emergent effects. Responsiveness, in resilience discourses, is increasingly seen as a real-time necessity: living with and being sensitive to problems and threats is understood to be the best way of ameliorating their impact (Evans and Reid 2014). Sensing as a mode of governance thus appears to have a lot in common with Deleuze's conceptualisation of a 'control society', where time is held constant: instead of a before (prevention) or an after (reaction) there is the continual modulation of responsiveness, an 'endless postponement' of a problem (Deleuze 1995, 179). The essence of entities, be they systems, societies or individuals becomes much less important than the emergent appearance of surface 'effects', which are to be modulated and responded to.

This is usefully highlighted in Stephanie Wakefield and Bruce Braun's work on the deployment of 'green infrastructure', which relies on the agency of non-human actors, such as the deployment of oysters as seawall infrastructure, to enable sensing that is grounded on the ontopolitics of responsivity rather than adaptation (Wakefield and Braun 2018). Thus non-human life is managed as a way of securing human life. The 'oystertecture' approach fits excellently with the ontopolitics of digital governance laid out here, as it seeks to respond to rather than adapt to climate change. This responsive approach is correlational rather than causal in its response to rising sea levels. Most importantly, Wakefield and Braun highlight the distinctiveness of this mode of governance, which rather than seeking to adapt and learn on the basis of causal relations that are oriented towards the future, has a very different temporality or approach to the future in that it seeks to 'ward it off', attempting to keep everything as it is by 'cancelling out or absorbing events' (emphasis in original) (Wakefield and Braun 2018). Rather than seeking to reform or adapt existing modes of infrastructure, digital governance seeks to maintain existing forms of infrastructure but to add other forms of sensing and responsivity. While modernist or causal understandings assumed a hierarchy of centralised reporting and adaptation, digital governance has a much flatter ontology of self-generated responses, whether at the level of society, community or the quantified self.

Thus, with digital modes of governance, there is no longer a 'line' of causality but a 'plane' of relationality – this shift is fundamental in terms of governance, which, as analysed above, no longer needs to assume a normative horizon or normative goals external to the actuality of the world. As Agamben has highlighted, the governance of effects can thereby be seen to be thoroughly depoliticised, as the tasks of governance are discursively derived 'empirically' from the world, rather than from human actors as subjects.

Notes

1 United Nations Global Pulse initiative website can be accessed at: http://www.unglobalpulse.org/.

2 The World Bank's OpenDRI webpages can be accessed at: https://www.gfdrr.org/opendri.

3 For information on the Data-Pop Alliance see: http://www.datapopalliance.org/; and for the Rockefeller Foundation: http://www.rockefellerfoundation.org/our-work/current-work/resilience.

4 Robert Cox (1981) prepared the ground, famously differentiating approaches that saw problems from a narrow status-quo perspective from those that sought to critically rethink the bigger picture.

5 On the importance of the normalising effects of insurance see, for example, Ewald (1991), Defert (1991), Dillon (2008).

6 He argued: 'If we anticipate catastrophes whose destructive potential threatens everybody, then the risk calculation based on experience and rationality breaks down. Now all possible, to a greater or lesser degree improbable, scenarios must be taken into consideration; to knowledge drawn from experience and science we must add imagination, suspicion, fiction and fear.' (Beck 2009, 53)

7 For the critics of the principle, which has been taken up in a number of ways in international policy documents, the problem was the paralysing aspects of 'possibilistic' thinking (see, for example, Sunstein 2002).

8 See also the analysis of Hurricane Katrina in Protevi (2009, 163–83).

9 Exemplified in the example of Frankenstein's failure to care for his creation, which then turned into a tragic monster. Latour (2011).

10 See, for example, Clark 2010; or Klein 2014, 1–3, which opens with the ironies of anthropogenic feedback loops, for example, when extreme hot weather, caused by the profligate burning of fossil fuels, melted the tarmac and grounded aircraft at Washington DC in the summer of 2012.

11 Latour (2013, 94–95); see also, Connolly (2013), Bennett (2010). Latour (2013, 112) echoes Connolly and Bennett on the cultivation of sensitivity: 'To become sensitive, that is to feel responsible, and thus to make the loops feedback on our own action, we need, by a set of totally artificial operations, to place ourselves *as if we were* at the End of Time.' (emphasis in original)

12 As Gilles Deleuze and Félix Guattari (2014, 11–22) note, tracing causal chains could only be a 'selective', 'artificial' and 'restrictive' procedure, 'overcoding' and reproducing its starting assumptions in a transcendent manner.

13 Deleuze (1988, 128) nicely captures the difference between transcendent and immanent approaches in his suggestion that transcendent approaches

introduce a 'dimension supplementary to the dimensions of the given'; i.e. ideas of goals, direction and causal connections, which separate the human subject from the object of governance. Whereas, on the plane of immanence: 'There is no longer a subject, but only individuating affective states of an anonymous force. Here [governance] is concerned only with motions and rests, with dynamic affective charges. It will be perceived with that which it makes perceptible to us, as we proceed.'

[14] Harman calls this 'occasionalism' and argues that Latour (2009, 228) provides the first known example of 'secular occasionalism', where there is no fixed way of explaining causation or the continuity of events. In ANT, nothing follows from anything else: 'Nothing is by itself either reducible or irreducible to anything else' (Latour 1993b, 169). The work of composing relations begins again 'every morning' (Latour et al. 2011, 76). Regarding complexity theory, see Chandler (2014a).

[15] As Charlotte Heath-Kelly (2016) notes, Big Data ontologies of complexity lead to universal rather than targeted surveillance parameters.

[16] Personal interview, researcher, Senseable City Lab, Massachusetts Institute of Technology, 30 March 2017.

[17] This form of governance through the modulation of effects can be usefully grasped in terms of Deleuze and Guattari's concept of 'machinic enslavement', derived from cybernetics, where responses are automated to manage or govern on the basis of maintaining equilibrium. In this process there is no distinction between using a machine and being part of the informational input to the machinic process: the process itself is more important than distinctions between entities or individuals. See Deleuze and Guattari (2014, 531–36); Lazzarato (2014, 23–34).

References

Agamben, Giorgio. 2014. 'For a Theory of Destituent Power.' *Chronos* 10, February.

Beck, Ulrich. 1992. *Risk Society: Towards a New Modernity*. London: Sage.

Beck, Ulrich. 2009. *World at Risk*. Cambridge: Polity Press.

Beck, Ulrich. 2015. 'Emancipatory Catastrophism: What Does It Mean to Climate Change and Risk Society?' *Current Sociology* 63 (1): 75–88.

Beck, Ulrich. 2016. *The Metamorphosis of the World*. Cambridge: Polity Press.

Bhaskar, Roy. 1998. *The Possibility of Naturalism: A Philosophical Critique of the Contemporary Human Sciences*, 3rd ed. Abingdon; Routledge.

Chandler, David. 2014a. *Resilience: The Governance of Complexity*. Abingdon: Routledge.

Chandler, David. 2014b. 'Beyond Good and Evil: Ethics in a World of Complexity.' *International Politics* 51 (4): 441–57.

Chandler, David. 2014c. 'Beyond Neoliberalism: Resilience, the New Art of Governing Complexity.' *Resilience: International Policies, Practices and Discourses* 2 (1): 47–63.

Clark, Nigel. 2010. *Inhuman Nature: Sociable Life on a Dynamic Planet.* Sage Publications, Kindle Edition.

Connolly, William E. 2013. *The Fragility of Things: Self-Organizing Processes, Neoliberal Fantasies, and Democratic Activism.* London: Duke University Press.

Cox, Robert W. 1981. 'Social Forces, States and World Orders: Beyond International Relations Theory.' *Millennium - Journal of International Studies* 10 (2): 126–155.

Defert, Daniel. 1991. '"Popular Life" and Insurance Technology.' In *The Foucault Effect: Studies in Governmentality*, eds. Burchell, Graham, Colin Gordon and Peter Miller, 211–33. Chicago: University of Chicago Press.

Deleuze, Gilles. 1988. *Spinoza: Practical Philosophy.* San Francisco: City Lights.

Deleuze, Gilles. 1995. 'Postscript on Control Societies.' In *Negotiations: 1972–1990*, 177–82. New York, NY: Columbia University Press.

Deleuze, Gilles and Felix Guattari. 2014. *A Thousand Plateaus.* London: Bloomsbury Academic.

Department for International Development, Foreign and Commonwealth Office and Ministry of Defence. 2011. *Building Stability Overseas Strategy.* London: DfID, FCO, MoD.

Dill, J. Gregory. 2003. 'Lodestone and Needle: The Rise of the Magnetic Compass.' *Ocean Navigator*, 1 January. Available at: http://www.oceannavigator.com/January-February-2003/Lodestone-and-needle-the-rise-of-the-magnetic-compass/. (accessed 14 May 2018)

Dillon, Michael. 2008. 'Underwriting Security.' *Security Dialogue* 39 (2–3): 309–32.

Evans, Brad and Julian Reid. 2014. *Resilient Life: The Art of Living Dangerously.* Cambridge: Polity Press.

Ewald, Francois. 1991. 'Insurance and Risk'. In *The Foucault Effect: Studies in Governmentality*, eds. Burchell, Graham, Colin Gordon and Peter Miller, 197–210. Chicago: University of Chicago Press.

Gillings, Michael. 2015. Comment: How Modern Life Has Damaged Our Internal Ecosystems. *SBS News*, 12 October. Available at: http://www.sbs.com.au/news/article/2015/10/09/comment-how-modern-life-has-damaged-our-internal-ecosystems. (accessed 14 May 2018)

Haraway, Donna. 1988. 'Situated Knowledges: The Science Question in Feminism and the Privilege of Partial Perspective.' *Feminist Studies* 14 (3): 575–99.

Haraway, Donna. 2015. 'Anthropocene, Capitalocene, Plantationocene, Chthulucene: Making Kin.' *Environmental Humanities* 6: 159–65.

Harman, Graham. 2009. *Prince of Networks: Bruno Latour and Metaphysics.* Melbourne: re.press.

Harman, Graham G. 2010. *Towards Speculative Realism: Essays and Lectures.* Winchester: Zero Books.

Heath-Kelly, Charlotte. 2016. 'Algorithmic Auto-Immunity in the NHS: Radicalisation and the Clinic.' *Security Dialogue* 48 (1): 29–45.

Johnson, Elizabeth R. 2017. 'At the Limits of Species Being: Sensing the Anthropocene.' *South Atlantic Quarterly* 116 (2): 275–292.

Kitchin, Rob. 2014. *The Data Revolution: Big Data, Open Data, Data Infrastructures & their Consequences.* Sage: London.

Klein, Naomi. 2014. *This Changes Everything: Capitalism vs. the Climate.* New York, NY: Simon & Schuster.

Latour, Bruno. 1993a. *We Have Never Been Modern.* Cambridge, MA: Harvard University Press.

Latour, Bruno. 1993b. *The Pasteurisation of France.* Cambridge, MA: Harvard University Press.

Latour, Bruno. 2004. *Politics of Nature: How to Bring the Sciences into Democracy.* Cambridge, MA: Harvard University Press.

Latour, Bruno. 2005. *Reassembling the Social: An Introduction to Actor-Network-Theory.* Oxford: Oxford University Press.

Latour, Bruno. 2011. 'Love Your Monsters.' *Breakthrough Journal* 2: 21–8.

Latour, Bruno. 2013. *Facing Gaia, Six Lectures on the Political Theology of Nature: Being the Gifford Lectures on Natural Religion, Edinburgh, 18th–28th of February 2013* (draft version 1 March 2013).

Latour, Bruno, Graham Harman and Péter Erdélyi. 2011. *The Prince and the Wolf: Latour and Harman at the LSE.* Winchester: Zero Books.

Lazzarato, Maurizio. 2014. *Signs and Machines: Capitalism and the Production of Subjectivity.* South Pasadena, CA: Semiotext(e).

Madrigal, Alexis C. 2014. 'In Defense of Google Flu Trends.' *The Atlantic,* 27 March. Available at: https://www.theatlantic.com/technology/archive/2014/03/in-defense-of-google-flu-trends/359688/ (accessed 14 May 2018)

Mayer-Schönberger, Viktor and Kenneth Cukier. 2013. *Big Data: A Revolution That Will Transform How We Live, Work and Think.* John Murray: London.

Merleau-Ponty, Maurice. 1989. *Phenomenology of Perception.* London: Routledge.

NIST. 2016. US National Institute of Science and Technology 'NIST Creates Fundamentally Accurate Quantum Thermometer', *NIST,* 15 March. Available at: https://www.nist.gov/news-events/news/2016/03/nist-creates-fundamentally-accurate-quantum-thermometer (accessed 14 May 2018)

Protevi, John. 2009. *Political Affect: Connecting the Social and the Somatic.* Minneapolis: University of Minnesota Press.

Radford, Tim. 2003. 'A Brief History of Thermometers.' *The Guardian,* 6 August. Available at: https://www.theguardian.com/science/2003/aug/06/weather.environment (accessed 14 May 2018)

Ramalingam, Ben. 2013. *Aid on the Edge of Chaos: Rethinking International Cooperation in a Complex World*. Oxford: Oxford University Press.

Ramalingam, Ben. et al. 2008. 'Exploring the Science of Complexity: Ideas and Implications for Development and Humanitarian Efforts.' *ODI Working Paper*, 285. London: Overseas Development Institute.

Sunstein, Cass R. 2002. 'The Paralyzing Principle.' *Regulation* (Winter): 32–37. Available at: http://object.cato.org/sites/cato.org/files/serials/files/regulation/2002/12/v25n4-9.pdf.

Tsing, Anna Lowenhaupt. 2015. *The Mushroom at the End of the World: On the Possibility of Life in Capitalist Ruins*. Princeton, NJ: Princeton University Press.

Venturini, Tommaso and Bruno Latour. 2010. 'The Social Fabric: Digital Traces and Quali-quantitative Methods.' In *Proceedings of Future En Seine 2009: The Digital Future of the City*, ed. Ewen Chardronnet, 87–101. Paris: Cap Digital.

Wakefield, Stephanie and Bruce Braun. 2018. 'Oystertecture: Infrastructure, Profanation and the Sacred Figure of the Human.' In *Infrastructure, Environment, and Life in the Anthropocene*, ed. Kregg Hetherington. Durham, NC: Duke University Press.

CHAPTER 3

Beyond Big Data Capitalism, Towards Dialectical Digital Modernity: Reflections on David Chandler's Chapter

Christian Fuchs

1. Introduction

David Chandler's chapter studies changes of onto-epistemology and govern-ance in the age of digitality and Big Data. He argues that the logic of dual-ism, reductionism, linear causation and mechanic determinism has advanced problems of society and is unable to give a proper response to the world's com-plexity. The implication is that we need a different kind of onto-epistemology that moves beyond dualism and enables new forms of governing society and the digital. David Chandler argues in this volume that the 'ontopolitical as-sumptions of digital governance can be usefully grasped in terms of actor net-work theory', and in this context he is particularly interested in Bruno Latour's works and new materialist theories in general, including the works of Donna Haraway and others. David Chandler says that these approaches allow us to move beyond dualism and to conceive the world and the digital as being

How to cite this book chapter:
Fuchs, C. 2019. Beyond Big Data Capitalism, Towards Dialectical Digital Modernity: Reflections on David Chandler's Chapter. In: Chandler, D. and Fuchs, C. (eds.) *Digital Objects, Digital Subjects: Interdisciplinary Perspectives on Capitalism, Labour and Politics in the Age of Big Data*. Pp. 43–51. London: University of Westminster Press. DOI: https://doi.org/10.16997/book29.c. License: CC-BY-NC-ND 4.0

co-relational, instead of as dualistic and based on linear causality. Big Data would be part of new correlational machines of sensing and seeing the world that have resulted in new forms of digital governance focusing on co-relation and correlation.

David Chandler's general approach is to search for and analyse onto-epistemologies that go, or claim to go, beyond dualism. He is in this context particularly interested in complexity theory and resilience studies. '[E]mergent or general complexity [...] appears to be the leading contender as an alternative ontological vision of the world' (Chandler 2014, 51). '[R]esilience-thinking claims to have the solution to the apparent conundrum of governing without assumptions of Cartesian certainty or Newtonian necessity' (Chandler 2014, 63).

2. (Post-)Modernity and (Post-)Modernism

I certainly agree that the dualist logic of subject/object, culture/nature, humans/technology, mind/body, society/economy, communication/work, reproduction/production, and so on, is a key aspect of an instrumental reason that has backfired and created global problems that society is not easily able to govern. But I am not convinced that it is theoretically feasible to term instrumental reason and dualism 'modernist binary understandings', 'modernist understandings of the world' or 'modernist divisions', and to characterise the alternative as 'non-modern ontologies' and post-epistemology.

The implication of such a terminology is that the alternative to modernity is either premodernity or postmodernity. A premodern onto-epistemology, as advanced for example by Martin Heidegger, often ends up in techno-pessimism that rejects any form of advanced technology use. For example, Heidegger saw newspapers, electronic communication and public transport as inauthentic forms of modernism that should be abolished (see Fuchs 2015). The other option, indicated for example by the term post-epistemology, is to see the alternative in a form of postmodernity.

Questioning binaries and determinism is certainly a feature of the works of postmodern thinkers such as Latour, Haraway, Lyotard, Baudrillard, Derrida, and Deleuze and Guattari. In postmodern thought, there is a stress on chance instead of design, deconstruction instead of totality, absence instead of presence, networks instead of hierarchies, indeterminacy instead of determinacy, immanence instead of transcendence, and so on. (See Table 1.1. in Harvey 1989, 43).

'[B]reaking through dualism appears to be the key to new materialism' and postmodern thought (Dolphin and van der Tuin 2012, 97). These approaches advance 'a monist perspective' (Dolphin and van der Tuin 2012, 85) that involves not only the flat ontology advocated by Chandler and others, but also what could be characterised as a new collapsism that collapses human/non-human, society/technology, the human/the machine, class/non-class binaries into one. Posthumanism collapses the human and the non-human and humanoid robots into the posthuman cyborg. Bruno Latour's Actor Network Theory collapses technology and society into the actant as the social. Deep Ecology and animal liberation theory collapse nature and society into an undifferentiated whole. Postmodernism collapses class/non-class into identity, and culture/ economy into culture. The consequence is that postmodernism has not just tried to displace and purge Marxist humanism from the academic world over the past decades, but has also been the ideology of capitalism's regime of flexible accumulation (Harvey 1989). There is a 'connection between this postmodernist burst and the image-making of Ronald Reagan, the attempt to deconstruct traditional institutions of working-class power (the trade unions and the political parties of the left), the masking of the social effects of the economic politics of privilege, ought to be evident enough' (Harvey 1989, 336). The danger of postmodern approaches is that proclaiming the 'farewell to modernity' can advance 'counter-Enlightenment in the garb of post-Enlightenment' (Habermas 1990, 5).

3. Dialectical Modernity

I agree with David Chandler that we need to move beyond dualist logic and analyse the world as a complex, dynamic whole. But postmodern thought lacks the necessary power of differentiation. Modernity is not the same as capitalism, instrumental reason and liberalism. Assuming the identity of these phenomena overlooks that modernity is in itself contradictory and contains the seeds of, and potentials for, post-capitalism.

Modernity is the project that aims at using knowledge 'for the pursuit of human emancipation and the enrichment of daily life' (Harvey 1989, 12). The type of modernity that is based on dualism, reductionism, mechanistic causality, positivism, instrumental reason, calculability, and determinism has backfired as a negative dialectic of the Enlightenment (Horkheimer and Adorno 1944/2002) and created a history of modern catastrophes.

But modernity is not just domination from above, but also manifests through hegemony as domination from below as well as resistance. This resistance to instrumental reason does not stand outside modernity but constitutes an alternative modernity. An alternative project can be based on the antagonistic features of modernity. Jürgen Habermas (1990) and Frederic Jameson (1991) agree that modernity is therefore incomplete. For Jameson (1991, 309-10), this means that postmodernity is more modern than modernity, whereas Habermas argues for a different, alternative modern project. Critical, dialectical modernity is an alternative to capitalist, instrumental modernity. Modernity is an unfinished project, because it lacks certainty and finitude and always remains open and developing. Modernity is always unfinished because it is an open, contradictory, dynamic societal formation.

I find the tradition of Hegelian and humanist Marxism a much more feasible approach than postmodernism. Postmodernists have often tried to present humanist and Hegelian Marxism as being part of the dualist tradition. But in reality, such versions of Marxism have advanced the onto-epistemology of dialectical modernity, in which categories and phenomena are identical and non-identical at the same time, posing a contradictory logic out of which dynamics, complexity and open development emerge. Hegel characterises the emergence of complexity and new properties as *Aufhebung* (sublation) taking place in an event, where contradictions (negations) are negated. Hegel describes the dialectical process as an open system of the encapsulated construction of triangles, so that a contradiction is sublated into a new emergent property that is itself part of a contradictory relation that constitutes the base of a new triangle that comes about through a further sublation, and so on. 'Something becomes an other, but the other is itself a something, so it likewise becomes an other, and so on ad infinitum' (Hegel 1830, §93). The logic of dialectical modernity is therefore complex, open and fractal in nature (see http://www.hegel.net/en/e-poster.htm; Fuchs 2003; 2004; 2008; Fuchs and Schlemm 2005). Dialectical modernity consists of different organisational levels that are constituted by encapsulated dialectical triangles that develop dynamically. Each triangle is a dialectic of subject and object. The more one zooms into this fractal dialectic, the more dynamic the system is. At its inner level there is constant change. The more one zooms out, the more continuity you will find. This encapsulated triangle structure is based on a dialectic of continuity and inner change/discontinuity. Human practice and praxis is the activity that produces society's dialectic and the changes at different organisational levels of this dialectic (Marcuse 1941a). It is an unsubstantiated prejudice often labelled against Hegelianism and Hegelian Marxism that they advance closure and determinism. Concepts of complexity theory such as emergence and bifurcation points can be seen as a manifestation of Hegelian dialectical logic and its principles such as *Aufhebung*, the negation of the negation, and the turn from quantity into new qualities (Fuchs 2003; 2008).

There are different ways of overcoming dualist logic. Postmodernism is one way, Hegelian humanist Marxism another. The two act as dialectical conversational poles. In some cases, they sublate each other and productively fuse into a new emergent whole – as is the case with the book you are holding in your hands or reading on your screen.

The dualisms of instrumental reason are at the foundation of capitalist domination that in a negative dialectic again and again turns against itself and so destroys capitalism's promises and produces crises and societal problems. Instrumental reason is the attempt to make society undialectical and one-dimensional. We never know when a major crisis will emerge, but we can be certain that as long as society is based on instrumental reason, sooner or later such a crisis will appear (Fuchs 2004). Immanuel Wallerstein has combined Marxist crisis theory and complexity theory, arguing that:

> The modern world-system in which we are living, which is that of a capitalist world-economy, is currently in precisely such a crisis, and has been for a while now. This crisis may go on another twenty-five to fifty years. Since one central feature of such a transitional period is that we face wild oscillations of all those structures and processes we have come to know as an inherent part of the existing world-system, we find that our short-term expectations are necessarily quite unstable. This instability can lead to considerable anxiety and therefore violence as people try to preserve acquired privileges and hierarchical rank in a very unstable situation. In general, this process can lead to social conflicts that take a quite unpleasant form (Wallerstein 2004, 77).

Wolfgang Streeck (2016) argues that the long phase of the complex world crisis that Wallerstein describes has resulted in a catastrophic crisis of capitalism. He says that capitalism's contradictions are exploding and that the system can no longer defer the crisis into the future by buying time. Streeck (12) confirms Wallerstein's analysis that capitalism has 'entered a period of deep *indeterminacy* – a period in which unexpected things *can* happen any time'. Streeck goes on to argue that we have entered a phase of prolonged chaos that he calls the interregnum – 'no new world system equilibrium à la Wallerstein, but a prolonged period of social entropy, or disorder' (13), in which social structures and institutions dissolve and leave society's 'members alone' (36), and the logic of the survival of the fittest rules. Streeck's position is in contrast to Wallerstein's somewhat defeatist. He sees the logic of indeterminacy as resulting in societal doom and gloom without a way out. Michael Hardt and Toni Negri (2017, 202) note that for Streeck 'all antagonistic subjects capable of challenging capitalist rule have now disappeared'.

In contrast to Streeck, Wallerstein sees uncertainty as a new principle of hope that should motivate political movements to attempt the impossible in pursuance of establishing a new system. Such optimism is based on the fact that the outcome of praxis is undetermined in bifurcation points and can intensify in unpredictable manners. Wallerstein implicitly advances a new notion of praxis that operates on the basis of relative chance, dialectical logic, and dialectical indeterminacy. 'The period of transition from one system to another is a period of great struggle, of great uncertainty, and of great questioning about the structures of knowledge. [...] And we must finally figure out how we can act in the present so that it is likely to go in the direction we prefer' (Wallerstein 2004, 89–90). Praxis faces uncertainty, but it is also the attempt to increase the likelihood of certain preferable options at bifurcation points.

4. Big Data Capitalism's Solutionism

Computing is embedded into the crises that have emerged from capitalism's contradictions. And arguably, it has to some degree made the occurrence of crises and catastrophes even more likely. Algorithmic trading, for example, has intensified the likelihood of financial crises. Together with the general logic of fictitious capital underpinning financial derivatives, it has made financial markets more unpredictable. User-generated fake news and fake online attention are forms of a semi-automatic online politics that uses social media bots and artificial intelligence. In the world of Big Data, it has become more difficult to discern which actions are initiated by humans and which by bots and algorithms. The conjunction of algorithmic politics and right-wing extremist ideology has increased the uncertainty and unpredictability of politics. Not many people thought that Donald Trump would become US president, but the polls' models of prediction failed: it was precisely this conjunction that won Trump the election (Fuchs 2018).

Big Data has not moved us towards dialectical modernity, but has rather tended to deepen the logic of mechanic determinism, reductionism and dualism, and the division of mental and manual labour that Alfred Sohn-Rethel (1978) considers characteristic of class societies, particularly capitalist ones. In contemporary capitalism, Big Data has been embedded into what Evgeny Morozov (2013) calls technological solutionism. Digital solutionism is based on the logic *to save everything, click here*. It assumes that digital technologies make society completely controllable, steerable and governable, and therefore provide a fix for global problems, economic and political crises, terrorism, crime and so forth.

The logic of technological solutionism is not new. It is a capitalist logic that Horkheimer (2004) called instrumental reason and Marcuse (1941b) technological rationality. Digital solutionism intensified and accelerated after the 9/11 attacks. Unable to respond to political complexity, governments advanced the solutionist ideology that large-scale data and online surveillance can predict, prevent and control terrorism and organised crime. The logic of determinism was thereby further extended and intensified. The surveillance society combines surveillance ideology, the surveillance state and surveillance capitalism (Trottier and Fuchs 2015). The rise of Big Data has added a new dimension to digital solutionism, advancing Big Data solutionism, which is the idea that Big Data sets can control, solve and overcome economic and political crises. Big Data capitalism does not overcome, but instead deepens the logic of dualism, determinism and linearity. It is an intensification of instrumental reason that has created new qualities of domination and exploitation. So for example, 'techniques and ideologies of Big Data make another appearance, promising that a greater, deeper analysis of data about past crimes, combined with sophisticated algorithms, can predict – and prevent – future ones. This is a practice known as "predictive policing", and even though it is just a few years old, many tout

it as a revolution in how police work is done. It is the epitome of solutionism'
(Morozov 2013, 182).

David Chandler hints at such a critique of Big Data solutionism when at the
very end of his chapter he argues, drawing on Giorgio Agamben, that digital and
Big Data governance can 'be seen to be thoroughly depoliticizing, as the tasks
of governance are discursively derived "empirically" from the world, rather than
from human actors as subjects'. The end of the story turns back against the main
thread of the story, which in a discursive logic typical for David's writings, creates
an openness and uncertainty regarding the whole story itself.

5. Towards Dialectical Digital Modernity

The escalation of the antagonisms inherent in capitalism's instrumental reason
has intensified the complexity, unpredictability and uncertainty of societal development. This phase of the deep economic, political and legitimation crisis
coincides with the rise of Big Data capitalism. Big Data technologies promise
to create certainty in a highly uncertain world, yet through their logic of digital
solutionism they exacerbate the crises. But pointing this out does not mean
that we should abolish digital technologies and revert to pre-modern technologies. It is also no way forward to try to create radically new postmodern technologies that completely break with the technologies we have. The digital technologies
we have are internally antagonistic. They advance solutionism and domination,
yet at the same time they contain new potentials for cooperation and liberation.
The point is that capitalism, class, power structures, domination and exploitation
have never allowed society and technology to become fully dialectical.

Again and again, modernity turns against itself and destroys its own potentials, calling forth catastrophes and crises. The point is then to shape technology and society differently and dialectically, so that digital objects and digital
subjects are no longer separated but, based on the logic of dialectical modernity, form a differentiated, complex unity in diversity. Our societal and digital
future is uncertain. But this does not mean that technology can determine or
compute the future. That society is complex, dynamic, open, non-linear, unpredictable and dialectical is an impetus for praxis as political hope that aims
at transforming the whole by perpetuating the system and trying to increase
the likelihood of certain potential development paths of our societal and digital
future. Such a future is not pre- or postmodern, but an alternative, dialectical
(digital) modernity that realises its own potentials. It is the revolt against capitalism in general, and the transcendence and sublation of digital capitalism in
particular. Such a society will also transform and sublate today's digital technologies, which means that it will abolish destructive technologies and technological qualities, preserve technologies of cooperation, reconstruct existing
technologies and create new dialectical technologies that transcend the logic of
instrumental reason.

References

Chandler, David. 2014. 'Beyond Neoliberalism: Resilience, the New Art of Governing Complexity.' *Resilience* 2 (1): 47–63.

Dolphijn, Rick and Iris van der Tuin. 2012. *New Materialism: Interviews & Cartographies*. Ann Arbor, MI: Open Humanities Press.

Fuchs, Christian. 2018. *Digital Demagogue. Authoritarian Capitalism in the Age of Trump and Twitter*. London: Pluto.

Fuchs, Christian. 2015. 'Martin Heidegger's Anti-Semitism: Philosophy of Technology and the Media in the Light of the Black Notebooks.' *tripleC: Communication, Capitalism & Critique* 13 (1): 55–78.

Fuchs, Christian. 2008. *Internet and Society: Social Theory in the Information Age*. New York, NY: Routledge.

Fuchs, Christian. 2004. 'The Antagonistic Self-Organization of Modern Society.' *Studies in Political Economy* 73: 183–209.

Fuchs, Christian. 2003. 'The Self-Organization of Matter.' *Nature, Society, and Thought* 16 (3) 281–313.

Fuchs, Christian and Annette Schlemm. 2005. 'The Self-Organisation of Society. Human Strategies in Complexity'. *Social Science Research Network*, Research Paper No. 16. Available at: http://ssrn.com/abstract=385284 (accessed 14 May 2018)

Habermas, Jürgen. 1990. *The Philosophical Discourse of Modernity*. Cambridge: Polity.

Hardt, Michael and Antonio Negri. 2017. *Assembly*. Oxford: Oxford University Press.

Harvey, David. 1989. *The Condition of Postmodernity: An Enquiry into the Origins of Cultural Change*. Oxford: Blackwell.

Hegel, Georg Wilhelm Friedrich. 1830. *The Encyclopaedia Logic (With the Zusätze)*, translated by Theodore F. Geraets, Wallis A. Suchting and Henry S. Harris. Indianapolis, IN: Hackett.

Horkheimer, Max. 2004. *Eclipse of Reason*. London: Continuum.

Horkheimer, Max and Theodor W. Adorno. 2002. *Dialectic of Enlightenment*. Stanford, CA: Stanford University Press.

Jameson, Frederic. 1991. *Postmodernism, or, The Cultural Logic of Late Capitalism*. Durham, NC: Duke University Press.

Marcuse, Herbert. 1941a. *Reason and Revolution. Hegel and the Rise of Social Theory*. Amherst, NY: Humanity Books.

Marcuse, Herbert. 1941b. 'Some Social Implications of Modern Technology.' In *Technology, War and Fascism: Collected Papers of Herbert Marcuse, Volume 1*, ed. Douglas Kellner, 39–65. London: Routledge.

Morozov, Evgeny. 2013. *To Save Everything, Click Here*. New York, NY: PublicAffairs.

Sohn-Rethel, Alfred. 1978. *Intellectual and Manual Labour: A Critique of Epistemology*. London: Macmillan.

Streeck, Wolfgang. 2016. *How Will Capitalism End? Essays on a Failing System*. London: Verso.

Trottier, Daniel and Christian Fuchs (eds.). 2015. *Social Media, Politics, and the State: Protests, Revolutions, Riots, Crime and Policing in the Age of Facebook, Twitter and YouTube*. New York, NY: Routledge.

Wallerstein, Immanuel. 2004. *World-Systems Analysis: An Introduction*. Durham, NC: Duke University Press.

CHAPTER 4

Karl Marx in the Age of Big Data Capitalism

Christian Fuchs

1. Introduction

Computers operate based on digital data. They convert information into streams of bits (zeros and ones) in order to store, process and transmit it. The logic of capitalist and bureaucratic administration has driven the development of computing. As a result of political-economic interests and needs and technological development, the volume, velocity and variety of data (Kitchin 2014, 68) have increased to a degree where quantity turns into a new quality. In short, we have seen the rise of Big Data. Increasingly, algorithms and digital machines are generating, collecting, storing, processing and assessing Big Data, and making decisions that sideline humans in economic, political and everyday life. This development has resulted in the emergence of a specific quality of digital capitalism: Big Data capitalism. Big Data capitalism requires that we assess how thought systems, forms of knowledge, political economy, governmentalities, materialities, infrastructures, practices, organisations, institutions, subjectivities, spaces (Kitchin 2014, 25), temporalities, and discourses and ideologies are

How to cite this book chapter:
Fuchs, C. 2019. Karl Marx in the Age of Big Data Capitalism. In: Chandler, D. and Fuchs, C. (eds.) *Digital Objects, Digital Subjects: Interdisciplinary Perspectives on Capitalism, Labour and Politics in the Age of Big Data*. Pp. 53–71. London: University of Westminster Press. DOI: https://doi.org/10.16997/book29.d. License: CC-BY-NC-ND 4.0

changing. The task of this chapter is to show how Karl Marx's theory matters for understanding and criticising Big Data capitalism's political economy.

The chapter first engages with why Marx matters today (Section 2), then introduces the notion of Big Data capitalism (Section 3), analyses digital labour's contradictions (Section 4), digital capitalism's crisis (Section 5), ideology today (Section 6), and concludes with some thoughts on alternatives to Big Data capitalism (Section 7).

2. Why Marx Matters Today

There are at least fourteen reasons why we need Marx today. As long as capitalism and class exist, his analysis remains absolutely crucial for understanding, criticising and changing society. Just as Marx analysed capitalism and society as historical, based on a dialectic of continuity and change, so his own approach is also subject to such a dialectic.

A first aspect of Marx's works that we need today is the analysis of the commodity form and capital. 'The wealth of societies in which the capitalist mode of production prevails appears as an "immense collection of commodities"' (Marx 1867/1976, 125). Neoliberal capitalism has resulted in the commodification of almost everything, including communication. In the world of digital commodities, we find the commodification of digital labour–power, digital content, digital technologies and online audiences. Information is non-rivalrous in consumption (as a resource, information is not used up when consumed). It is difficult to exclude others from access. Information can be easily copied. It is therefore an antagonistic commodity type that can be turned into a commodity, but that can also relatively easily resist commodification and be turned into a common good. Digital capitalism faces a contradiction between digital capital and the digital commons.

Second, Marx can inform our understanding of the exploitation of labour today. 'The proletarian is merely a machine for the production of surplus-value, the capitalist too, is merely a machine for the transformation of this surplus-value into surplus capital' (Marx 1867/1976, 742). The proletariat today takes on new forms, including precarious labour – such as the unpaid labour of interns and shadow workers, whose labour may not resemble more familiar forms of labour, but which nevertheless produces value – and workers in the international division of digital labour (IDDL) (Fuchs 2014; 2015).

Third, Marx analysed the globalisation of capitalism. Capital 'must nestle everywhere, settle everywhere, establish connexions everywhere' (Marx and Engels 1848/2010, 486–487). Since the late twentieth century, capitalism has become more global in comparison to its Fordist development stage, and has entered a new stage of imperialist capitalism.

Fourth, Marx matters today for understanding capitalism's crisis. He stressed that the capitalist economy and capitalist society's contradictions again and again produce crises. 'The fact that the movement of capitalist society is full of contradictions impresses itself most strikingly on the practical bourgeois in the changes of the periodic cycle through which modern industry passes, the summit of which is the general crisis' (Marx 1867/1976, 103).

Fifth, Marx's stress on the dialectic of technology and society helps us to understand contemporary technologies. He worked out this analysis in *Capital Vol. 1*'s Chapter 15 (*Machinery and Large-Scale Industry*) and *The Grundrisse*'s *Fragment on Machines* (Fuchs 2016c, Chapter 15 & appendix 2). Marx's analysis of technology is based on Hegel's dialectic of essence and existence. In the machinery chapter in *Capital Vol. 1*, he argues that 'machinery in itself shortens the hours of labour, but when employed by capital it lengthens them; [...] in itself it lightens labour, but when employed by capital it heightens its intensity; [...] in itself it is a victory of man over the forces of nature but in the hands of capital it makes man the slave of those forces; [...] in itself it increases the wealth of the producers, but in the hands of capital it makes them into paupers (Marx 1867/1976, 568–569). Figure 1 visualises some of the dialectics of technology in capitalism.

Sixth, Marx's analysis of the general intellect matters today. The notion of general intellect indicates that 'general social knowledge has become a direct force of production' (Marx 1857/1858/1973, 706). Universal labour produces the general intellect. 'Universal labour is all scientific work, all discovery and invention' (Marx 1894/1981, 199). Knowledge, communication and technology thereby become common goods.

Marx anticipated the emergence of the information economy. The capitalist profit imperative creates the need to increase productivity. Technological

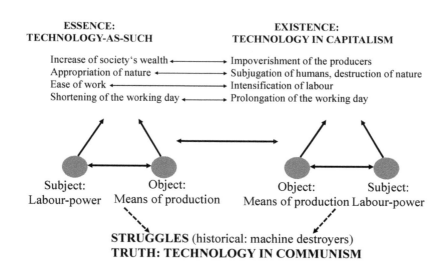

Figure 1: Marx's analysis of the dialectics of technology in capitalism.

progress progressively increases the relevance of science, technology and knowledge in production. At one stage of capitalist development, quantity turns into the new quality of informational capitalism.

Seventh, Marx matters for understanding digital capitalism. In the *Grundrisse*, he conceptually anticipated the Internet, arguing that institutions 'emerge whereby each individual can acquire information about the activity of all others and attempt to adjust his own accordingly […] Interconnections […] [are established] through the mails, telegraphs etc.' (Marx 1857/1858/1973, 161). This formulation anticipates the Internet as a global system of information, communication and social networking.

The eighth dimension of Marx's works that is crucial for understanding contemporary capitalism's political economy is the antagonism between productive forces and relations of production. 'The contradiction between the general social power into which capital develops and the private power of the individual capitalists over these social conditions of production develops ever more blatantly, while this development also contains the solution to this situation, in that it simultaneously raises the conditions of production into general, communal, social conditions. This transformation is brought about by the development of the productive forces under capitalist production and by the manner and form in which this development is accomplished' (Marx 1894/1981, 373).

In digital capitalism, there is an antagonism between networked digital productive forces and class relations. Networked digital technologies create new forms of commodification and exploitation, and new problems for accumulation. However, digital information as a commodity also has features that resist commodification. Digital capitalism is grounded in an antagonism between digital commons and digital commodities. Digitalisation shapes, and is shaped by, the 'antagonism between the social cooperation of the proletariat and the (economic and political) command of capital' (Negri 2017, 25).

The ninth reason why Marx matters today is that his theory, along with various approaches in the tradition of Marxist theory, allows us to ground a critical theory of communication and language (Fuchs 2016a, 2016c). He says, for example, that 'Peter only relates to himself as a man through his relation to another man, Paul, in whom he recognizes his likeness' (Marx 1867/1976, 144). Communication is the way that humans relate to each other symbolically in order to interpret the social world, make sense of each other, construct joint meaning and transform social reality. Lukács' *Ontology of Social Being*, Raymond Williams's cultural materialism, and other Marxist theory approaches allow the construction of dialectical critical theories of communication that pose alternatives to Habermas's dualist theory of communication and Luhmann's instrumental systems theory of communication (Fuchs 2016a).

Tenth, Marx makes us think about the notions of the base and the superstructure, which pose the question of how to reflect on the role of communication in capitalism. Marx reminds us that it is crucial to think about how economy/

society, work/communication, capital/power, labour/ideology, body/mind, physical/mental work, production/reproduction are related. The dualities of society and capitalism are simultaneously identical and non-identical. They form dialectics. Raymond Williams has 'solved' the base/superstructure problem in a materialist and dialectical manner. Williams (1977) argues that there is an identical economic moment of all social systems and subsystems of society: humans produce sociality through the communication processes. Communication is the process of the social production and reproduction of sociality and society. At the same time, each societal subsystem and social system also features a non-identical moment: these are emergent, non-economic qualities.

Ideology and fetishism form the eleventh dimension of Marx's relevance today. In commodity fetishism, the 'definite social relation between men themselves' assumes 'the fantastic form of a relation between things' (Marx 1867/1976, 165). In political fetishism, the nation is a fetish: nationalism is the ideology that constructs fictive ethnicity (Balibar and Wallerstein 1991, 49, 96–100). In the realm of the media, advertising fetishises the commodity form and ideological tabloid journalism fetishises domination and exploitation. We have experienced the rise of new nationalisms and xenophobia directed against immigrant workers and refugees. Nationalism distracts from class contradiction by portraying capital and labour as non-contradictory and united in 'one nation'. Marx, in his analysis of authoritarianism, coined the notion of 'Bonapartism' that entails the ideological project 'to unite all classes by reviving for all the chimera of national glory' (Marx 1871/2010, 330).

Twelfth, Marx is a role model for critical journalism and critical public intellectuals. Thirteenth, Marx stresses the importance of social struggles for a better society. His humanism was practical. He speaks of 'the categorical imperative to overthrow all relations in which man is a debased, enslaved, forsaken, despicable being' (Marx 1844/2010, 182). Today, there are discussions about the role of digital technologies as tools for social struggle. Practical humanism is related to the fourteenth dimension: Marx foregrounds the need for alternatives, namely social systems that transcend the profit imperative and focus on human cooperation.

3. Big Data Capitalism

The rise of Big Data capitalism stands in a broader societal – economic, political, ideological – context. In the economy, we have experienced the neoliberal commodification and privatisation of (almost) everything, including data and communication(s). In the political system, a surveillance-industrial complex has emerged. This political–economic complex has been accompanied by an ideology that promotes the idea that surveillance technologies will prevent and detect crime and terrorism. Surveillance ideology has helped create a culture of control, fearmongering, scapegoating, suspicion, competition and individualisation.

The collection, storage, control and analysis of Big Data stands in the context of political-economic interests that aim at the economic and political control and targeting of individuals. They are targeted as consumers and as potential terrorists and criminals. Edward Snowden has revealed the existence of a global communication surveillance system that secret services use to monitor and analyse communication flows in real time. The companies implicated in this surveillance system include AOL, Apple, Facebook, Google/YouTube, Microsoft, Paltalk, Skype/Microsoft, and Yahoo!.

C. Wright Mills argued in 1956 that there is an 'ever-increasing interlocking of economic, military, and political structures' (Mills 1956, 8). In this context, he spoke of the existence of a power elite. Today, the power elite makes use of a surveillance-industrial complex in order to exert control. In the surveillance-industrial complex, users make data public or semi-public on the Internet. Corporations commodify this data and users' activities to accumulate capital. Secret services and the police aim to gain access to the Big Data flows in order to securitise data and society. In doing so, they partly outsource surveillance to private security services, for whom surveillance is a profitable business. The NSA subcontracts surveillance to more than 2,000 private security companies. In the surveillance-industrial complex, surveillance capital and the surveillance state are fused together. Big Data means Big Brother power and big capitalist business.

Marx speaks of surveillance labour as how the 'work of directing, superintending and adjusting becomes one of the functions of capital' (1867/1976, 448). Foucault, who states that 'we live in a society where panopticism reigns' (Foucault 1994, 58), goes on to argue that the 'panoptic mechanism basically involves putting someone in the center – an eye, a gaze, a principle of surveillance – who will be able to make its sovereignty function over all the individuals [placed] within this machine of power' (Foucault 2007, 93–94). The surveillance-industrial complex shows that around 'the concept of power […], Marx and Foucault coincide' (Negri 2017, 184) and that 'capital and power […] become unified […] and constitute a chiasm between two contradictory actions that are forced to join together and yet are intransitive' (Negri 2017, 12).

Some scholars in the field of surveillance studies claim that surveillance has become post-panoptic, and that digital surveillance has not resulted in a digital panopticon. They stress that surveillance has become decentralised, and argue that Foucault's panopticism should be theoretically smashed. Such approaches disregard the emergence of surveillance technologies' decentralised centralism. Decentralised surveillance technologies collect Big Data in many places. This data is networked and controlled by two central panoptic collective actors: capital and the state.

Big Data capitalism and algorithmic power could result in the world turning into a huge shopping mall in which humans are targeted by ads almost everywhere, and where commercial logic colonises society. In the world of Big Data, algorithms that use instrumental logic for calculating human needs can automate human activities and decision-making in order to meet those needs. The problem is that algorithms and machines do not have ethics and morals. Data commodification means the emergence of new social inequalities, and intensifies the exploitative tendencies of the Internet. Big Data entails a 'Big Data divide' (Andrejevic 2014) in respect to data ownership and data control. Big Data also features new types of rational discrimination and cumulative disadvantage (Gandy 2009). Big Data's logic of digital positivism overlooks that technology is no fix for social and political problems. Big Data surveillance's logic of categorical suspicions abolishes the presumption of innocence; instead, a presumption of guilt emerges, based on the principle 'You're a criminal and terrorist until proven innocent'– this despite the fact that most terrorists do not communicate their plans online. Günther Anders (1980, 221) stresses surveillance's totalitarian character: 'As surveillance devices are used routinely, the main premise of totalitarianism is already created and, with it, totalitarianism itself'. Surveillance and surveillance ideology are often embedded into law and order politics, resulting in fascist potentials being advanced. Big Data means that massive amounts of data are stored on servers and transmitted over the Internet, which under the current energy regime means an exacerbation of environmental problems. E-waste is being dumped into developing countries.

In 2012, data centres used electricity equalling the output of 30 nuclear power plants (Glanz 2012). Running the Internet accounts for about 10% of all electricity produced globally (De Decker 2015). Outsourcing data and software use, and crowdsourcing labour to the Cloud, can increase unemployment and precarious labour.

The rise of Big Data in research has resulted in new approaches such as computational social science and digital humanities. These are forms of Big Data positivism. Such research obtains large amounts of funding, and is obsessed with quantification. Big Data analytics entails the danger that the 'convergence of social-scientific methods toward those of the natural sciences is itself the child of a society that reifies people' (Pollock and Adorno 2011, 20). Big Data positivism is an 'immunization of the [Internet] sciences against philosophy' (Habermas 1971, 67). Computer science colonises the social sciences and humanities. The danger is that computational social science brings about the death of theory and roots out critical qualitative, theory-oriented research. Georg Lukács (1971, 88) warned in this context that mathematics and positivism reduce qualities to quantities that 'can be calculated' and reify human activities. The digital machine that organises Big Data creates a new form of reification that destroys qualities, dialectics, critique and non-instrumental action. We need alternatives to Big Data analytics; we need critical digital media studies instead of computational social science.

4. Digital Labour's Contradictions

In 2016, Google made profits of US$19.5 billion and was the world's twenty-seventh largest transnational company. In the same year, Facebook registered profits of US$ 10.2 billion and was the world's 188th largest global corporation[1]. But not all social media corporations are as profitable. Twitter reported losses of US$ 456.9 million in 2016[2]. In the US economy, the share of profits in the GDP was 24.8% and the share of the wage sum 53.1% (Fuchs 2015, Chapter 5). Facebook's wage share (i.e. the share of the wages it paid from its revenues) was 11.0%. Why are the company's wages so low in comparison to the total US economy, and its profits so high? The social media economy is based on the exploitation of users' unpaid digital labour. Marx (1885/1978) described the capital accumulation cycle in the form $M - C .. P .. C' - M'$. In the social media economy, this cycle changes into $M - C .. P1 (v1, c) .. P2 (v2=0) .. C' - M'$. The platforms are products (P1) that are not commodities, but a 'free lunch'. Personal data (P2) is a commodity generated by users' digital labour that is sold to advertising clients who are enabled to present targeted ads on users' profiles.

Toni Negri argues that we need 'a new theory of labour value as a common potentiality' (Negri 2017, 29). Marx stresses that technological and capitalist development has resulted in the emergence of the collective worker: 'With the progressive accentuation of the cooperative character of the labour process, there necessarily occurs a progressive extension of the concept of productive labour, and of the concept of the bearer of that labour, the productive worker. In order to work productively, it is no longer necessary for the individual himself to put his hand to the object; it is sufficient for him to be an organ of the collective labourer, and to perform any one of its subordinate functions' (Marx 1867, 643–644). Marx also speaks of the collective worker as an 'aggregate worker': 'An ever increasing number of types of labour are included in the immediate concept of productive labour, and those who perform it are classed as productive workers, workers directly exploited by capital and subordinated to its process of production and expansion' (Marx 1867, 1039).

Marx argues that the cooperative character of labour requires an extension of the concept of productive labour. It is not just the unpaid labour time connected to wage-labour that is exploited and productive, but also the unwaged labour that contributes to the production of commodities and capital accumulation. Expressions of this insight have been made independently of each other in, among other fields, autonomist theory, socialist feminism, and audience labour theory.

In autonomist theory, the concept of the social worker, 'a new working class' that is 'now extended throughout the entire span of production and reproduction' (Negri 1988, 209) creates an 'interconnection between productive labour and the labour of reproduction' (Negri 1988, 209). Socialist feminism stresses orthodox Marxism's common assumption that 'women in domestic labor are not productive' (Dalla Costa and James 1973, 31). This assumption denies 'women's potential *social* power' (6). Domestic and reproductive labour 'produces not merely use values, but is essential to the production of surplus value' (31). It produces a commodity 'unique to capitalism: the living human being – 'the labourer himself' (6). Dallas Smythe's audience labour theory argues that audiences of advertising-funded media are unpaid audience workers conducting labour that creates an audience commodity. The 'material reality under monopoly capitalism is that all non-sleeping time of most of the population is work time. [...] Of the off-the-job work time, the largest single block is time of the audiences, which is sold to advertisers' (Smythe 1977, 3).

Digital labour on commercial social media is in certain respects different from audience labour on commercial broadcast media. Social media uses targeted advertising that is based on a Big Data commodity. Audiences make meanings out of content. Social media users also create social relations, content and data. Users' digital labour on social media is based on prosumption (productive consumption), constant surveillance of personal data, targeted and personalised advertising, predictive algorithms and algorithmic auctions. Facebook and Google are the world's largest advertising agencies utilizing such labour and the harvesting of the Big Data commodity of audience information.

Digital labour is alienated digital work organised in an international division of digital labour that entails the slave-labour of miners extracting minerals that form the physical foundations of digital tools, Taylorist assemblage labour, e-waste labour, software engineering, various forms of online labour, users' labour, and so on. (Fuchs 2014, 2015, 2017b).

In the United States, the average reproductive labour time per week per person was 44.53 hours in 2015 (for detailed data on the following calculations, see Fuchs 2017a). The average annual hours of wage-labour were 1,778. 232 billion total hours of wage-labour were performed, of which 113 billion were surplus labour hours, and 119 billion were necessary labour time. The traditional rate of surplus value is calculated as the relationship of the surplus labour time of wage labour (s) to its necessary labour time (v). In monetary terms, it is calculated as the relationship of total annual profits (p) to total wages (v). In the case of the US economy, the traditional rate of surplus value in 2015 was 0.942. But the classical formula does not take unwaged labour into account. According to statistics, 579 billion hours of unpaid reproductive labour hours were performed in the USA in 2015. The organic composition of labour (the corrected rate of surplus value) can be calculated in the following formula (Fuchs 2017a):

Organic composition of labour =

$$\frac{\textit{Wage labour's unpaid labour time + Unwaged labour's unpaid labour time}}{\textit{Paid labour time}}$$

Such an effect of capital is not just to increase wage labour's unpaid labour time, but also to increase the unpaid labour time of unwaged labour. Reproductive labour is productive because it is a form of unpaid, surplus labour time. Capital exploits wage labour and reproductive labour. The organic composition of labour in the USA in 2015 was (579 + 113) / 119 = 5.8 (Fuchs 2017a). Per waged hour of labour, 5.8 hours of unpaid reproductive labour were performed. Reproductive labour made up 83.7% of all unpaid labour time, and 16.3% of labour's surplus labour time.

In the same year of 2015, the average reproductive labour time in the USA was 44.5 hours per week per person. On average, 4.9 hours were spent watching advertisements, and 12.4 hours using commercial social media (Fuchs 2017a). Audience labour and users' digital labour constitute significant shares of reproductive labour time. Moreover, reproductive labour is gendered. In the US, women on average conduct 60% of reproductive labour (Fuchs 2017a). Facebook's algorithm uses racist and sexist logic segmenting market data using crude distinctions, generalisations and assumptions. Users in poorer countries, and poorer users in general, are treated as being less valuable consumers, i.e. as being less likely to purchase advertised commodities when clicking on ads (Fuchs 2017a).

Digital capitalism deepens exploitation while at the same time creating new foundations for autonomous realms that transcend the logic of capitalism. It creates the foundations for new relations of production that germinate within capitalism. With digitalisation, 'the commodity becomes increasingly transparent' (Negri 2017, 25) and 'there begin to emerge sectors that are increasingly sensitive to the autonomy of social cooperation, to the self-valorisation of proletarian subjects' (Negri 2017, 25). Digital capitalism is founded on an antagonism between the digital commodity created by digital labour on the one side, and the digital commons on the other.

Open access publishing is a good example of digital antagonism. Open access is to a certain degree a reaction to the high profit rates of academic publishing corporations, and the monopolisation tendencies in this industry. In 2016, Reed Elsevier achieved a net profit before tax of £1.934 billion and revenues of £6.895 billion. Thus its profit rate was 1.934/(6.895–1.934) = 39.0%. In the same year, Springer made profits of €296.4 million and revenues of €833.1 million. Its profit rate was 296.4/(833.1–296.4) = 55.2%[3]. Such profit rates are extremely high. They are achieved by the sale of expensive bundles of article subscriptions, databases and journals to libraries, and content access to individuals.

Universities and the academic system use public funding to a significant degree. Academic knowledge is a commons that is 'brought about partly by the cooperation of men now living, but partly also by building on earlier work' (Marx 1894, 199). Monopoly capital privatises and commodifies the academic commons. Open access is a counter-reaction to monopoly publishing capital.

'Open access (OA) literature is digital, online, free of charge, and free of most copyright and licensing restrictions' (Suber 2012, 4). The majority of open access projects are non-profit and run by academics or academic associations. A minority of open access projects are for-profit. They achieve profits by article and book processing charges (APCs, BPCs). Authors pay high publishing charges (sometimes thousands of €/£/$) for publication of their works. APCs and BPCs are like going to a restaurant where you pay for being allowed to cook and eat your own meal. In the Diamond Open Access Model, not-for-profit, non-commercial organisations, associations or networks publish material that is made available online in digital format, is free of charge for readers and authors and does not allow commercial and for-profit re-use (Fuchs and Sandoval 2013).

On March 20, 2017, the Directory of Open Access Journals listed 9,423 open access journals. 1,866 of these used the CC-BY-NC-ND licence, 1,328 CC-BY-NC, 522 CC-BY-NC-SA. A total of 3,716 (39.4%) did not allow commercial re-use. 5,134 (54.5%) did not use APCs[4]. These data indicate the existence of digital academic commons that are autonomous of capital.

There is a variety of political positions on open access (Fuchs and Sandoval 2013). The policy and industry perspective argues that 'open access is a great new business model'. The trade union perspective holds that 'open access is constituted by voluntary non-resource projects that destroy the jobs of publishing workers'. The radical open access perspective says that 'non-profit open access requires struggles against capitalist publishing that mobilises resources'.

Radical open access can only work properly by achieving material support in the form of funds from foundations and the public, help from volunteers, universities acting as open access publishing houses, and universities and research councils establishing policies that favour publishing in OA journals.

Lawrence & Wishart (L&W) is the publisher of *Marx and Engels Collected Works*. The Marxists Internet Archive (MIA, https://www.marxists.org) is an open access library of classical Marxist texts, including Marx and Engels's writings. In 2014, a conflict arose between L&W and MIA about whether or not Marx and Engels's works should be available online in open access format.

L&W argued that 'infringement of this copyright has the effect of depriving a small radical publisher of the funds it needs to remain in existence. [...] [MIA] is reproducing the norms and expectations not of the socialist and communist traditions, but of a consumer culture which expects cultural content to be delivered free to consumers, leaving cultural workers such as publishers, editors and writers unpaid'. MIA disagreed, and said that the Internet '*is a new media for information*. Specifically, the history of the workers movement should in fact be 'free.' [...] The point of any communist publishing house, which the MIA lives up to, is to assure the widest distribution of these works, not, again, to restrict them. That is the opposite of communist publishing'.

The conflict is one between the digital commons-Left and the copyright-Left. It is an expression of the antagonism between networked digital productive forces and alternative projects' operation within capitalism. Making Marx's and Engels's works available online is not simply an economic, but also a political question. These works should be accessible online without payment for political reasons. Wide accessibility is a good foundation for making Marxist ideas a material force, and the Internet is an excellent medium for this task. Because of the 'Streisand effect', copyright enforcement is counterproductive on the Internet. Competition between left-wing projects is self-defeating. The Left should concentrate on cooperation that challenges for-profit corporate publishing. Cooperation could also entail the struggle for and development of alternative forms of funding (public funding, donation models, charges for commercial re-use, making works available open access once a specific level of donations is achieved, and so forth).

5. Digital Capitalism's Crisis

Paul Mason (2015) connects Marx's theorem of the Law of the Tendency of the Rate of Profit to Fall, Schumpeter's long wave theory, and the analysis of digital media. The result is a breakdown theory of capitalism, a new version of Henryk Grossmann's breakdown theory of capitalism in the digital age. Grossmann (1992, 119) argued that 'the capitalist system inevitably breaks down due to the relative decline in the mass of profit' (Grossmann 1992, 119). Mason writes that information technology results in zero marginal costs of information. As a result, the rate of profit would fall until capitalism breaks down and post-capitalism emerges (see Fuchs 2016b).

Such analyses disregard how class struggle influences the rate of profit and surplus value. The Marxian rate of profit is calculated the following way:

$$Rate\ of\ profit = \frac{s}{c + v}$$

s ... surplus value, profit
c ... constant capital
v ... variable capital

By dividing the fraction's enumerator and the denominator by variable capital, we get the following transformation:

$$Rate\ of\ profit = \frac{\frac{s}{v}}{\frac{c}{v} + 1}$$

s/v ... Rate of surplus value
c/v ... Organic composition of capital

The rate of surplus value measures the intensity of labour exploitation, and the organic composition of capital measures the technology and resource intensity of production. Since the 1970s, computerisation has had ambivalent, contradictory effects on the rate of profit. It has increased both the organic composition of capital and the rate of surplus value. These two ratios have contradictory effects on the rate of profit. A rise of the organic composition decreases the rate of profit, a rise of the rate of surplus value increases it. Capitalist class struggle against the working class has decreased the wage share (the share of wages in the GDP). The total effect has been that in many countries, and at the global level, the general profit rate has fluctuated. The fluctuation has encouraged financialisation, which increases the volatility of the economy. The relative drop in wages has resulted in an increase of household debts and a weakening of purchasing power. The 2008 crisis was an expression of neoliberal finance capitalism's accumulated contradictions. Ever since, the economic crisis in many parts of the world has also turned into an ideological crisis of liberalism, giving rise to authoritarian ideology, nationalism and, to a certain degree, authoritarian capitalism.

6. Ideology Today

Commodity producers do not relate to each other directly. Exchange value means the exchange of particular quantities of commodities in the form x commodity A = y commodity B (e.g. 1 banana = £0.15). The social relations of production are not visible in the produced and purchased commodities, which is what Marx terms commodity fetishism. A commodity is 'a social hieroglyphic' (Marx 1867/1976, 167). 'The emergence and diffusion of ideologies appears as the general characteristic of class societies' (Lukács 1986, 405, translation from German).

Nationalism is an ideology that treats the nation as a political fetish object. Nationalism veils class relations. It presents capital and labour as united by a (fictive) national interest. '[N]ation and nationhood are central components of fascist political discourse' (Woodley 2010, 185). '[F]ascism must *itself* be understood as a political commodity: [...] fetishization of communal identities which conceal the true nature of the commodity' (Woodley 2010, 17–18). Fascism is 'a populist ideology which seeks, through a mythology of unity and identity, to project a 'common instinctual fate' (uniform social status) between bourgeois and proletarianized groups, eliding the reality of social distinction in differentiated class societies' (Woodley 2010, 17). Capitalist crisis can produce fascism, which is why we cannot rule out that the new nationalisms will turn into new fascisms and a new world war.

Figure 2 shows a model of right-wing authoritarianism (see Fuchs 2018 for more details). This model uses authoritarian leadership, nationalism, the friend/enemy-scheme, patriarchy and militarism to distract attention from class structures.

Donald Trump is a typical example of right-wing authoritarianism. He is not just a politician and a capitalist, but also a media personality who uses Twitter and reality TV to spread ideology and brand himself. Social media is a realm

Figure 2: A model of right-wing authoritarianism.

of symbolic, communicative and ideological struggle. In the information age, the realm of online communication is an important domain of class struggle. With more than 30 million followers on Twitter, more than 20 million likes on Facebook, and more than 7 million followers on Instagram, Trump uses social media as a tool for spreading right-wing authoritarian ideology.

On 5 September 2016, US-Americans celebrated Labor Day. Trump posted a video on Twitter and Facebook, in which he addressed American workers (see

http://twitter.com/realDonaldTrump/statuses/772798809508372480, https://t.
co/RNl7cfzkmN). In the video, he says:

> The American worker built the foundation for the country we love and
> have today. But the American worker is getting crushed. Bad trade deals
> like NAFTA and TPP, such high and inexcusable taxes and fees on small
> businesses that employ so many good people. This Labor Day, let's honour
> our American workers, the men and women who proudly keep America
> working. They are the absolute best anywhere in the world. There is
> nobody like 'em. I'm ready to make America work again and to make
> America great again. That's what we are going to do on November 8.

This passage contains several ideological elements. It presents US-Americans
as a mythic collective. It constructs a unified national interest of capital and
labour. He presents the US nation as being under attack by foreign enemies.
Social conflict is portrayed as a conflict between nations, which deflects attention from class conflicts. Trump's use of Twitter makes evident how nationalism works as political fetishism. Rosa Luxemburg argues in this context that
nationalism is a 'misty veil' that 'conceals in every case a definite historical content' (Luxemburg 1976, 135). '[B]lood, community, folk, are devices for hiding
the real constellation of power' (Neumann 1994/2009, 464).

7. Alternatives

The twenty-first century is reaching a historical bifurcation point characterised by turbulence and an intensification of political polarisation. The future is
uncertain. We could head towards hyper-neoliberal capitalism, authoritarian
capitalism, fascism, the total destruction of the Earth and the annihilation of
humanity in a nuclear world war, or an alternative society of the commons.

In their tetraology *Empire, Multitude, Commonwealth, Assembly* Michael
Hardt and Antonio Negri (2000, 2004, 2009, 2017) describe a stage in capitalist development in which global capital (the Empire) faces a new working
class (the multitude). New common potentials emerge that could become the
foundation of a society of the commons, the commonwealth. Commonwealth
is, however, just one possible outcome of twenty-first-century society's development. There could also be negative developments such as a new fascism or
the end of humanity. Which option prevails depends on how social struggles
will develop. The truth of what Rosa Luxemburg wrote in 1918 has today again
become very urgent: 'In this hour, socialism is the only salvation for humanity'
(Luxemburg 1971, 367).

Right-wing authoritarian movements advance particularistic politics of nature, of the social, and of communication. In respect to nature, they fetishise national identity, the family, and conservative traditions, and see immigrants and
global identity as environmental problems disrupting the nation. Right-wing

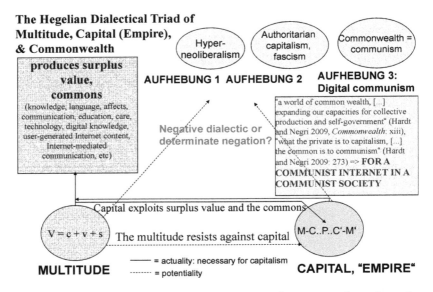

Figure 3: The contradictory development options of society resulting from the antagonism between the capitalist empire and the multitude.

authoritarianism's social policies are a combination of neoliberal ideology that propagates survival of the fittest and a national-'socialist' rhetoric that reserves welfare for the autochthonous, national population. In respect to communication, right-wing authoritarianism combines conservative techno-pessimism that sees traditional values under threat on the Internet and argues in favour of law-and-order control of the Internet, with a neoliberal techno-capitalist ideology that celebrates the corporate media and the corporate Internet.

Progressive forces are today often split and fragmented. The commons consist of social, natural and communicative commons. All of these commons have become increasingly commodified and privatised. Left-wing parties and movements predominantly struggle for the defence of the social commons, Green movements for the defence of the natural commons, and tech movements for the defence of the communicative commons. In order to challenge right-wing authoritarianism, progressive forces should learn from the failures of the Left in the 1920s when various factions, especially Social Democrats and Communists, opposed each other and did not unite against the fascist threat. We need a united political front against right-wing authoritarianism where the defence of the social, natural and communicative commons becomes one movement associated with one progressive party and an associated movement. Social democracy needs a renewal in the form of social democracy 2.0; a movement for socialist democracy and democratic socialism. To the convergence of capital and right-wing authoritarianism, the only feasible answer is left-wing convergence into an internationalist progressive movement (see Figure 4).

Figure 4: Political convergence of movements for the commons.

In respect of communications, the perspective of the commons-based society stands for the advancement of the digital commons, platform cooperatives, and a public-service Internet. Democratic communications shape and are shaped by 'an association of free men, working with the means of production held in common, and expending their many different forms of labour-power in full self-awareness as one single social labour force' (Marx 1867, 171).

Franz L. Neumann (1957, 294–295) stresses that in situations of crisis, it is important that academics act as critical public intellectuals: 'Hence there remains for us as citizens of the university and of the state the dual offensive on anxiety and for liberty: that of education and that of politics. Politics, again, should be a dual thing for us: the penetration of the subject matter of our academic discipline with the problems of politics […] and the taking of positions on political questions. If we are serious about the humanization of politics; if we wish to prevent a demagogue from using anxiety and apathy, then we – as teachers and students – must not be silent. […] We must speak and write'.

Notes

[1] Data sources: SEC-filings for the year 2016, forms 10-K (Alphabet, Facebook); Forbes 2000 list of the world's biggest public companies.
[2] Data source: Twitter SEC-filing, form 10-K for the year 2016.
[3] Data source: Reed Elsevier Investor Relations, Annual Reports, https://www.relx.com/investors/annual-reports
[4] For a significant share, there was no data available, which means that the actual rate of journals not using APCs was actually higher.

References

Andrejevic, Mark. 2014. 'The Big Data Divide.' *International Journal of Communication* 8: 1673–1689.

Anders, Günther. 1980. *Die Antiquiertheit des Menschen 2. Über die Zerstörung des Lebens im Zeitalter der dritten industriellen Revolution.* Munich: C. H. Beck.

Balibar, Étienne and Immanuel Wallerstein. 1991. *Race, Nation, Class.* London: Verso.

Dalla Costa, Maria and Selma James. 1973. *The Power of Women and the Subversion of the Community.* 2nd ed. Bristol: Falling Wall Press.

De Decker, Kris. 2015. 'Why We Need a Speed Limit for the Internet.' *Low-Tech Magazine,* 19 October 2015.

Foucault, Michel. 2007. *Security, Territory, Population.* Basingstoke: Palgrave.

Foucault, Michel. 1994. *Power.* New York, NY: New Press.

Fuchs, Christian. 2018. *Digital Demagogue: Authoritarian Capitalism in the Age of Trump and Twitter.* London: Pluto.

Fuchs, Christian. 2017a. 'Capitalism, Patriarchy, Slavery, and Racism in the Age of Digital Capitalism and Digital Labour.' *Critical Sociology* 43, DOI: https://doi.org/10.1177/0896920517691108.

Fuchs, Christian. 2017b. *Social Media: A Critical Introduction.* London: Sage. 2nd edition.

Fuchs, Christian. 2016a. *Critical Theory of Communication.* London: University of Westminster Press.

Fuchs, Christian. 2016b. 'Henryk Grossmann 2.0: A Critique of Paul Mason's Book 'PostCapitalism: A Guide to Our Future'.' *tripleC: Communication, Capitalism & Critique* 14 (1): 232–243.

Fuchs, Christian. 2016c. *Reading Marx in the Information Age. A Media and Communication Studies Perspective on 'Capital Volume I'.* New York: Routledge.

Fuchs, Christian. 2015. *Culture and Economy in the Age of Social Media.* New York: Routledge.

Fuchs, Christian. 2014. *Digital Labour and Karl Marx.* New York: Routledge.

Fuchs, Christian and Marisol Sandoval. 2013. 'The Diamond Model of Open Access Publishing: Why Policy Makers, Scholars, Universities, Libraries, Labour Unions and the Publishing World Need to Take Non-Commercial, Non-Profit Open Access Serious. *tripleC: Communication, Capitalism and Critique* 11 (2): 428–443.

Gandy, Oscar H. 2009. *Coming to Terms with Chance: Engaging Rational Discrimination and Cumulative Disadvantage.* Farnham, UK: Ashgate.

Glanz, James. 2012. 'Power, Pollution and the Internet.' *New York Times Online,* 22 September 2012.

Grossmann, Henryk. 1992. *The Law of Accumulation and Breakdown of the Capitalist System. Being also a Theory of Crises.* London: Pluto.

Habermas, Jürgen. 1971. *Knowledge and Human Interest.* Boston, MA: Beacon Press.

Hardt, Michael and Antonio Negri. 2000. *Empire*. Cambridge, MA: Harvard U.

Hardt, Michael and Antonio Negri. 2004. *Multitude: War and Democracy in the Age of Empire*. London: Penguin.

Hardt, Michael and Antonio Negri. 2009. *Commonwealth*. Cambridge, MA: The Belknap Press.

Hardt, Michael and Antonio Negri. 2017. *Assembly*. Oxford: Oxford University Press.

Kitchin, Rob. 2014. *The Data Revolution*. London: Sage.

Lukács, Georg. 1971. *History and Class Consciousness*. Cambridge, MA: MIT Press.

Lukács, Georg. 1986. *Zur Ontologie des gesellschaftlichen Seins*. Zweiter Halbband. Georg Lukács Werke, Band 14. Darmstadt: Luchterhand.

Luxemburg, Rosa. 1971. *Selected Political Writings of Rosa Luxemburg*. New York, NY: Monthly Review Press.

Marx, Karl. 1894/1981. *Capital Volume III*. London: Penguin.

Marx, Karl. 1885/1978. *Capital Volume II*. London: Penguin.

Marx, Karl. 1871/2010. The Civil War in France. In *Marx and Engels Collected Works (MECW), Volume 22*, 30–59. New York: International Publishers.

Marx, Karl. 1867/1976. *Capital Volume I*. London: Penguin.

Marx, Karl. 1857/1858/1973. *The Grundrisse*. London: Penguin.

Marx, Karl. 1844/2010. 'Contribution to the Critique of Hegel's Philosophy of Law.' Introduction. In *MECW, Volume 3*, 175–206

Marx, Karl and Friedrich Engels. 1848/2010. 'Manifesto of the Communist Party.' In *MECW, Volume 6*, 477–519. New York: International Publishers.

Mason, Paul. 2015. *PostCapitalism: A Guide to Our Future*. London: Allen Lane.

Mills, Charles Wright. 1956. *The Power Elite*. Oxford: Oxford University Press.

Negri, Antonio. 2017. *Marx and Foucault*. Cambridge: Polity.

Negri, Antonio. 1988. *Revolution Retrieved: Selected Writings on Marx, Keynes, Capitalist Crisis and New Social Subjects 1967–83*. London: Red Notes.

Neumann, Franz. 1957/2017. 'Anxiety and Politics'. *tripleC: Communication, Capitalism and Critique* 15 (2): 612-636

Neumann, Franz. 1944/2009. *Behemoth: The Structure and Practice of National Socialism, 1933–1944*. Chicago, IL: Ivan R. Dee.

Pollock, Friedrich and Theodor W. Adorno. 2011. *Group Experiment and Other Writings*. Cambridge, MA: Harvard University Press.

Smythe, Dallas W. 1977. 'Communications: Blindspot of Western Marxism.' *Canadian Journal of Political and Social Theory* 1 (3): 1–27.

Suber, Peter. 2012. *Open Access*. Cambridge, MA: The MIT Press.

Williams, Raymond. 1977. *Marxism and Literature*. Oxford: Oxford University Press.

Woodley, Daniel. 2010. *Fascism and Political Theory: Critical Perspectives on Fascist Ideology*. Abingdon: Routledge.

CHAPTER 5

What is at Stake in the Critique of Big Data? Reflections on Christian Fuchs's Chapter

David Chandler

1. Introduction

In his chapter, Christian sets out a powerful overall analytic of the relevance of a critical theory approach for understanding and engaging with the context and alternatives to Big Data capitalism. Here, Big Data plays a fundamental role in the surveillance society, which potentially constitutes a new form of totalitarian controlling ideology: 'The digital machine that organises Big Data creates a new form of reification that destroys qualities, dialectics, critique, and non-instrumental action.' Against this dehumanising ideological control, Christian argues that we require a Marxist critical humanism to put the human back at the centre of the world. I shall not engage with this chapter at the formal level of Marxist argumentation, and have a lot of time for Marxist critical humanism; where I differ from Christian is as to the relevance of these ideas in our contemporary moment and their usefulness as a way of engaging with and critiquing 'Big Data capitalism'.

How to cite this book chapter:
Chandler, D. 2019. What is at Stake in the Critique of Big Data? Reflections on Christian Fuchs's Chapter. In: Chandler, D. and Fuchs, C. (eds.) *Digital Objects, Digital Subjects: Interdisciplinary Perspectives on Capitalism, Labour and Politics in the Age of Big Data.* Pp. 73–79. London: University of Westminster Press. DOI: https://doi.org/10.16997/book29.e. License: CC-BY-NC-ND 4.0

2. Critical Marxism

Firstly, I would like to put Marxist critical humanism into context. Perhaps the classic critical work on the problem of digitalisation in capitalist modernity is the one that established the reputation of critical theory and the Frankfurt School: Theodor Adorno and Max Horkheimer's *Dialectic of Enlightenment* (1947). For Adorno and Horkheimer, modernist thinking was dehumanising: the Enlightenment was problematic in denaturalising the world and the human, and in reducing, universalising, and equalising the experience of the world. For critical theory, the Enlightenment was problematic and oppressive rather than liberating. The Enlightenment view of reason contained its own seeds of destruction. Enlightenment was seen as a history of the separation of humanity from nature through the power of rationality – based on the subsumption of difference to the rule of equivalences. This cast the Enlightenment as a totalitarian project with no inherent limits (Adorno and Horkheimer, 1997: 6), very much along the lines of the presentation in Christian's chapter. So, for Adorno and Horkheimer: 'Bourgeois society is ruled by equivalence. It makes the dissimilar comparable by reducing it to abstract quantities' (1997, 7).

> What was different is equalized. That is the verdict which critically determines the limits of possible experience. The identity of everything with everything else is paid for in that nothing may at the same time be identical with itself. Enlightenment… excises the incommensurable… [u]nder the levelling domination of abstraction. (1997, 12–13)

For this Marxist critical theory approach, rather than being a process of progress and reason, the Enlightenment was seen as a machinic, deadening, reduction of the world and of the human individual. For Adorno and Horkheimer, this was a world with no possibility of an outside, as everything was subsumed into equivalence through conceptual abstraction (1997, 16). In other words, this meant that nothing new could ever occur as 'the process is always decided from the start'; even unknown values could still be put into equations, dissolving the world into mathematics. Everything new was thus already predetermined, producing a world of 'knowledge without hope' (Adorno and Horkheimer 1997, 27–28). Similarly, as Christian argues, Big Data capitalism subsumes everything to the laws of market equivalences or to algorithmic surveillance.

Thus, for this line of critique, the (pre-)history of Big Data capitalism is a long one, starting with the earliest attempts to bring the outside under control through the extension of equivalence, Mauss's gift economy and pre-modern magic and sacrifice being early versions of the exchange of non-equivalents (Mauss 2002). The performative exchange of non-equivalents then led to the reflection of equivalence in thought – conceptual subsumption – through the ratio, i.e. the proportion of conceptual equivalence. Under capitalism this process was formalised further, in both practice and thought, through money

as the universal equivalent of exchange and through the abstractions of democracy and universal rights, and the development of science and the digital
(Sohn-Rethel 1978). The modernist project was thus one of the extension of the
imaginary of rationalist and bureaucratic control, and with this development
came an intensification of subject/object and human/nature binaries.

Christian's chapter is a true inheritor of the critical project in its portrayal of
Big Data capitalism as the apogee of all that is dehumanising and problematic
in modernity – from peak capitalism, to peak fascism to peak dehumanisation. The Enlightenment project thus apparently reaches its peak in Big Data
capitalism with the equivalence of everything through the market and digital
algorithmic regulation. Critical theory and its inheritors seek to respond by
challenging the dominance of this modernist ideology; questioning hierarchies
of nationalism and fascism established upon the basis of the cuts and distinctions of Eurocentric or modernist forms of reason, with their growing distinction between Man and Nature; and seeking to contest the telos of progress and
the rationalising grounds upon which equivalences and subsumptions of difference are established. For Christian,

> Big Data capitalism and algorithmic power could result in the world
> turning into a huge shopping mall in which humans are targeted by ads
> almost everywhere, and where commercial logic colonises society. In
> the world of Big Data, algorithms that use instrumental logic for calcu-
> lating decisions and human needs can automate human activities and
> decisions. The problem is that algorithms and machines do not have
> ethics and morals.

For this critical Marxist approach, it is the political struggle against Enlightenment or modernist thought – which lacks a soul, its machinic totalitarianism being without 'ethics and morals' – which is the emancipatory aspect of
the contradictions and crises seen to be manifested in Big Data capitalism. The
critical approach seeks to resolve the problem by bringing man back to the
world and rejecting the homogenising, commodifying and calculating gaze of
modernity.

3. Big Data and Modernity

However, the difficulty of squeezing the critique of Big Data into the critical
theory denunciation of modernity is that critical theory approaches are forced
to evade the non-modern epistemological claims of Big Data and the modes of
governance they call forth (focusing on Big Data as an ultra-modernist framing
of politics and governance). One aspect that stands out about Christian's 'left'
critique of Big Data is precisely the way he ties it to a long history of modernist drives and understandings in order to maintain a critical approach and the

relevance of Karl Marx. While critical of modernist drives to equalise, commodify and control, Christian makes little distinction between Big Data as a methodological approach and Big Data as just another word for more of the same. Where this breaks down is that it reduces Big Data to data. I would suggest that while the modernist positivist assumptions of data have their dangers and problems (see Hacking, 1990), Big Data is claiming something different (and is thereby differently dangerous and differently problematic). This difference reflects the ways politics and governance have changed over the last century, highlighting the collapse of confidence in modernist and Enlightenment approaches.

Big Data claims to provide an insight into the 'actual', rather than working at a level of modernist knowledge based upon representation or abstraction. Big Data capitalism as a mode of governance relies on an 'actualist' or surface view of appearances, rather than focusing on causal relations, where continuities over time are crucial to establishing trajectories of linear and non-linear causation. Thus Big Data claims to transform our everyday reality and our immediate relation to the things around us. It claims to do this by making visible unseen but existing processes and effects through 'datafication'. The process of Big Data 'seeing' through datafication is straightforward in theory, although work on perfecting the correlations required is more complicated. For example, if search terms put into Google correlated with processes in the world, such as shopping intentions, flu outbreaks or increases in conflict tensions, then these processes in the world could be 'datafied' i.e. they could be seen indirectly through the algorithmic detection and analysis of these terms via Google. This would work in the same way as a canary in the coalmine to sense poisonous gases, as a real-time indicator enabling responses.

It is this 'datafication' of everyday life that leads to a very specific form of its 'commodification', and it is this process which lies at the heart of the relational interactions at the core of what we are calling 'Big Data capitalism': a way of accessing reality by bringing interactions and relationships to the surface and making them visible, readable and thereby governable, rather than seeking to understand hidden laws of causality (Anderson 2008; Cukier and Mayer-Schöenberger 2013). Big Data as a mode of governance thus relies upon increasing the field of vision through the power of correlation. This ability to 'see' better through datafication is imagined to allow the modulation or regulation of processes and thereby to perpetually 'ward off', 'cancel out' or 'absorb' crises or breakdowns (Wakefield and Braun 2018). In this imaginary, it would be as if time slowed down, making a shock or crisis governable. For a contemporary example, as I write, see how this can be applied to slow and perceive the 'blur of colour' of horse racing (Wood 2017).

Hopefully, the analogy of 'seeing' the present in slow-motion enables us to grasp that datafication is not about problem-solving through reduction and abstraction, but about the particular and the analogue, sensing changes in context which would otherwise go unseen. So, while data can be understood as digital – in terms of binary code – the world itself becomes more analogue or less differentiated in terms of distinctive properties or essences of objects. Big Data is concerned with the surface of the 'actual', not the ontological nature of being or the processes of emergence in complex causal interactions. The 'knowledge' generated is therefore not something fixed or that can be stored and re-used, but is about 'seeing' the flux or flow of change through mechanisms of correlation. Thus the governance mode of Big Data capitalism is enabled through a different type of 'knowledge', one that is more akin to the translation or interpretation of signs than that of understanding chains of causation (Esposito 2013).

In science and computer sciences, this increase in data gathering possibilities and the development of computational capacity has enabled analysts to talk of a 'fourth paradigm' of knowledge production (beyond theory, experiment and simulation) (Pietsch 2013, 2). Thus Big Data appears to lack certain attributes of the modernist 'production process' of knowledge, and appears as less mediated by subject-centred conceptual apparatuses. As Rob Kitchin highlights, Big Data is unique in that its construction is often not part of a conscious process of knowledge production: the data is often already there, in social media or other electronic processes of data capture, and it is the discovery of correlations which is the key innovation (Kitchin 2014, 2). Thus, it is argued: 'Big Data analytics enables an entirely new epistemological approach for making sense of the world; rather than testing a theory by analysing relevant data, new data analytics seek to gain correlational insights "born from the data"' (Kitchin 2014, 2).

4. Conclusion

This is a point of fundamental importance regarding a critical stance regarding the rise of Big Data. It would appear that, to take a 'left' approach of critique, Big Data has to be seen as a modernist problematic, one that calls forth and intensifies modes of governance of top-down 'command-and-control'. But it is possible to take a different approach, one that engages critically with discourses of Big Data, not because these discourses represent a 'peak' modernist abstraction, but rather on the grounds of an epistemological rejection of modernist claims of causal processes and the potential for the direction and control of human knowledge. Seeing what exists and responding to it is a poor substitute for understanding and being able to apply knowledge to change what exists. Big Data discourses accept the world as it is, and facilitate adaptation to it, reducing the human to any other factor to be modulated and regulated. Rather than follow a modernist approach which artificially exaggerates the divide between human and non-human or subject and object, Big Data approaches seek to bypass these crucial distinctions entirely.

In this respect, the epistemological claims of Big Data and their ontological or metaphysical underpinning reflect the contemporary exhaustion of modernist and Enlightenment thought. In fact, for many critical theorists who lack Christian's critical Marxist approach, the problem of Big Data is precisely that it does not live up to its claims of removing the human from epistemic claims (boyd and Crawford 2012). Rather than critiquing modernity for its 'soullessness' and for man's separation from the world, contemporary critique wishes to take this further. The modernist episteme is critiqued today, not because it is alienating and dehumanising, but from the opposite standpoint that it is too humanist or human-centred. It is for this reason that Christian's chapter goes against the stream of Big Data critique in its demand for the human to be returned to a world of meaning that has been denied it by modernist rationalism and instrumentality.

References

Adorno, Theodor and Max Horkheimer. 1947/1977. *Dialectic of Enlightenment.* London: Verso.

Anderson Chris. 2008. 'The End of Theory: The Data Deluge Makes the Scientific Method Obsolete.' *Wired Magazine* 16 (7): 23 June. Available at: http://archive.wired.com/science/discoveries/magazine/16-07/pb_theory (accessed 14 May 2018).

boyd, danah and Kate Crawford. 2012. 'Critical Questions for Big Data: Provocations for a Cultural, Technological, and Scholarly Phenomenon.' *Information, Communication, and Society* 15 (5): 662–679.

Cukier, Kenneth and Viktor Mayer-Schöenberger. 2013. 'The Rise of Big Data: How It is Changing the Way We Think About the World.' *Foreign Affairs* May/June. Available at: http://m.foreignaffairs.com/articles/139104/kenneth-neil-cukier-and-viktor-mayer-schoenberger/the-rise-of-big-data (accessed 14 May 2018).

Esposito, Elena. 2013. 'Digital Prophecies and Web Intelligence.' In *Privacy, Due Process and the Computational Turn: The Philosophy of Law meets the Philosophy of Technology,* edited by Mireille Hildebrandt and Katja de Vries. Abingdon: Routledge.

Hacking, Ian. 1990. *The Taming of Chance.* Cambridge: Cambridge University Press.

Kitchin, Rob. 2014. 'Big Data, New Epistemologies and Paradigm Shifts.' *Big Data and Society* 1 (1): 1–12.

Mauss, Marcel. 2002. *The Gift: The Form and Reason for Exchange in Archaic Societies.* London: Routledge.

Pietsch, Wolfgang. 2013. 'Big Data: The New Science of Complexity.' 6th Munich-Sydney-Tilburg Conference on Models and Decisions, Munich, 10–12 April 2013, Philsci Archive, University of Pittsburgh. Available at: http://philsci-archive.pitt.edu/9944/ (accessed 14 May 2018).

Sohn-Rethel, Alfred. 1978. *Intellectual and Manual Labour: A Critique of Epistemology*. Atlantic Highlands, NJ: Humanities Press.

Wakefield, Stephanie and Bruce Braun. 2018. 'Oystertecture: Infrastructure, Profanation and the Sacred Figure of the Human.' In *Infrastructure, Environment, and Life in the Anthropocene*, edited by Kregg Hetherington. Durham, NC: Duke University Press.

Wood, Greg. 2017. 'Bookmakers to Embrace "Big Data" to Shift Racing's Betting Landscape.' *The Guardian*, 6 October.

CHAPTER 6

Seeing Like a Cyborg? The Innocence of Posthuman Knowledge

Paul Rekret

1. Introduction

Posing a connection between philosophy and biography is an exercise fraught with predicaments, not least of which is the determinist connection one risks between life and thought.[1] Keeping this proviso in mind, if we can nevertheless assume that ontological statements are somehow associated with the subject positions of their authors, then it bears insisting that assessments of theoretical paradigms not forego analysis of authors' motivations. Appraisals of theory ought not shrink from examining the desires a theory expresses, the cognitive or analytical needs it aims to fulfil, and the reasons it might pursue certain lines of inquiry and not others. Where theory seeks to formulate judgements about its own present, such questions are especially instructive since the political stakes are all the more immediate. It is with this in mind that I'd like to examine what counts among the more prominent delineations of the current epoch: those accounts of the 'posthuman' which look primarily to contemporary technological developments as the basis for articulations of a fundamental

How to cite this book chapter:
Rekret, P. 2019. Seeing Like a Cyborg? The Innocence of Posthuman Knowledge. In: Chandler, D. and Fuchs, C. (eds.) *Digital Objects, Digital Subjects: Interdisciplinary Perspectives on Capitalism, Labour and Politics in the Age of Big Data.* Pp. 81–94. London: University of Westminster Press. DOI: https://doi.org/10.16997/book29.f License: CC-BY-NC-ND 4.0

transformation of existential experience.[2] My choice of focus is motivated by a belief that such theories tend to neglect the entrenched global divisions in access to the rewards, and exposure to the perils, that recent technological advancements imply, along with the continuity of historical structures of inequality this entails. In this context I propose recalling the peculiar conditions from which our conceptions of digital experience are forged, namely contemporary regimes of private property. Not only might this prove valuable for reflection upon the historical horizons of our social theories, but it might also help us to understand the impulses that animate them.

2. Eroding Boundaries

Remaining with the question of history, it is noteworthy that the assembly of theories at issue here cohere around a periodising move. This is a diagnosis of contemporary transformations in subjective experience formulated in terms of the obsolescence of a bounded anthropocentrism that is seen as the hallmark of modern and postmodern philosophising. On this view, ecological crisis is taken to intensify the sense that human existence is entangled with a complex infrastructure, a growing ability to manipulate biological processes at molecular level is taken to challenge distinctions between nature and artifice, while advances in digital knowledge production enable the automation of a growing breadth of cognitive processes. Together these processes are read as evidence against the notion that thought is a discrete property of the human. While transformations at the level of the ecological, biological and digital are seemingly disparate, they are afforded a certain coherence insofar as they coalesce around a figure of 'hybridity', signalling technological mutations of the human species that erode the symbolic binaries constitutive of modern thought. As divisions between the natural and the cultural, the mind and the body, and the human and the technological all grow increasingly difficult to maintain, so too, it follows, do the anthropocentric terms by which social theory tends to operate. The new state of hybridity, the argument goes, has disrupted the modern ideal of an abstract, rational subject, autonomous over and against the world.

Putting the figure of hybridity momentarily aside, it is worth noting that on a theoretical level posthumanism consolidates around what it sees as the exhaustion and inability to respond to the new state of hybridity by an earlier 'linguistic turn' associated with Martin Heidegger, Ludwig Wittgenstein, and more recently, Jacques Derrida and Michel Foucault, amongst others.[3] Needless to say, the poststructuralist critique of the subject holds an important place in theories of the posthuman, but its emphasis upon language or discourse is nevertheless regarded as inadequate for reflecting upon the digital mediations by which thinking is increasingly conditioned. In this regard the posthumanist's line of reasoning is relatively straightforward. The poststructuralist critique of modern philosophy can be characterised by its critique of the epistemic violence wrought upon the world by a subject endowed with the capacity for rational thought who excludes all those 'others' he poses as incapable of autonomous reasoning: women, the mad, the subaltern, animals, and so on.[4] This is an ethical position that, to one degree or another, posthumanist theorists also tend to adopt. Yet they also seek to extend it hyperbolically so that the difference between these standpoints grows rather stark. The poststructuralist gesture is centred on undermining the authority and self-certainty of the subject by dispersing it to the unstable media of his knowledge – whether conceived as discourse, différance, or power/knowledge – which precede him and which he can never master. Pivotal to the posthumanist argument, however, is the claim that even this dispersal remains all too anthropocentric a set of claims insofar as it is centred upon the way *social* constructions condition and mediate subjectivity. Even if poststructuralists posit thought as finite and seek to undermine the mind's mastery over the world, the argument goes, they continue to posit the centrality and ontological autonomy of the *human* as the medium of thought. This further entails giving methodological and political priority to human actors, a consequence which exhibits the persistence of modern thought's anthropocentric hierarchy.

3. The Claim to Hybridity

In what counts as something of an *ur*-text for such assertions, Donna Haraway's 'A Cyborg Manifesto' (1991) looks to technological developments in synthetic biology, bio-informatics, and cybernetics to articulate the 'cyborg' as reflective of an increasingly prevalent hybrid of machine and organism. Haraway's point is that, as the human body is increasingly structured by its connections with cybernetics or with biotechnology, the boundaries definitive of the human are increasingly dislocated. Hybridity thus triumphs as modern dualisms erode. Or, as she writes, '[h]umans are always congeries of things. We are not self-identical' (Haraway 1991, 181). It would not be overstating Haraway's influence to say that the arguments made in 'A Cyborg Manifesto' have been paradigm forming. Indeed, their impact is rivalled only by a book published two years later by the French anthropologist Bruno Latour. While *We Have Never Been Modern* generated parallel, if at times distinct, lines of inquiry, Latour (1993, 2) nevertheless echoes Haraway's central argument when he declares the post-Cold War era to be defined by the 'proliferation of hybrids'. In a further resonance, Latour's opening illustration of such hybridity, the freezing of human embryos, is also drawn from biotechnology. The cryopreserved organism can, for both thinkers, stand in for a broader process whereby hybridity undermines the modern critical projection of clear and distinct ontological zones of what counts as human and what does not.

Despite the undeniably heterogeneous and complex research programmes that Haraway and Latour developed from these basic insights, our concern here is with the widespread adoption of the claim that we inhabit an age of hybridity. The view that the subject has been eroded in the current epoch is an ontological contention that increasingly shapes an expansive theoretical paradigm and is, moreover, often taken as self-evident. But it is worth remarking that this is an odd claim – at least where it implies a relation between ontology and history – for it insinuates that, in general, while existence itself is defined by hybridity, this only becomes self-evident in an epoch where technological change makes its manifestation undeniable. To twist a well-known phrase, history here becomes the midwife of ontology, where the hybrid entities that emerge from bio- and enhancement technologies bear the weight of actualising the ontological assertion that the human never was an integral, autonomous being exercising control over itself or its surroundings in the first place. Yet such a claim so often denotes a move that seeks to rescue technological advancements – which are often the product of destructive capitalist compulsions, if not explicitly militarist impulses – for progressive theoretical ends. It follows that it falls upon the theorist's ontological speculations to salvage and reimagine the technological for emancipatory purposes, a task which can only be accomplished where the deeper truths about existence which these processes harbour can be discerned. It is in this way that the posthumanist can be said to collapse ontological speculation into ethico-political argument, since it is the affirmation of hybridity and concordant critique of anthropocentrism that acts as the starting point for ethical and political thought in this context (Rekret 2016). Besides producing a peculiar oscillation between history and ontology, the critique of anthropocentrism can sometimes effect a sort of theoretical narcissism which places the theorist at the endpoint of an eschatology wherein the true nature of existence is only discernible from the historical instant at which they find themselves.

4. The Head and the Hand

At this point, it is necessary to take a step back to examine the parameters of this figure of hybridity. Putting aside ontological assessments, it is significant that while posthumanist theory's diagnosis of the present is founded upon meticulous consideration of recent social and technological transformations, this tends to come at the expense of an assessment of longer continuities. This is to say that much of what counts as posthumanist theorising tends to forego a thorough accounting of the material conditions for the emergence of the symbolic dualisms (nature/culture, mental/material, mind/body, human/technological) of modernity in the first place.[5] This lacuna invites a survey of the attempts that have been made to provide just such an account. Taking our cue from a critical theoretical tradition concerned with the ways that the emergence of capitalism has mediated our cognitive categories allows us to situate the dualisms in question as inseparable from processes of dispossession and enclosure.

One of the more emphatic versions of such a claim originates in Alfred Schmidt's (1971) proposal that the dualist conception of man and nature be viewed through the prism of the history of a real interaction. Schmidt here reflects a broader field of scholarship that sees the early generalisation of wage labour as conditioning a perception of 'nature' as an object of conscious and planned human interventions. Once labour is separated from its means so that its relation to production is mediated by the wage, any abstract unity between humanity and nature is severed. This entails that capital ultimately reverses the hierarchy between man and nature so that the latter is no longer conceived as an object prevailing over a subject.

Schmidt's fecund insight into the historical conditions for a 'thought' that takes itself as acting autonomous upon the world can inform our analysis further if we bring it to bear on the history of philosophy more directly. In this context, in her history of the gendered and racialised nature of processes of primitive accumulation, Silvia Federici (2004, 138–40) reads Descartes' institution of an ontological division between purely mental and purely physical domains as inseparable from a mechanical view of the body suitable to the ongoing suppression of pre-capitalist forms of community. A reason that posed the body as an 'intelligible' object, as Federici (2004) has it, could subordinate it to uniform and predictable forms of action, that is, to capital's discipline over labour. Moreover, this separation of the mental and the sensuous went hand in hand with a separation of women from the knowledge of reproduction and their consequent constitution as natural reproducers of labour (Federici 2004; Mies 1998; Merchant 1983).

This reading of the relationship of Cartesian thought to the violent history of the origins of capitalism is not far removed from a line of thought in Michel Foucault's (2013, 45–73) *History of Madness*. It is well known that in that book Foucault relates Descartes' *a priori* exclusion of madness from the process of reasonable thought to the seventeenth-century confinement of the homeless and unemployed in asylums as a means of regulating unemployment. At the very least, not unlike Federici, Foucault understands thought's becoming autonomous – and so the foundations of the modern subject – through the lens of anti-capitalist struggle.

A not dissimilar intuition is also apparent in Alfred Sohn-Rethel's (1978) critique of modern epistemology. Putting aside his main lines of argument around the material sources of cognitive abstraction, in Sohn-Rethel's reading of Descartes the latter's positing of the world-in-itself as *res extensa* is tied directly to the limitations and frictions of capitalist control over artisanal production.[6] Here the modern philosophical project of grounding thought as autonomous from the world is related to the bourgeois need for a mental labour autonomous from material labour. That is, the separation of the head and the hand is viewed as crucial to capital's ultimate control over artisanry through automation insofar as the latter is grounded upon a form of knowledge whose sources are not sensuous (Sohn-Rethel 1978, 113, 122, 141).

How can these accounts of the history of the mental and sensual dimensions of experience inform our understanding of contemporary concepts of hybridity? At a minimum, they suggest that the conditions for what Latour calls the 'modern constitution' are inseparable from processes associated with capital accumulation. This further implies that any argument for the suspension of the boundary between them must confront the ways by which capital mediates thought. In the balance is a question of whether thought seeks to avow the objective constraints upon it, and whether or not it owns up to the dimensions of historical experience that condition it. Admittedly, this may initially appear a dubious claim, inasmuch as the variety of posthumanist scholarship of interest here is explicitly a politically progressive enterprise centred upon a critique of patriarchy, racial hierarchy, capitalism, and especially the pursuit of profits and war, to which technological innovation tends to be directed.[7] But the resignation from an assessment of capital's role in the history of the mediation of our relation to the world not only puts into question contemporary historico-ontological assessments regarding the state of hybridity, it also poses still further questions. For if capital's mediations are patently not only still present, but more intensive and expansive than ever, then it bears interrogating whether the divisions and separations to which capital compels existence might not in fact be fully reflected in the notion of hybridity.

5. Ontological Surgery

It is undeniable that technological developments, whether frozen embryos, the coding of DNA, or the manipulation of biological processes at the level of molecular fragments, erode or undermine boundaries between what is natural and what is artificial. In this sense, the posthumanist's historical narrative grasps an increasingly prevalent aspect of contemporary experience. But it does so at an ontological level that may not offer a picture faithful to the full breadth of contemporary experience. To follow a line of argument proposed by Marilyn Strathern (2005), when examined at another level of practice, namely the epistemology that dominates contemporary regimes of intellectual property – constituting as this does the grounds of much of our knowledge of the world – the boundaries or dualisms in question here are not only seen not to have been breached, but the boundary between them grows ever wider. Strathern's point is that, insofar as contemporary bio-technological and technological development is governed by an expansive process of the enclosure of knowledge, it is premised upon a conceptual relation to the world conceived as a collection of 'natural' phenomena standing apart from an autonomous will that modifies it in order to produce 'inventions'.[8]

Not unlike claims outlined by theorists of posthumanism, and Haraway (1991) especially, Strathern diagnoses a 'natural' world that is increasingly understood and related to as information or code. But whereas the posthumanist takes this as evidence of an erosion of the boundary of the natural and tech-nological, from Strathern's perspective it entails the opposite. For not only are 'natural' sources of information transformed into products that come to be governed by intellectual property laws, but these in turn enable the 'dis-covery' of further potential sources of information, and accordingly, facilitate renewed conceptions of natural processes awaiting transformation and com-modification by the labour of the human mind. What is considered 'nature' thus not only grows in scope, but the more it does so, the more extensively is it consumed by an intellectual property regime which makes scientific insights the objects of privatisation (Strathern 2005, 102). This is the case even where agreements such as the 1992 Convention on Biological Diversity seek to pro-tect indigenous practices from patenting by recognising that knowledge may be embedded in practice. Such well-intentioned safeguards do not represent a challenge to contemporary processes of capital accumulation, but instead merely entail, Strathern writes elsewhere, intellectual property's inclusion or 'hybrid embrace' of pre-modern (or alter-modern) practices as further forms of exclusive resources (Strathern 1999, 184).[9] It turns out that even sensuous forms of knowledge can be abstracted as objects in the current paradigm. Or, to put it starkly, everything is a commodity or else commodifiable, and this is a stance grounded upon a view of nature as an abstract object manipulated and transformed by autonomous subjects.

Its worth repeating that theorists of posthumanism are not naive to the role that private property plays in knowledge production, nor are they blind to the role that capital plays in the production of the contemporary hybridities they observe.[10] Capitalism is often explicitly considered inseparable from new understandings of life or humanity. However, returning to Strathern's argu-ment, this belies a view of processes associated with capitalism through the lens of ontological speculation. That is, capitalism is said to produce new fields of 'difference', new 'complexity', or non-human or de-individualising abstract conceptions of life (Haraway 1997, 57; Braidotti 2013, 60).[11] These sorts of for-mulations, whereby capital is viewed as reflecting a deeper ontological state of hybridity, overlook what legal theorist Sheila Jasanoff (2012) calls, echoing Strathern, the 'ontological surgery' that intellectual property operates upon the world, and that moreover, is conditional of the boundary erosions in question. This omission refracts our earlier claims about the history of capitalism inso-far as the posthumanist neglect of the *a priori* epistemic distinction between nature and artifice is reflected in these theories' bounded view of the subject's relation to the contemporary world.

These claims are partly echoed by other, longstanding criticisms which view valorisations of 'cyborg', hybridity, or posthuman, as disavowing global divi-sions of labour. The argument here is that bodies hinged to assembly lines, farm tools or brooms have long functioned as machines in exchange for a wage, as indentured labour, or as chattel slaves (Wilkie 2011; Fernandez & Malik 2002). To point this out not only puts in question the posthumanist periodisation for an epoch of hybridity, but also the sorts of ethics that it tends to occasion. For one thing, it implies that the human relation to the machine has a more complex history than recent attempts to valorise or criticise technological change tend to allow. For another, it suggests that posthumanism offers a politics that speaks to the experience of the consumers of digital and bio-technological advances but not necessarily to its producers. Where consuming subjects might have the meaning and boundaries of their agency troubled by technological change, this refers to a form of autonomy that has never been the property of most of the world's people in the first place. The latter claim is put into stark relief when we consider, as Jessop (2007) shows, that 97% of the world's patents and 80% of R&D funding are located in OECD countries. In this light, contemporary technoscience amounts to the reorganisation of the separation of an autonomous mind exercising authority over a world conceived as separate and natural. Such a division of labour implies the pervasiveness of the modern dualism of mind and world, albeit reorganised by contemporary technoscience upon a global, neo-colonial scale.

6. The Innocence of Knowledge

The insights garnered from Schmidt, Federici, Sohn-Rethel and others imply that when we understand the division of the mental and material or social and natural in purely ontological terms, we overlook the imbrications of social struggle to which our own categories are subjected. Ironically, this tendency to indifference, on the part of ontological speculation, to the material genesis of its categories reproduces the very Cartesian binary it claims has been eroded. This is so not only insofar as the modern dualisms are seen to persist in practice where ongoing global processes of the enclosure of ideas and inventions are concerned, but it further implies, as I have claimed elsewhere, a view of the mind as innocent of any imbrication with those practices (Rekret 2016).

   With this in mind, I'd like to return to my opening query to pose the question of what function this posthuman economy of the innocence of knowledge serves. What sort of desire does the now widespread ontological claim to the obsolescence of the modern dualisms in the face of an expansive state of hybridity express? For it's worth pointing out that claims to innocence are themselves never innocent, but always deployed in particular contexts and to particular purposes. To what end then does intellectual postponement of an interrogation of thought's material conditions by an ontology of hybridity function? One conduit to these questions involves looking back to what is likely the initial modern formulation of epistemic innocence in John Locke's theory of knowledge. Reflecting on Locke's epistemology will permit us to glimpse the way in which claims to epistemic innocence are always embedded in a political context, and to begin to set the parameters of a further appraisal of the posthumanist argument.

When he posed the mind as a *tabula rasa* Locke (2000) did so as a means of grounding a hypothetical process of building reason from experience.[12] On Locke's formulation, epistemic innocence, for which he posited the child as a privileged vessel, offered direct access to objects in the real world, and thus evaded what was most problematic about accrued knowledge and language (Rose 1984). In her incisive assessment of Locke's argument, Joanne Faulkner (2011a) points out that in posing human knowledge as essentially innocent, Locke offered a powerful rejoinder to medieval morality, and the doctrine of original sin in particular. To pose the mind as a blank slate served an early modern middle class need for freedom from the entrenched values of feudal society. Accordingly, Locke's scepticism and the notion of epistemic purity that underlies it amounts, on Faulkner's reading, to a bourgeois imaginary that rejects tradition as a source of authority and hierarchy. In her appraisal Faulkner (2011a) goes on to show how, in posing the child's mind as a privileged instance of the claim that ideas are not innate but the result of intercourse with the world, Locke also exhibits a fundamental tension within any claim to the innocence of thought. On the one hand, the child functions as a source of critical knowledge, one that repudiates superstition and prejudice. On the other hand, Locke makes clear that precisely because it is innocent and thus liable to corruption, the child requires the adult's control and discipline. As such, the child offers an assertion of humanity's essential innocence, while at the same time allowing the loss of control and ignorance that innocence implies to be projected and disowned. In other work Faulkner (2011b, 69–70) relates this unstable inclusion of innocence to liberal political philosophy and to the simultaneous valorisation and repression of the natural that early incarnations of the social contract implied. She explains that Locke permits 'nature' to persist in the *polis* both as a check on state power and as a fantasy of original enjoyment. But the natural 'childhood of humanity', embodied in the peasant or colonial subject or the child itself, also poses a risk to a mature modern contractual order since it implies the failure to enclose and 'improve' the land and to assume the industrious character demanded of the citizen of civil society. In this sense, Locke's formulation of innocence serves the bourgeois imagination with a narrative accounting for the legitimacy of its power along with a means of disowning the loss of control the quality of innocence risks.

Does Locke's mobilisation of innocence on behalf of an ascendant merchant class shine any light upon posthumanism's own impulses? After all, as we have already affirmed, the posthumanist argument is usually grounded upon speculation as to how largely nefarious technological developments might be repurposed to emancipatory ends. Notwithstanding these commitments, the question here bears on the deeper issue of whether posthumanist theories of hybridity reflect or reduce the historical dimensions of existential experience. On this point the evidence marshalled above suggests, following Strathern and others, that a retraction of reflexivity occurs where thought displaces epistemological reflexivity for ontological speculation. It remains to ask, then, why the claim to hybridity has been so predominant in the humanities and social sciences in recent years.

7. Posthuman Anxieties

Crucially, for feminist scholarship especially, posthumanism addresses a looming anxiety that the poststructuralist critique of the subject, given its emphasis on the social construction of gender, left untouched and unscathed underlying essentialist biological conceptions of sex.[13] In this context notions of hybridity can be mobilised to challenge received notions of both cultural *and* biological convention. This can be seen as a significant critical intervention where the poststructuralist assessment of the discursive construction of gender circumvents more difficult questions of biology itself. Remaining with the issue of the social theorist's relation to the biological sciences, it is also worth noting that the narrative of 'hybridity', and the focus upon scientific and technical change it implies, proposes renewed engagement with the natural sciences for humanities scholars reeling from the Sokal 'hoax' and the broader delegitimation of continental philosophy this scandal stood in for, as well as broader cultural and institutional attacks upon traditional liberal arts pursuits.[14]

While this is all certainly the case, there seems to be a deeper underlying logic to the popularity of the posthumanist paradigm, one which ultimately involves the pose of epistemic innocence these theories imply. Recall that for Locke epistemic purity served to undermine the legitimacy of feudal knowledge and aristocratic power while at the same time projecting the loss of control such a purity implied upon the abject subjects of early modern society. Similarly, in the case of what we have seen of the posthumanist's circumvention of the issue of thought's mediation to the world by private property, the rhetoric of hybridity permits the articulation of a critique of capitalism and commodification that can nevertheless celebrate capital's achievements. It only does so, however, by ignoring a much thornier problem: that capital might direct or subsume those technological developments down to their very core. A full accounting of these questions is not possible here, but suffice it to say that the possibility of extracting emancipatory content from new technological developments is a much more vexing problem than the figure of hybridity permits.[15] Even more disturbing, posthumanism disavows the anxiety that our concepts themselves might also be inseparable from processes associated with contemporary capitalism. Ours is an epoch where concern over capitalist manipulation of cognitive performance is widespread, and where worry and discomfort over the manipulation of what we think and feel, whether by the algorithms organising web platforms or drug therapies designed to increase and extend cognitive performance or prevent mental breakdown, is pervasive. In this context, it would seem that to avoid asking how thought is conditioned and limited by its social context in the name of an account focused upon the erosion of the hierarchies governed by modern 'man' offers a therapeutic to both theorists and consumers of the products of contemporary capitalism. This is a therapy that permits the expression of critical perspectives on contemporary technological development, all the while *containing* that critique so that it need not look back to its own, possibly compromised, subject-position, or indeed, its own forms of consumption. In this sense, the risk of ontologies of 'hybridity' is that they reproduce the withdrawal from, or delegation of, critical thought that is characteristic of a world increasingly governed by processes of automation and algorithmic organisation.

Notes

[1] I would like to thank Nicholas Beuret and Simon Choat for their critical comments on drafts of this essay.

[2] By posthumanist I refer to a particular strand of critical theorising. It is important to distinguish this from theories of the 'posthuman' grounded upon normative critique of the dehumanising effects of technology such as Fukuyama (2002) and Habermas (2003). For an overview of 'critical' posthumanism, see Badmington (2003) and Herbrechter(2013).

[3] On this point see Coole & Frost (2010); Braun & Whatmore (2010); Bryant, Harman & Srnicek (2011).

[4] On this point see Rekret (2018a).

[5] Latour (1991) is exceptional amongst the thinkers of the ontological or posthuman turn in question here insofar as he attends to the historical origins of what he calls 'the modern constitution'. Drawing on Shapin and Schaffer (1985), it is ironic that Latour presents a mostly discursive story of the separation of the natural and social in the seventeenth century, one that overstates a controversy over the terms of the scientific and the political to the much broader terms of the natural and the social. In doing so, it hyperinflates the relative importance of historical personae, in this case Boyle and Hobbes. For a convincing critique of Latour's history of modernity see Pels (1995), Jacob (1995) & Choat (2017).

[6] For a broader accounting of Sohn-Rethel's argument see Rekret and Choat (2016). The argument in this section is developed more extensively in Rekret (2016; 2018c).

[7] It ought to be noted that Latour is an exception here insofar as his own politics can be characterised as anti-socialist liberal pragmatism. Much of the ontological speculation that takes inspiration from his work is more explicitly concerned with an emancipatory politics. For a critical assessment of Latour in this regard see Noys (2011).

[8] Ian Hacking's (1998) critique of Haraway parallels Strathern's. Hacking argues that as developments in medical technology imply that we increasingly

treat bodies as assemblages of replaceable parts, so we intensify rather than transcend the Cartesian framing of existence.

9   On this point, see also Parry (2004); Helmreich (2009); Brand & Görg (2008).

10 It is worth insisting that Haraway's work has not only been crucial to shaping a progressive Science and Technology Studies research paradigm, but she has explicitly situated her work within a socialist tradition. Neither Haraway's political commitments nor her research as a whole are at issue here. Rather, this essay is interested in the ontology of hybridity upon which a whole paradigm of social theory rests and which emanates from her work.

11 Similar claims are found across a range of work. See for instance Latour (1988), Connolly (2013), Barad (2007).

12 I draw in this section on arguments first outlined in Rekret (2018a).

13 On this point see Parisi (2008).

14 For an overview of the Sokal hoax in the context of the 'culture wars' see Guillory (2002).

15 For instance, see the exchange between Alberto Toscano (2011; 2014) and Jasper Bernes (2013) around logistics.

References

Badmington, Neil. 2003. 'Theorising Posthumanism.' *Cultural Critique* (53), Winter: 10–27.

Bensaid, Daniel. 2002. 'A New Appreciation of Time.' In *Marx for Our Times: Adventures and Misadventures of a Critique*, translated by George Eliot, 69–94. London: Verso.

Bernes, Jasper. 2013. 'Logistics, Counterlogistics and the Communist Project.' *Endnotes* (3) September: 172–201.

Braidotti, Rosi. 2013. *The Posthuman*. Cambridge: Polity Press.

Brand, Urich and Christoph Görg. 2008. 'Post-Fordist Governance of Nature: The Internationalisation of the State and the Case of Genetic Resources.' *Review of International Political Economy* 15(4): 567–89.

Braun, Bruce and Sarah J. Whatmore. 2010. *Political Matter: Technoscience, Democracy, and Public Life*. Minneapolis: University of Minnesota Press.

Bryant, Levi, Graham Harman and Nick Srnicek (eds.). 2011. *The Speculative Turn*. Melbourne: Re-Press.

Choat, Simon. 2017. 'Science, Agency and Ontology: A Historical-Materialist Response to New Materialism.' *Political Studies*.

Connolly, William. 2013. *The Fragility of Things: Self-Organizing Processes, Neoliberal Fantasies, and Democratic Activism*. Durham and London: Duke University Press.

Coole, Diana and Samantha Frost. 2010. *New Materialisms: Ontology, Agency, and Politics*. Durham and London: Duke University Press.

Faulkner, Joanne. 2011a. 'Innocents and Oracles: The Child as Figure of Knowledge and Critique in the Middle Class Philosophical Imagination.' *Critical Horizons* 2(3), 20: 323–46.

Faulkner, Joanne. 2011b. *The Importance of Being Innocent: Why We Worry About Children*. Cambridge: Cambridge University Press.

Federici, Silvia. 2004. *Caliban and the Witch: The Body and Primitive Accumulation*. New York: Autonomedia.

Fernandez, Maria and Suhail Malik. 2002. 'Whatever Happened to the Cyborg Manifesto?' *Mute*, 10 July. Available at: http://www.metamute.org/editorial/articles/whatever-happened-to-cyborg-manifesto (accessed 14 May 2018).

Foucault, Michel. 2013. *History of Madness*. London: Routledge.

Fukuyama, Francis. 2002. *Our Posthuman Future: Consequences of the Biotechnology Revolution*. London: Profile Books.

Guillory, John. 2002. 'The Sokal Affair and the History of Criticism.' *Critical Inquiry* 28(2), Winter: 470–508.

Habermas, Jürgen. 2003. *The Future of Human Nature*. Cambridge: Polity Press.

Hacking, Ian. 1998. 'Canguilhem Amid the Cyborgs.' *Economy and Society* 27: 202–16.

Haraway, Donna. 1991. *Simians, Cyborgs, and Women: The Reinvention of Nature*. London: Routledge.

Haraway, Donna. 1997. *Modest_Witness@Second_Millenium: FemaleMan_Meets_OncoMouse: Feminism and Technoscience*. New York and London: Routledge.

Helmreich, Stefan. 2009. *Alien Ocean: Anthropological Voyages in Microbial Seas*. London: University of California Press.

Herbrechter, Stephan. 2013. *Posthumanism: A Critical Analysis*. London: Bloomsbury.

Jacob, Margaret C. 1998. 'Reflections on Bruno Latour's Version of the Seventeenth Century.' In *A House Built on Sand: Exposing Postmodern Myths About Science*, edited by Noretta Koertge. Oxford: Oxford University Press.

Jessop, Bob. 2007. 'Knowledge as a Fictitious Commodity: Insights and Limits of a Polanyian Perspective.' *Reading Karl Polanyi for the 21st Century: Market Economy as Political Project,* edited by Ayşe Buğra and Kaan Ağartan. London: Palgrave Macmillan.

Jasanoff, Sheila. 2012. 'Taking Life: Private Rights in Public Nature.' In *Lively Capital: Biotechnologies, Ethics, and Governance in Global Markets*, ed. Kaushik Sunder Rajan, 155–83. Durham and London: Duke University Press..

Latour, Bruno. 1988. *The Pasteurization of France*, translated by Alan Sheridan. Cambridge and London: Harvard University Press.

Latour, Bruno. 1991. *We Have Never Been Modern*. Cambridge, MA: Harvard University Press.

Locke, John. 2000. *An Essay Concerning Human Understanding*. London: Routledge.

Malatino, Hilary. 2017. 'Biohacking Gender.' *Angelaki* 22 (2): 179–90.

Merchant, Carolyn. 1983. *The Death of Nature: Women, Ecology and the Scientific Revolution*. London: Harper and Row.

Mies, Maria. 1998. *Patriarchy and Accumulation on a World Scale: Women in the International Division of Labour*. London: Palgrave MacMillan.

Noys, B. 2012. *The Persistence of the Negative: A Critique of Contemporary Continental Theory*. Edinburgh: Edinburgh University Press.

Parisi, Luciana. 2008. 'The Nanoengineering of Desire.' In *Queering the Non/Human*, eds. Noreen Giffney and Myra J Hird. Aldershot: Ashgate.

Parry, Bronwyn. 2004. *Trading the Genome* New York, NY: Columbia University Press.

Pels, Dick. 1995. 'Have We Never Been Modern? Towards a Demontage of Latour's Modern Constitution.' *History of the Human Sciences* 8 (3): 129–41.

Rekret, Paul. 2018a. 'The Posthumanist *Tabula Rasa*'. *Research in Education: Policy, Theory and Practice*, 101(1):25-29.

Rekret, Paul. 2018b. 'The Head, The Hand, and Matter: New Materialism and the Politics of Knowledge.' *Theory, Culture & Society*

Rekret, Paul. 2018c. *Derrida and Foucault: Philosophy, Politics, Polemics*, London and New York: Rowman & Littlefield.

Rekret, Paul. 2016. 'A Critique of New Materialism: Ethics and Ontology.' *Subjectivity* 9(3): 225–245.

Rekret, Paul and Simon Choat. 2016. 'From Political Topographies to Political Logics: Post-Marxism and Historicity.' *Constellations: An International Journal of Critical and Democratic Theory* 23(2): 281–291.

Rose, Jacqueline. 1984. *The Case of Peter Pan, Or, the Impossibility of Children's Fiction*. London: Palgrave Macmillan.

Schmidt, Alfred. 1971. *The Concept of Nature in Marx*. Translated by Ben Fowkes. London: New Left Books.

Shapin, Steven and Simon Schaffer. 1985. *Leviathan and the Air-Pump: Hobbes, Boyle, and the Experimental Life*. Princeton: Princeton University Press.

Sohn-Rethel, Alfred. 1978. *Intellectual and Manual Labor: A Critique of Epistemology*. London: Macmillan Press.

Strathern, Marylin. 2005. *Kinship, Law and the Unexpected: Relatives are Always A Surprise*. Cambridge: Cambridge University Press.

Strathern, Marylin. 1999. *Property, Substance and Effect: Anthropological Essays on Persons and Things*. London: The Athlone Press.

Toscano, Alberto. 2011. 'Logistics and Opposition.' *Mute*, 9 August. Available at: http://www.metamute.org/editorial/articles/logistics-and-opposition (accessed 14 May 2018).

Toscano, Alberto. 2014. 'Lineaments of the Logistical State.' *Viewpoint*, 28 September. Available at: https://www.viewpointmag.com/2014/09/28/lineaments-of-the-logistical-state/ (accessed 14 May 2018).

Wilkie, Robert. 2011. *The Digital Condition: Class and Culture in the Information Network*. New York: Fordham University Press.

CHAPTER 7

Posthumanism as a Spectrum: Reflections on Paul Rekret's Chapter

Robert Cowley

1. Introduction

Paul Rekret explicitly intends to 'take a step back to examine the parameters' of posthuman thinking. He challenges the assumption that knowledge generated by posthuman theorising somehow straightforwardly or 'innocently' reflects the contemporary world. Instead, he treats posthumanism as a particular 'story' produced in, and reproduced through, specific circumstances. He proposes that posthumanism might not emancipate us from the dilemmas which it addresses, so much as normalise the conditions of their production.

In order to establish a critical distance from posthumanism, then, Rekret emphasises its contingency. There is good reason to suppose that his analysis will resonate with those those already uncomfortable with broader tendencies towards 'hybrid thinking'. We might hypothesise, however, that Rekret will be less likely to provoke dialogue with posthumanist thinkers themselves, for whom

How to cite this book chapter:
Cowley, R. 2019. Posthumanism as a Spectrum: Reflections on Paul Rekret's
    Chapter. In: Chandler, D. and Fuchs, C. (eds.) *Digital Objects, Digital Subjects:
    Interdisciplinary Perspectives on Capitalism, Labour and Politics in the Age of Big
    Data*. Pp. 95–100. London: University of Westminster Press. DOI: https://doi.
    org/10.16997/book29.g. License: CC-BY-NC-ND 4.0

'critical distance' is more a problem to be overcome than a useful diagnostic strategy, and contingency is an explicitly celebrated virtue.

In what follows, I suggest that this problem of incompatibility need not be construed in such stark terms. To reach this conclusion, I first reflect further on the reasons for, but also question the extent of, posthumanism's appeal. Relatedly, I go on to propose that posthumanism may more usefully be thought of as a spectrum, than a discrete mode of thinking.

2. Situating the Appeal of Posthumanism

It has become clichéd to observe that Donna Haraway's (1985) famous image of the cyborg has only gained resonance over time. It is surely in large part due to the wide spread of digital technology that Haraway's vision, of the tendency for contemporary scientific and technological developments to blur the edges of the human, strikes us as so prescient. The digital is no longer the direct concern only of distant corporate technicians; its presence in everyday life no longer seems optional. Rather, it seems uncontroversial – even banal – to suggest that we have become reflexively aware that our actions, from the moment we wake up, are digitally mediated. This change is one of several contemporary conditions which collectively shape a 'posthuman' sensibility, on which Rekret reflects critically in his chapter.

This sensibility, in Rekret's definition, is characterised primarily by an ontological privileging of 'hybridity'. And, for those who follow contemporary theorising in the humanities or social sciences, it is difficult to ignore the spread of various forms of hybrid thinking. The desire to decentre human agency seems widespread. Some random examples might include: the recent embrace of assemblage theory in urban theory; the growing enthusiasm for placing objects at the centre of historical research; and the trend even for anthropologists to speculate on the social agency of plants, fungi and microbes (Kirksey and Helmreich 2010). The primacy of human ability to think rationally 'about' and act 'on' the world has been eroded by notions of the entanglement of cognitive processes, and expectations of variously dispersed agency. As Timothy Morton puts it, there is a growing understanding that humans are 'no longer in the centre of the universe, but we are not in the VIP box beyond the edge, either' (Morton 2013, 13). Potentially, then, posthumanism not only describes the written output of a certain set of scholarly writers, but also the wider appeal of a certain ontological orientation across the academy, and perhaps beyond.

To understand this appeal, it may be helpful to think of posthumanism as performing three inter-related roles:

(1) it draws on and reverberates with an existing, dispiriting story relating to the end of modernity;

(2) it reframes this story in optimistic terms;

(3) it thereby offers the prospect of a hopeful way forwards.

The end of modernity is dramatised most conspicuously in widespread expectations of global climate changes, mocking the idea that humans are, or can be, in control of the world. The 'anthropocene' presents us with both the 'bizarre situation, in which we have become potent enough to change the course of the Earth yet seem unable to regulate ourselves' (Hamilton 2017, vii–viii), and the unsettling prospect that 'over this century humans will, in full knowledge of what we are doing, irreparably degrade the conditions of life on our home planet' (ibid, 37). And yet, this dispiriting dilemma is inherited from postmodern theories *about* the world – a mode of thinking from which posthumanism claims to distance itself. Rosi Braidotti, for example, specifically opposes the use of theory 'as a tool to apprehend and represent reality' (Braidotti 2013, 5). The ideal of cognitive distance is devalued when 'The boundaries between the categories of the natural and the cultural have been displaced and to a large extent blurred' (Braidotti 2013, 3). Thus, while posthumanism reverberates with existing narratives of loss, to articulate a widespread sense of confusion, it does not pose as a set of detached observations: its stories are presented as emerging from the world.

In its diagnostic mode, then, posthumanism does not aim to impose an analytical framework on the world, but instead to relate what the world seems to be telling us. Simultaneously, however, this reframing of our understanding adopts a celebratory register (Chandler 2018), which envigorates what Rekret calls an affirmative 'ethico-political' argument. Thus, Haraway's cyborg was presented in a playful 'manifesto'. For Braidotti, the 'posthuman predicament' is 'an opportunity to empower the pursuit of alternative schemes of thought, knowledge and self-representation' (Braidotti 2013, 12). Jane Bennett's influential book ends indicatively with 'a litany, a kind of Nicene Creed for would-be vital materialists' (Bennett 2010, 122). The broader celebratory project here is captured well by the goal of Kohn's 'anthropology of life': 'neither to do away with the human nor to reinscribe it but to open it' (Kohn 2013, 6). In short, posthuman hybrid thinking reworks existing critiques of human exceptionalism into an optimistic sense of expanded agency, and then dwells on the generative ethical and political implications of this sensibility.

3. Questioning the Appeal of Posthumanism

Rekret's response is to treat posthumanism, in effect, as a contingent discourse – even if he shies away from that term. In mobilising the discursive category of the 'posthuman', he might be accused of conflating a variety of bodies of theory which in fact proceed as much in contestation as in concert. However, his definition does not rest on a delineation of the *boundaries* of this field: his intention is not to specify which thinkers do and do not fall into this category. Rather, his definition relates to certain tendencies present across a broad range of current thinkers – whether or not they self-identify as posthumanists. This is an uncontroversial mode of definition: the mutual debts among relevant authors have been mapped out elsewhere – both by sceptical commentators (see, for example: van Ingen, 2016), and explicitly in the texts themselves.

More problematically, a strategy that involves defining and labelling discursive trends may not be the best way to win friends. It implies a certain distancing; it performatively positions the labeller outside the body of discourse in question. This move may seem threatening to those living through a given discourse, who feel they are narrating their condition in a neutral way. Those who have been the victims of injustice, illness, or climate change, may feel bemused, or significantly offended, by commentaries treating the resulting afflictions as socially constructed 'stories' (Hacking 2000). Indeed, from a posthumanist perspective, Rekret's 'retreat' into discourse may seem irresponsibly relativistic, and indicative of poststructuralist tendencies, which – as Rekret notes – are precisely what posthumanism is attempting to go beyond. Braidotti, for example, clearly asserts that 'The posthuman subject is not ... poststructuralist, because it does not function within the linguistic turn or other forms of deconstruction' (Braidotti 2013, 188). In parallel, as if to preempt the charge that posthumanism's generative potential is constrained by the specificity of the conditions of its emergence, Braidotti insists only on its relevance to the contemporary world. Posthumanism inoculates itself by transforming contingency into a positive attribute, in rejection of universalist aspirations. One might, then, conclude that there is little possibility of Rekret's critique speaking to posthumanists themselves, since it depends on such an alienating method.

At the same time, the reach of posthumanist thinking should not be exaggerated. Although it responds to a contemporary dilemma, the sensibility of this dilemma is inevitably uneven. This reflection began by rehearsing the idea that we have come increasingly to 'see like a cyborg' in our post-modern, digitally mediated, anthropocenic era. But who is this 'we'? Certainly, for the educated and affluent, who are more likely to follow technological developments in the media, it would seem difficult to be unaware of a wider set of concurrent advances in robotics, artificial intelligence, big data, genetic engineering, and other fields, which collectively disrupt received notions of the boundaries of the 'human' and, by extension, previous assumptions about human agency. However, those on the prosperous side of the 'digital divide' may forget the specificity of their own conditions. 'We' might be surprised that, even in a wealthy country such as the UK, 13% of adults have never used the internet (Office for National Statistics 2014). Furthermore, if it is permissible to view posthumanism in discursive terms, as tending to frame and represent reality in certain ways, there is no reason to suppose that its stories will always be 'decoded' (Hall, 1992) in the same way. Thinking about the triple appeal of posthumanism, as I have proposed above, already opens up several positions on a spectrum of possible responses. This is the case even after we exclude those 'aggressive nihilists' (Connolly 2017) who, for personal gain, cynically refute the significance of the dilemmas which posthumanism addresses.

First, at one end of this spectrum, sit a range of actors not afflicted with a sense of loss of the modern. Some of this group are 'still' premodern; for others, the dualisms of modernity are comfortably in place. This need not imply naivety on their part: engineers and technology innovators, for example, generally seem happy to acknowledge that solutions often have unexpected consequences, yet retain faith in the possibility of learning lessons and improving techniques over time. Policy-makers seem fully aware that plans can rarely be enacted in a linear way (van Assche and Verschraegen 2008), but still presume that a process of approximate societal steering is better than none at all. Belief in 'progress' more generally is still widespread, and may more typically be understood in incremental, iterative terms, rather than as megalomaniac ambition. For this group, there is no strong sense of disillusionment with which posthuman thinking can reverberate. The 'we' that frets over the demise of human exceptionalism might be a smaller constituency than its inhabitants imagine.

A more ambiguous middle position might be imagined. Here, posthumanism's diagnostic role is positively received, but a pragmatic choice is made to proceed in traditional ways regardless. For those who act within particular disciplinary spheres, engaging with posthumanism may make little sense at the level of everyday practice. Natural scientists may be fully aware of – and even enthusiastically curious about – new discoveries which fundamentally call modernist assumptions into question, even while the 'cultural performances' of their day jobs depend on 'a strong view of the human agent and of nature as consisting of nonagentic objects of understanding' (Connolly 2017, 100). Thus, in Rekret's terms, it seems quite feasible to buy into posthumanism's 'speculative ontology' without embracing its 'ethico-political project'.

It is the third position, however, which would seem to be in Rekret's main line of fire. This describes a more active embrace of this project: here, an awareness of the world's hybridity becomes a source of optimism, and is translated somehow into action or new frameworks for everyday thinking.

4. Conclusion

Is it likely, then, that Rekret's argument will tend to fall on deaf ears among those who most actively embrace the logics which he critiques? While he proceeds by emphasising the contingency of the conditions giving rise to posthuman thinking, posthumanists themselves acknowledge and celebrate contingency. The possibility of 'stepping back' from the subject matter, furthermore, is epistemologically excluded from posthumanist theorising, insofar as the latter refuses to view the world from a cognitive distance. If this means taking sides, then the force of Rekret's argument might be expected to diminish precisely as the appeal of posthuman 'hybridity' spreads.

This incompatibility invokes a wider set of questions around the relevance of critique to 'non-representational' thinking of different types. And yet, I have suggested here not only that the prevalence of the posthuman sensibility is un-even (and limited), but that we should expect its reception – even among sym-pathetic audiences – to vary significantly. And perhaps the audience of 'third position' posthumanists is somewhat chimerical: posthuman writers them-selves are not so arrogant as to position their own ethico-political proposals as definitive; their real-world acolytes no doubt display reflexivity to varying degrees. To point to this variety and unevenness is not to undermine Rekret's 'method': he does not define posthumanism as a discrete body of thought, but rather mobilises some of its common tendencies for heuristic purposes. Rather, it opens up the possibility – which Rekret does not explicitly deny – that more satisfactorily reflexive forms of 'hybrid thinking' might be developed in future.

References

Bennett, Jane. 2010. *Vibrant Matter: A Political Ecology of Things*. Durham, NC: Duke University Press.

Braidotti, Rosi. 2013. *The Posthuman*. Malden, MA: Polity Press.

Chandler, David. 2018. *Ontopolitics in the Anthropocene: An Introduction to Mapping, Sensing and Hacking*. Abingdon: Routledge.

Connolly, William E. 2017. *Facing the Planetary: Entangled Humanism and the Politics of Swarming*. Durham: Duke University Press Books.

Hacking, Ian. 2000. *The Social Construction of What?* Cambridge, MA: Harvard University Press.

Hall, Stuart. 1992. 'Encoding/decoding.' In *Culture, Media, Language*, (eds.) Stuart Hall et al. 128–38. London: Routledge.

Hamilton, Clive. 2017. *Defiant Earth: The Fate of Humans in the Anthropocene*. Cambridge: Polity Press.

Haraway, Donna. 1985. 'A Manifesto for Cyborgs: Science, Technology and Socialist Feminism in the 1980s.' *Socialist Review* 80: 65–107.

Kirksey, S. Eben and Stefan Helmreich. 2010. 'The Emergence of Multispecies Ethnography.' *Cultural Anthropology* 25 (4): 545–76.

Kohn, Eduardo. 2013. *How Forests Think: Toward an Anthropology Beyond the Human*. Berkeley, CA: University of California Press.

Morton, Timothy. 2013. *Hyperobjects: Philosophy and Ecology After the End of the World*. Minneapolis: University of Minnesota Press.

Office for National Statistics. 2014. Internet Access Quarterly Update: Q1 2014. Statistical bulletin. https://www.ons.gov.uk (accessed 16 November, 2017).

van Assche, Kristof and Gert Verschraegen. 2008. 'The Limits of Planning: Nik-las Luhmann's Systems Theory and the Analysis of Planning and Planning Ambitions.' *Planning Theory* 7 (3): 263–283.

van Ingen, Michiel. 2016. 'Beyond The Nature/Culture Divide? The Contradic-tions of Rosi Braidotti's *The Posthuman*'. *Journal of Critical Realism* 15 (5): 530–542

SECTION II

Digital Labour

CHAPTER 8

Through the Reproductive Lens: Labour and Struggle at the Intersection of Culture and Economy

Kylie Jarrett

1. Introduction

The intersection of the digital with our work and leisure, and the blurring of these two categories, has become an increasingly significant field of inquiry in Big Data capitalism. Digital labour studies – in which this nexus is explored – is fast becoming a field of its own, incorporating analyses of workers in the platform-mediated gig economy, users of social media, social media influencers, and the ways in which various work practices are being re-shaped by digital technologies. The importance of this field lies in how the dynamics it traces – such as the centrality of immaterial/affective labour, precarious and exploited work conditions and the social factory – are emblematic of wider trends in contemporary capitalism.

In early 2016, I published *Feminism, Labour and Digital Media: The Digital Housewife*, which contributes to this debate by arguing a case for using Marxist

How to cite this book chapter:
Jarrett, K. 2019. Through the Reproductive Lens: Labour and Struggle at the Intersection of Culture and Economy. In: Chandler, D. and Fuchs, C. (eds.) *Digital Objects, Digital Subjects: Interdisciplinary Perspectives on Capitalism, Labour and Politics in the Age of Big Data*. Pp. 103–116. London: University of Westminster Press. DOI: https://doi.org/10.16997/book29.h. License: CC-BY-NC-ND 4.0

feminist theories of domestic work to explain the economic and cultural logics of consumer labour in digital media. By 'consumer labour,' I mean the myriad ways in which our cultural products are expropriated and alienated from us when we upload them to platforms, but also how our data is the cornerstone of surplus value generation for digital media companies. The book sought to address what I considered a fruitless debate about whether such work is alienated and exploited or socially meaningful and a site for self-actualisation. In *The Digital Housewife*, I argue that domestic work, as conceptualised by Marxist feminists, gives us a model of work that is both these things – integral to capitalism for its productive and reproductive capacity, but always potentially outside these same dynamics. Domestic work is labour that straddles the cultural and the economic, and thus, I argue, it gives us a mechanism for understanding forms of digital labour that perform the same feat of gymnastics.

My book is quite narrowly targeted at a particular theoretical concern – and personal bugbear – and focuses on only a limited range of digital labour practices in making its case. Nevertheless, the central principles from which its arguments are drawn have begun growing in importance in the study of digital labour and capitalism more broadly. In this chapter, I want to move away from the specific argument in my book and instead focus on this wider context. I will engage with wider conversations about activism, struggle and critique into which its argument has entered, and attempt to identify contexts where the emphasis on alternative labour histories and the politics of social reproduction that animates my book brings important critical insight. Along the way, I'll describe some elements of *The Digital Housewife*, but mostly as a means of illustrating what bringing reproductive work into view can do for our understanding of contemporary capitalism and its sites of struggle. I will do this by focusing on three key areas: history, value and subjects.

2. History

One of the orienting feminist concepts in my book is that the social factory has a longer history than is usually ascribed to it in studies of digital capitalism. The argument is often made that we live in times marked by a peculiar saturation of the whole of existence with the dictates of capital – the real subsumption of life that constitutes Mario Tronti's (1973) social factory. This is often attributed to the conditions of post-Fordism and the information-intensive industries of Big Data capitalism. There is often an implicit assumption that the circumstances of the social factory are new.

However, for anyone who is not a white, cis-, het- man, it is difficult to see precisely what is novel about the conditions in which all of life is subsumed into capital. Private domestic space and interpersonal relations, including sexual activity, have historically been considered outside capital, providing arenas in which autonomous self-making could happen, and where Marx's species-being could be realised. In white hetero-patriarchal contexts this has long been equated with the private, domestic space of the nuclear family (Berlant and Warner 1998; England 1993; Osucha 2009). Yet women, people of colour, and LGBTQ+ have never experienced such contexts as places of autonomy or agency but rather as venues of (en)forced and uncompensated work, as well as situations of domination and surveillance. Moreover, as Marxist feminists such as Dalla Costa and James (1975), Federici (2004), Mies et al. (1988) and Davis (1983) assert, gender, raced and sexed being and the organisation of labour are intimately related, placing human subjectivity at the core of capitalist accumulation. Taking these perspectives into account, the absorption of the whole of life – the existence of a social factory – is a fundamental, if not foundational, part of the capitalist narrative.

An example of this longer history of the social factory that I have explored (Jarrett 2017) is the effective slave labour system of the Magdalene Laundries in Ireland between 1922 and 1937. These laundries were carceral institutions where women believed dangerous to the middle-class 'stem-family system' (Inglis 1997, 13) through sexual activity outside of patriarchal marriage, deemed 'unproductive' through poverty (Buckley 2016), or otherwise considered unruly by behavioural norms of the day were sent for penance and re-education into domestic labour discipline. Women slaved in abject conditions in these nun-run commercial, but non-profit, laundries for no pay, typically for years.

The Magdalene Laundries, though, are not merely an aberration of Irish Catholicism, but must be read as part of a society-wide social, cultural, legal and political machinery supporting a state economic agenda to get men – but specifically men – back to work in a very weak economy (Daly 1995). This was achieved through an aggressive re-instatement of the gendered division of labour, both materially – in the forms of regulations controlling women's labour and political rights – and culturally, through sermonising, cultural products and the disciplining effect of institutions like the Laundries. These sites enforced women's domesticity by disciplining and policing women's bodies, sexuality and 'souls,' exacting penance to ensure alignment with their constrained economic roles. Based on a 'thematic of sin' (Inglis 1997) and regimes of shame, the cultural logics that animated these institutions and which gave legitimacy to their economic effects did not end at the Laundry gate. They were also articulated in the sensibilities of all in Irish society, as evidenced by claims that key advocates of the Magdalene system were women (Crowley and Kitchen 2008). The Laundries, and their embedding in everyday Irish society, exemplify the idea of the social factory – a society, a cultural fabric and individual embodied subjectivities formed by an economic agenda.

Such examples of the long history of capitalist logics manifesting in non-market contexts suggest that if we are to understand labour in Big Data capitalism, it is vital to recover and incorporate labour histories that do not belong to white men in industrialised labour (see also Fuchs 2017). As Alan Sears (2016, 139) summarises, different members of the working class 'face different forms of autonomy and coercion based on their location within dominant divisions of labour organised around differentiated processes of dispossession'. To understand capitalism holistically we therefore need to know more about the histories (and present experiences) of women, people of colour, trans or LGBTQ+ people, and people with disabilities, whose experiences in capital are marked by saturated regimes of precariousness and oppression. The overt relationship of these subaltern labour conditions to the immersive politics of the social factory suggests that they usefully map the experiences of oppression found in the precarious social factories of Big Data capitalism.

One suite of labour experiences we need to engage with more effectively and extensively is that of paid and unpaid sex work, which Morgane Merteuil (2017) has argued offers valuable insight into contemporary labour relations in Big Data capitalism. Using camming – webcam-based sex work – as her example, she describes a relationship between the dynamics of sex work and platforms such as Uber or Taskrabbit. Platforms, Merteuil argues, function similarly to pimps in that they broker exchanges between worker and client, take a cut of any profits, and also provide certain rules for how labour is to be performed. Merteuil argues that rather than the digital housewife that I propose, it is the digital whore that provides the best model for understanding labour in platform economies.

But the analogy runs deeper than the neat comparison between platforms and pimps. If we examine the long history of sex work, in particular by women and women of colour, we see very blurry distinctions between intimacy and economy, between paid and unpaid work, between agency and control. When your core business is to 'marry well,' then even unpaid sex with your life partner has an economic logic. It is the common and ongoing negotiations of these boundaries in interpersonal, legal, political and economic contexts that may reveal much about the politics of labour in the digital economy, in which distinctions between what we consider legitimate commodification are similarly unfixed and mutable. The unequal power relations that shape heterosexual marriage and which make unpaid sexual labour, like much labour for platforms, an effect of non-market social and economic coercion, may also be useful to consider in unpacking the dynamics of exploitation in Big Data capitalism.

Another issue raised by recognising this wider context of the social factory is the question of what precisely is new about labour in Big Data capitalism. If it is not the case that it uniquely requires and/or produces the saturation of life by capitalist principles, then what is its particularity? Is it a question of an increased intensity or extensity of capitalism's exploitative and alienating tendencies? Is it merely a matter of enhanced visibility as new mechanisms of quantification, such as the workplace tracking technologies explored by Phoebe Moore (2017), materialise existing practices of capture? Or is there some other substantive difference in how labour is manifested in Big Data capitalism? We must know more about the particular qualities of contemporary work if we are to properly critique this labour and, more importantly, identify sites into which we may intervene.

I reiterate, though, that in tracing this difference we must not found our distinction in the work of white cis-, het-, men working in industrialised labour, but look to sexed, raced, gendered and sexualised labour practices as well. It is in these 'alt' labour histories that we find not only difference but continuity with how work is constructed today, and so they may provide fruitful avenues for critique but also models for struggle. As Isabell Lorey suggests, we need to not only interpret precarity as a mechanism for securing domination, but also take 'subjective experiences of precaritization [as a] starting point for political struggles' (2015, 6). Understanding how women, people of colour, people in the Global South, trans, queer or disabled people have laboured in, but also resisted, conditions of oppression can tell us much. In survival – in what Rema Hammami calls 'the politics of subaltern persistence' (2016, 172) – we may find the forms of action we need today.

3. Value

Working with a longer history of the social factory, and with histories of work that are marked by their apparent non-market and cultural dimensions, also shifts focus in relation to what is valuable in capitalism. This is part of what I am calling 'the reproductive turn' in digital labour studies, where emphasis is not only on processes of commodification but also on how value, or things that are *of value* to capitalism, are generated through uncommodified dimensions of capitalist exchange. It is a direction that explores, as Nancy Fraser (2014, 61) has advocated, the 'indispensable background condition for the possibility of capitalist production.'

The key model for understanding consumer labour that I have advocated is that described by Leopoldina Fortunati (1995) in *The Arcane of Reproduction*. Fortunati insists that domestic work is integral to capitalism and not a mere subsidiary – reproducing workers is a necessary part of the production cycle. She argues, though, that the work of unpaid domestic labour is not directly exploited but instead involves a multi-phased process of incorporation involving the production of inalienable goods. Fortunati describes how the unpaid housewife's labour generates uncommodified or non-fungible products such as food and healthcare that are consumed by the paid worker. At this point, these products are transformed into labour-power and only then can they be converted into something with exchange value (labour-time). In this model, domestic labour is at a step removed from commodity production. This does not mean, however, that the uncommodified phase is outside capitalism; it remains an integral part of its long value chain. Fortunati's argument allows us to see how value can be extracted from labour even without its abstraction and commodification. When applied to forms of labour in Big Data capitalism, this model requires consideration of a greater range of activities that produce commodifiable outputs but also allows for multiplicity and contradiction in the nature of goods produced across that value chain.

A growing body of studies of digital labour, particularly those concerned with gendered or racialised activity, also look simultaneously at the economic and non-economic dimensions of digital labour, emphasising dimensions of subject formation alongside the economic frameworks of digital platforms. What is important, though, is that these studies do not assume that the social relations and uncommodified dimensions of these exchanges of labour and/ or goods are somehow outside capitalism. Rather they emphasise how they interact, in particular noting the disciplining functions of the uncommodified exchanges of these sites – for instance, how affectively charged interactions between users can be valuable to capitalism in providing normative pressures that underpin the desire to contribute this labour.

This focus on longer value chains and the possibilities of contradiction and multiplicity along them is prevalent in the work of Julia Velkova (2016), who has explored the politics of gift and commodity relations in the open source animation community, Blender. Her work (Velkova and Jakobsson 2015; see also Jarrett 2015a) draws on the biography of objects (Appadurai 1986; Kopytoff 1986), and suggests tracking how the economic relations associated with a cultural good change over time and as it circulates in different social relations. Velkova notes this multiplicity using the example of Blender, describing how exchanges of labour and software between the company and the open source community were sometimes conceived and construed as gifts, and at other times as commodity exchanges. What Velkova also notes, though, is that at all times, and regardless of their form, these exchanges were entrenching the hierarchical structures that sustained and supported the capitalist enterprise at the core of Blender. In effect, she usefully describes how the practices of gifting, both from producers and the open source user community, demonstrate multiplicity, but also the conservative, reproductive qualities of non-market exchanges within capitalism.

As I have noted before (Jarrett 2015b), what I refer to as 'the reproductive turn' is arguably not a turn at all, but really a *re*turn to the frameworks that guided early Cultural Studies, particularly as it emerged out of the Birmingham School, where economics and culture or identity were always conceived as mutually informing. As Velkova's study emphasises, it is important to a full critique of digital labour and contemporary capitalism to grasp this inter-relationship, to refuse the false binary between culture/society/identity and economics, and to explore the idea of value in broad terms.

Beyond my field of Internet research, the renewal of this perspective is crucial as we try to understand contemporary politics such as the 'aggrieved entitlement' (Kimmel 2013) of the alt-Right in the US (and arguably Donald Trump's election). Just as we cannot understand historical race relations in the

US without due consideration of its economic basis and its social and personal impacts, we cannot grasp the contemporary politics of online misogyny, renewed European fascism or Islamophobia without exploring the intersections of precarity economics with the historic privileges of masculinity and whiteness. It has certainly not been helpful – as was the tenor of my social media in the immediate aftermath of Trump's election – simply to denounce others as 'liberals' for their emphasis on identity politics, or to reduce everything to questions of class. The two cannot be so simply differentiated, and simplistic and unproductive binaries cannot move our critique toward positive change. Struggles for equality and justice are better served when we integrate our economic and identity critiques, examining how these dimensions of society intersect in politicising, valorising and exploiting difference (Alcoff 2006; Fraser 2014). In the contemporary moment, unless we look at the longer immaterial value chains of capitalism where the entitlement of certain actors is produced and reproduced, and where that promise has been betrayed and made unstable, we cannot come to grips with Trump, the growing threat posed by fascist and racist political parties, or even with Brexit.

A focus on the economic logics of social reproduction and the reproduction of economic logics is also important if we are to identify points of struggle most relevant to the precarious conditions of Big Data capitalism. Silvia Federici (2012) says that the ways we produce and reproduce consciousness – identity politics and ideological critique in the reproductive sphere – become point zero for political activism. Because social reproduction is both the production of desired human qualities and an accommodation to the market, this means reproductive work is always in tension, involving a 'potential separation, and it suggests a world of conflicts, resistances, and contradictions that have political significance' (2012, 99). It is in cracking open and moving between and against these contradictions – in refusing to reproduce regressive embodied interpretive horizons (Alcoff 2006) – that resistant political consciousness may develop.

Nick Srnicek and Alex Williams (2016) argue that an old-fashioned Gramscian counter-hegemonic project is essential to challenging the politics of platform capitalism. Intervention in ideology happens, they say, through transforming mediated political discourse and the material instantiations of those ideas: culture and economics. Physical infrastructures such as housing and urban design, as well as reproductive institutions such as the education system or the family, need to be rethought and remade in order to challenge consent to the neoliberal hegemony. Fundamentally, this project requires changing our suite of tools for self-making, including, and especially, how we articulate the concept and practices of work and living. This suggests that rather than opposing identity politics to capitalist and economic critique, the task is to mobilise these politics to articulate new critical subjects, drawing on the affective and economic excess that inheres to reproductive work to articulate awareness of oppression and alternative modes of being, thinking and doing.

By digging deep into and transforming reproductive activities we can forge a counter-hegemonic project.

4. Subject

This leads directly into the final point that emerges from applying reproductive lenses to labour in Big Data capitalism, which is how this application changes our conceptualisation of the labouring subject and, in doing so, changes our modes of politics. If we assume that the social factory has a long history – and, as feminists have argued, one that precedes the origins of capitalism – then our critique cannot end when we identify the real subsumption of life. We must assume that this is a feature of all of life in capitalism, albeit differently articulated across social groups. But we must also recognise that this capitalist-inflected activity doesn't necessarily reproduce capitalism. This means we need to move our critique of labour in Big Data capitalism away from the alienation of species-being – one of the four forms of alienation described by Marx (1961/2013) in the *Economic and Philosophic Manuscripts* – which has become almost a default critique in studies of digital labour, at least in media studies (Jarrett 2016b).

Not only does this emphasis on the impact of digital media on self-making reproduce the framework of false consciousness, it is also predicated on a subject that is gendered, raced and sexed. The concept of alienation from species-being is not universally applicable. Arguably it relies on a humanist subject – a self-possessed, singular individual for whom the alienation generated by capitalism is a formative tragedy (Eisenstein 1979; Braidotti 2013). But for women, and all other people constituted as 'other,' such a state of autonomy and singularity has never been attributed nor achieved either within capitalism or without. The entrenchment of power relations and systems of domination based in dimensions other than class has historically delimited the capacity to articulate 'species-being' for certain actors. For many subjects, alienation *is* the condition of existence – hybrid, queer, trans subjectivities, for instance – so a politics that seeks simply a return to, or seats its political subjectivity in, a coherent, pre-lapsarian species-being becomes exclusive and potentially genocidal.

This critique has two implications. It suggests, as James Reveley (2013) has argued, the need to focus more on the more material dimensions of alienation – products, other workers, nature – in our critiques of Big Data capitalism. This draws attention to how digital labour practices may have negative impacts on other workers or citizens, reproduce cycles of waste and obsolescence, or perpetuate other inequalities or social and environmental damage typical of the capitalist system. Shedding a critique of digital labour based in self-possession, and instead focusing on the dimensions of material dispossession and degradation, would manifest a more useful and nuanced critique of digital labour.

Secondly, this critique allows for the mobilisation of the subjects of Big Data capitalism in terms of their relationality and multiplicity, rather than their autonomy. This, in turn, enables politics that are intersectional and fluid. I am continually drawn back to Chela Sandoval's description of the tactical, liminal and differential subjectivities of US third-world feminism 'with the capacity to de- and recenter, given the forms of power to be moved' (2000, 58). This is the 'methodology of the oppressed', whose locus of possibility is not any one ideology but works with and through these differences, adapting tactically to power. These are also the dynamic politics of queer discomfort– of not fitting – described by Sara Ahmed (2004), that has long been the activist terrain of the subaltern. Rather than seeking remedy in a return to a mythic unified form of agency or by acting against a singular experience of class oppression, refusing the primacy of the humanist subject allows for this kind of engagement through points of difference and commonality, including that of class location.

Eschewing the singular coherence of the political and economic subject allows us to generate coalitional action directed at the ways in which we are all made vulnerable (Butler 2004; Butler et al. 2016; Fotopolou 2016) by Big Data capitalism, building temporary unions across race, gender, class, ability, sex and sexuality to resist those politics. Such a focus on how alliances are built through shared feelings of precariousness not only explains the generation of the political action of multitude (Hardt and Negri 2005), but also offers a mechanism for activating those politics.

We may also use the excessive effects of Big Data capitalism to achieve this activation. A moment in my social media use while preparing the preliminary paper that lead to this chapter illustrates how activism and precariousness can walk hand in hand. In the space of three minutes on my Facebook feed, I received three updates that spoke of shared struggle and the capacity to use social media within a counter-hegemonic project. The first, shared by a friend in France, showed the story of Fatima Hajiji, a 16-year-old Palestinian girl shot and killed by Israeli forces in Jerusalem. Appearing directly below this were Irish media reports of Dublin and Sligo City Councils voting to fly the Palestinian flag over their offices in solidarity with the Palestinian people. A few moments later, an Italian friend shared a link to the 'When I See Them, I See Us' video, which links the US Black Lives Matter cause to that of people in Occupied Palestine. The histories and present experiences of Palestinian, Irish and African American people are fundamentally different, but they intersect through respective vulnerabilities to colonial imperialism and capitalist necropolitics. In this example we can see alliances being established, not from singularity but in a solidarity based in shared precariousness. We also see the (potential) activation of critical political subjects aided by the visibility and networks provided by Big Data capitalism. Even though the mechanisms of capture enrolled by Facebook are encompassing and exhaustive, there remain gaps in the reproductive logics of the interface that can be exploited to speak back to power.

It would be absurd, though, to claim that such sharing of ideas through a commercial platform is tantamount to real political change – my likes do not impact lived conditions in the Gaza strip, for instance – or to claim that social media created these alliances. These are not my points. What this example does articulate, though, is the capacity to document, distribute and amplify the existence of counter-politics in ways reminiscent of the consciousness-raising activities of second-wave feminist activism or the abolitionist meetings of earlier periods. We can see similar disruptions in reproductive patterns in Jack Qiu's (2016, this volume) descriptions of the use of social media by Chinese Appconn workers to articulate discursive change and then to organise material, oppositional practices and solidarity amongst workers. These are all interventions that refuse the easy reproduction of class and identity status and are, in part, about building new subjectivities.

In my own politics, similar uses of social media are found in the Irish Repeal movement – a broad coalition of over 100 groups campaigning for a referendum to repeal the eighth amendment to the Irish Constitution that denies bodily autonomy to pregnant people. Among many material actions, the expression of this movement's politics across various media also seeks to produce new critical subjects by making abortion visible as a lived experience in Ireland, breaking apart the reproduction of silence and shame with which abortion is associated on the island, and uniting groups with disparate politics through shared recognition of the ways in which the Constitution and Irish laws render certain bodies – female, trans, raced, LGBTQ+, asylum seeker bodies – more vulnerable than others. Despite the varied political and ideological positions of each group or individual, the movement comes together under the badge 'Repealers,' as evidenced in the moving, grassroots hashtag campaign #knowyourrepealers that trended in September 2016. If, as Srnicek and Williams contest, both the immaterial and material dimensions of hegemony need to be systematically challenged to bring about effective political change, the Repeal movement shows how the reproductive capacity of digital media – its ability to (in)form critical subjects and shape actions – can be enrolled in the articulation, building and mobilisation of alliances to effect social change.

5. Conclusion

There are a lot of threads in this chapter, and they seem to have taken us very far from my short book. Little more than a theoretical framework for understanding digital users' labour, *The Digital Housewife* seems removed from the broad political concerns raised in this chapter. However, just as digital labour has a greater analytical importance because it exemplifies trends associated with Big Data capitalism, so too do the ideas and frameworks upon which my book draws. The more I (and others) reflect upon the political and economic circumstances of contemporary capitalism, the more resonance is found in the cultural economy of the reproductive sphere. This perspective suggests that labour and life are entwined in complex ways in Big Data capitalism, but articulates this complexity in a manner that is productive for thinking and acting in resistance. It allows for work, paid and unpaid, to be simultaneously cultural and economic – to be neither fish nor fowl – and to see in this hybridity the means through which to understand it better – a crucial preliminary step in breaking it apart to use for other ends.

To achieve this, though, requires proper attention to both the arenas of social reproduction and the stratification of capitalist dispossession. Only by eschewing the false binary between productive and reproductive labour can we generate a holistic picture of how Big Data capitalism organises us as economic units and as individual subjectivities; this is the mechanism through which we can adequately envision the dialectic (Ferguson 2016; Fraser 2014). This in turn gives us the political ground from which to generate a critique of capitalism that does not merely reproduce inequalities and exclusions. From an understanding of the differential distribution of labour and how that is reproduced across all social systems we can see more clearly the labour processes that are of value to capitalism and how these may not only exist in formal labour settings. Different places and modes for intervention into capitalism – such as articulating the politics of reproductive rights as an identity marker – can subsequently open up.

The politics, concepts and framework that I am articulating here are not new. Indeed, much of this paper – and indeed the point of the *Digital Housewife* book itself – is merely foregrounding long-standing queer, feminist, decolonial and Cultural Studies' critiques of economic determinism. The call to focus on social reproduction that is at its core merely echoes the crucially important work of feminist, queer and race activists in expanding the nature of class composition. However, this is really the point. Big Data capitalism may be new, but capitalism and inequality are not. Valuable critiques from feminists, race and queer theorists or activists addressing the complexity of a culturally saturated economic system already exist and demand centrality in our responses to Big Data capitalism. In drawing on these experiences – on these differential labour histories and the insight of a reproductive lens – we may also find valuable tools for today's struggle.

References

Ahmed, Sara. 2004. *The Cultural Politics of Emotion*. New York: Routledge.

Alcoff, Linda Martín. 2006. *Visible Identities: Race, Gender, and the Self*. New York: Oxford University Press.

Appadurai, Arjun. 1986. 'Introduction: Commodities and the Politics of Value.' In *The Social Life of Things: Commodities in Cultural Perspective*, ed. Arjun Appadurai, 3–63. Cambridge: Cambridge University Press.

Berlant, Lauren and Michael Warner. 1998. 'Sex in Public.' *Critical Inquiry* 24 (2): 547–66.

Braidotti, Rosi. 2013. *The Posthuman*. Cambridge: Polity.

Buckley, Sarah-Anne. 2016. 'The Catholic Cure for Poverty.' *Jacobin*, May 27, https://www.jacobinmag.com/2016/05/catholic-church-ireland-magdalene-laundries-mother-baby-homes/

Butler, Judith. 2004. *Precarious Life: The Powers of Mourning and Violence*. London: Verso.

Butler, Judith, Zeynep Gambetti, and Leticia Sabsay eds. 2016. *Vulnerability in Resistance*. Durham: Duke University Press.

Crowley, Una and Rob Kitchin. 2008. 'Producing 'Decent Girls:' Governmentality and the Moral Geographies of Sexual Conduct in Ireland (1922–37).' *Gender, Place and Culture* 15 (4): 355–72.

Dalla Costa, Mariarosa and Selma James. 1975. *The Power of Women and the Subversion of the Community*. 3rd edition. London: Falling Wall Press.

Daly, Mary E. 1995. 'Women in the Irish Free State 1922–39: The Interaction Between Economics and Ideology.' *Journal of Women's History* 6/7 (4/1): 99–116.

Davis, Angela Y. 1983. *Women, Race and Class*. New York: Vintage Books.

Eisenstein, Zillah R. 1979. 'Developing a Theory of Capitalist Patriarchy and Socialist Feminism.' In *Capitalist Patriarchy and the Case for Socialist Feminism*, ed. Zillah R. Eisenstein, 5–40. New York: Monthly Review Press.

England, Paula. 1993. 'The Separative Self: Androcentric Bias in Neoclassical Assumptions.' In *Beyond Economic Man: Feminist Theory and Economics*, ed. Marianne A. Ferber and Julie A. Nelson, 37–53. Chicago: University of Chicago Press.

Federici, Silvia. 2004. *Caliban and the Witch: Women, the Body and Primitive Accumulation*. New York: Autonomedia.

Federici, Silvia. 2012. *Revolution at Point Zero: Housework, Reproduction and Feminist Struggle*. Oakland, California: PM Press.

Ferguson, Susan. 2016. 'Intersectionality and Social-Reproduction Feminisms: Toward an Integrative Ontology.' *Historical Materialism* 24 (2): 38–60.

Fortunati, Leopoldina. 1995. *The Arcane of Reproduction: Housework, Prostitution, Labour and Capital*. Translated by Hilary Creek. New York: Autonomedia.

Fotopolou, Aristea. 2016. *Feminist Activism and Digital Networks: Between Empowerment and Vulnerability*. London: Palgrave Macmillan.

Fraser, Nancy. 2014. 'Behind Marx's Hidden Abode: For an Expanded Conception of Capitalism.' *New Left Review* 86: 55–72.

Fuchs, Christian. 2017. 'Capitalism, Patriarchy, Slavery, and Racism in the Age of Digital Capitalism and Digital Labour.' *Critical Sociology*, Online First. DOI: https://doi.org/10.1177/0896920517691108.

Hammami, Rema. 2016. 'Precarious Politics: The Activism of "Bodies That Count" (Aligning with Those That Don't) in Palestine's Colonial Frontier.'

In *Vulnerability in Resistance*, eds. Judith Butler, Zeynep Gambetti, and Leticia Sabsay, 167–90. Durham: Duke University Press.

Hardt, Michael and Antonio Negri. 2005. *Multitude*. London: Penguin.

Inglis, Tom. 1997. 'Foucault, Bourdieu and the Fields of Irish Sexuality.' *Irish Journal of Sociology* 7: 5–28.

Jarrett, Kylie. 2017. 'Le Travail Immatériel dans l'Usine Sociale: Une Critique Féministe.' *Poli: Politique de l'Image* 13: 12–25.

Jarrett, Kylie. 2016a. *Feminism, Labour and Digital Media: The Digital Housewife*. New York: Routledge.

Jarrett, Kylie. 2016b. 'Queering Alienation in Digital Media.' *First Monday* 21 (10). DOI: http://dx.doi.org/10.5210/fm.v21i10.6942

Jarrett, Kylie. 2015a. "Let's Express our Friendship by Sending Each Other Funny Links Instead of Actually Talking": Gifts, Commodities and Social Reproduction in Facebook.' In *Networked Affect*, eds. Ken Hillis, Susanna Paasonen and Michael Petit, 203–219. Cambridge: MIT Press.

Jarrett, Kylie. 2015b. 'Devaluing Binaries: Marxist Feminism and the Value of Consumer Labour.' In *Reconsidering Value and Labour in the Digital Age*, eds. Eran Fisher and Christian Fuchs, 207–223. Basingstoke, Hampshire: Palgrave Macmillan.

Kimmel, Michael. 2013. *Angry White Men: American Masculinity at the End of an Era*. New York: Nation Books.

Kopytoff, Igor. 1986. 'The Cultural Biography of Things: Commoditization as Process.' In *The Social Life of Things: Commodities in Cultural Perspective*, ed. Arjun Appadurai, 64–91. Cambridge: Cambridge University Press.

Lorey, Isabell. 2015. *State of Insecurity: Government of the Precarious*. Trans. Aileen Derieg. London: Verso.

Marx, Karl. 1961/2013. 'Economic and Philosophic Manuscripts.' In *Marx's Concepts of Man: Including Economic and Philosophical Manuscripts*, Erich Fromm and Karl Marx, 73–215. Translated by T. B. Bottomore. London: Bloomsbury.

Merteuil, Morgane. 2017. 'The Digital Whore: Cyber Sexual Labour and Social Reproduction.' Unpublished conference paper, Historical Materialism, New York, 21–23 April.

Mies, Maria, Veronika Bennholdt-Thomsen and Claudia von Werlhof. 1988. *Women: The Last Colony*. London: Zed Books.

Moore, Phoebe. 2017. *The Quantified Self in Precarity: Work, Technology and What Counts*. Abingdon: Routledge.

Osucha, Eden. 2009. 'The Whiteness of Privacy: Race, Media, Law.' *Camera Obscura* 24 (1): 67–107.

Qiu, Jack Linchuan. 2016. *Goodbye iSlave: A Manifesto for Digital Abolition*. Urbana, Chicago: University of Illinois Press.

Reveley, James. 2013. 'Understanding Social Media Use as Alienation: A Review and Critique.' *e-Learning and Digital Media* 10 (1): 83–94.

Sandoval, Chela. 2000. *Methodology of the Oppressed*. Minneapolis: University of Minnesota Press.

Sears, Alan. 2016. 'Situating Sexuality in Social Reproduction.' *Historical Materialism* 24 (2): 138–163.

Srnicek, Nick and Alex Williams. 2016. *Inventing the Future: Postcapitalism and a World Without Work*. Revised edition. London: Verso.

Tronti, Mario. 1973. 'Social Capital.' *Telos* 17: 98–121.

Velkova. Julia. 2016. 'Open Cultural Production and the Online Gift Economy: The Case of Blender.' *First Monday* 21 (10). DOI: http://dx.doi.org/10.5210/fm.v21i10.6944

Velkova, Julia and Peter Jakobsson. 2015. 'At the Intersection of Commons and Market: Negotiations of Values in Open-Sourced Cultural Production.' *International Journal of Cultural Studies* 20 (1): 14–30.

CHAPTER 9

Contradictions in the Twitter Social Factory: Reflections on Kylie Jarrett's Chapter

Joanna Boehnert

On 2 November 2017 two of New York City's local digital news sites, The Gothamist and DNAinfom, were shut down by owner Joe Ricketts. All articles and information generated since 2009 vanished from the sites – to be archived elsewhere in less accessible format. 115 people lost their jobs. The destruction of the news companies along with the documentation of local history was instigated by Ricketts as an unsubtle response to an event just one week earlier: when reporters at DNAinfo and Gothamist had voted to unionise. Twitter exploded as another source of local news disappeared and union organising was dealt a symbolic blow.

On 3 November 2017 interdisciplinary artist Mary Boo Anderson posted a new version of the 'expanding brain' meme on Twitter (see https://twitter.com/whoismaryboo/status/926469404199653376, Figures 1 and 2). The sequential series of four images and text linked her experience as a Twitter user to the collapse of digital platforms after the unionisation of content creators. The text also references Anderson's own feelings of enjoying making content for Twitter

How to cite this book chapter:
Boehnert, J. 2019. Contradictions in the Twitter Social Factory: Reflections on Kylie Jarrett's Chapter. In: Chandler, D. and Fuchs, C. (eds.) *Digital Objects, Digital Subjects: Interdisciplinary Perspectives on Capitalism, Labour and Politics in the Age of Big Data*. Pp. 117–123. London: University of Westminster Press. DOI: https://doi.org/10.16997/book29.i. License: CC-BY-NC-ND 4.0

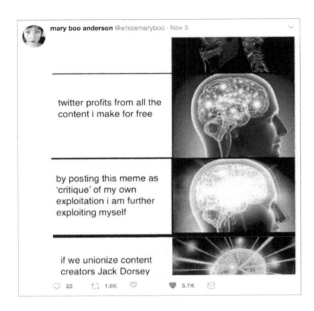

Figures 1 and 2: Mary Boo Anderson @whoismaryboo Twitter post, 3 November 2017.

while simultaneously feeling exploited by Twitter profiting from her labour and even from her critique of this exploitation. In the last frame, she speculates about unionising content creators and having Twitter CEO Jack Dorsey shut down 'this garbage site'.

Anderson's artwork powerfully captures what Kylie Jarrett describes as contradictions of digital labour in the social factory of digital media. In *Feminism, Labour and Digital Media: The Digital Housewife* (2016) Jarrett argues that we can better understand the role of digital media users in the digital economy by using feminist analysis of social reproduction. Jarrett's essay in this book, 'Through the Reproductive Lens: Labour and Struggle at the Intersection of Culture and Economy', expands ideas she developed in *The Digital Housewife* to reflect on the wider context of the politics of social reproduction, speculating on alternative digital media practices. In this short commentary, I use Anderson's artwork to reflect on how Jarrett's ideas can help us understand recent dramatic changes on Twitter.

In describing how ideas and even identities and subjectivities are generated by communicative labour in society (i.e. 'the social factory') Jarrett illustrates how unpaid labour in capitalism is beset by tensions, working simultaneously in oppressive and liberatory ways. I am interested in how these contradictions manifest on Twitter, and what can be done to encounter, break and possibly transform the most troubling tensions. My concern here is with the specific ways in which Twitter is designed to function, the strategies it uses to achieve its goals and the social consequences of these priorities. The social factory concept, an autonomist Marxist concept that describes how capitalism not only directs our economic lives but also expands its alienating, expropriating and commodifying logics into the social domain, is the foundation of this analysis.

The expanding brain meme (i.e. four sequential images of an embodied brain, accompanied by textual content on a variety of themes) had been used over the course of 2017 to imply the evolution of an individual's intellectual capacities. It suggests progress from the reptilian brain to a state with expanded cognitive capacities and even cosmic spiritual insights. Normally, the meme is used in an ironic or semi-ironic manner. Anderson's expanded brain meme is harnessed to highlight her conflicted feelings of liking Twitter but also feeling exploited by the platform, her ideas on disrupting this exploitation, and her vision of being 'set free' by Jack Dorsey's abolition of Twitter.

Twitter occupies a strategic position in the digital media ecosystem. It has gained a massive user base (roughly 330 million active users) due to the platform's facilitation of user interaction in ways that bring good ideas from the margins into prominence. This design amplifies good ideas (Anderson's tweet got over 7000 likes and retweets in the first few days) and disrupts power hierarchies in communication channels and traditional news outlets. Unfortunately, however, things seem to be changing on Twitter in ways that could have a profound impact on the role it plays in facilitating marginalised opinions.

On the same day that Anderson made her artistic intervention, the BBC reported that Twitter has published new rules. Twitter user Tim Peterson noted a specific change: 'Twitter removed its belief 'in speaking truth to power' from its rules' (@petersontee, 3 November 2017). Paterson published screenshots of the new and old Twitter Rules. Twitter has removed 'We believe in freedom of expression and in speaking truth to power' and replaced it with 'We believe in freedom of expression and open dialogue'. The implications of this shift in priorities will become evident over time, but the change inevitably signals an adjustment in priorities and allegiances. Many users have already noted that recent changes in the ways Twitter operates diminish its traditional value.

In November 2017, Twitter changed tweet length from 140 characters to 280 characters, and dramatically transformed the look and feel of the platform. A core distinguishing feature of Twitter has always been its requirement that users express themselves clearly and succinctly. The change in character length altered not only individual tweets but the experience of Twitter feeds, which are no longer easily scrollable. It now takes longer to engage with multiple tweets. This change comes on the back of other modifications. Recently the 'like' feature was changed to function in a similar way to a 'retweet'. This reduces Twitter users' options to use 'likes' and 'retweets' for different purposes. I am not the only user who is concerned that the platform I rely on to access news and analysis is no longer operating in ways that originally made it so attractive.

Mary Boo Anderson's expanding brain meme links Twitter users/content producers to the journalists from the two recently deleted digital new sites (DNAinfo and The Gothamist). Ricketts wrote a blog in September 2017 titled 'Why I'm Against Unions at Businesses I Create', where he said: 'I believe unions promote a corrosive us-against-them dynamic that destroys the esprit de corps businesses need to succeed'. In describing how the value of his company comes from his own entrepreneurial skills and the capital that he personally generated on Wall Street, Ricketts is articulating a mainstream ideological position. In stark contrast to this view, Jarrett's Marxist feminist analysis describes how a wide variety of work enables capitalist profits to take place.

Capitalism depends on many different types of labour, including a vast amount of unpaid labour and reproductive labour. Jarrett's digital housewife metaphor links feminist theory on women's reproductive work to digital work. Both Twitter users and the journalists who lost their jobs can be understood as digital workers who share information and contribute precarious or unpaid cognitive and communicative labour that adds value to digital platforms. The issue of the boundary of valuation is at the crux of the ideological divide in capitalism and in digital capitalism. This has been the case since Marx described the collective labourer or *Gesamtarbeiter* (Fuchs 2017, 4). Christian Fuchs explains that 'in a software company, not just the software engineers who produce the software commodity, are productive workers, but also the secretaries, cleaners, janitors, accountants, marketers, etc. Productive labour produces surplus-value' (2017, 4). Where Ricketts sees value as narrowly created by a stock broker and entrepreneur, the feminist Marxist argument describes all the other labour that sustains communities of people but is exploited in capitalist structures.

In her new text, Jarrett considers Morgane Merteuil's (2017) argument that the digital whore metaphor more accurately describes the extent of capture of the subjective domain in platform economies subject to capitalist logics. If the social emerges from the result of human activities that are the result of relationships largely structured by capitalism, then subjectivities under capitalism are all in profoundly conflicted space. The structures that dominate our lives encourage specific identification and ideological affiliations. The whore metaphor captures how capitalism envelops the intimate spaces of so many people – but especially the most oppressed constituencies.

Jarrett argues that while some media theorists consider the exploitation of labour in digital media as a new feature of the digital economy, 'for anyone who is not a white, cis-, het- man, it is difficult to see precisely what is novel about the conditions in which all of life is subsumed into capital' (2018, 104). Since people in persecuted groups have had to struggle the hardest against various types of oppression, their vantage points can more clearly reveal contradictions in capitalism and digital capitalism. These struggles highlight the tensions in digital media as users experience both agency and pleasure – in having access to more critically engaged news sources; in forming global communities with like-minded people; in having marginalised voices amplified; in the humour (lols) shared, and so on – and exploitation and anxiety – from the increasingly precarious nature of various types of labour; from fake news; from the 'alt-right' and other reactionary movements on social media; from online harassment, and so on. Just as unpaid domestic work has enabled the reproduction of capitalist relations from the start of capitalism, so unpaid digital work enables digital capitalism. But there are serious problems, not just with the injustices inherent in this dynamic, but with the robustness of the structures we depend on for the reliable news that is fundamental to democratic processes.

Like many digital news platforms, DNAinfo and the Gothamist were struggling financially. Digital media platforms are driven by the value of user data and advertising. Twitter has never managed to leverage these in the ways Facebook has done. Platform capitalism has created data-based social relations that have 'fundamentally altered the landscape of capital accumulation and property relations' (Cole 2017). Matthew Cole references Nick Srnicek's (2017) definition of one of the core attributes of platforms, i.e. 'proprietary architecture that mediates interaction possibilities' (2017) and claims that 'the most important asset for platforms is their intellectual property – company software, algorithms, and user data' (2017). It is this intellectual property that enables platforms to mediate exchanges between their users. The problem is that it is not evident that these platforms and the social relations that they establish can

support reliable news and the basic information necessary to enable democratic decision-making in ways that do not lean towards authoritarian and
reactionary political positions. Jarrett describes digital platforms within capitalism's modes of accumulation as having an antagonistic relationship to the
social domain (2016, 3, 33). Troubling digital capitalism by focusing on these
antagonisms and the dialectical relationships between the alienating and actualising tendencies of digital labour creates space for deeper interventions.

Straddling these tensions, Twitter can be understood as the embodiment of
the acceleration of polarised positions. My personal experience of Twitter is
often educational and liberatory. Other Twitter users have expanded my understanding of race, gender, class, economics and other issues that have impacted
my IRL activism, research and friendships. Twitter offers a means to interpret
and respond to political events, and participate in debates and conversations
on a global scale. Yet these experiences, and any associated tenuous feelings of
agency, are precarious. Twitter has facilitated access to news, analysis, commentary and humour from sources that were not easily accessible in the pre-digital
era. And yet even though Twitter users make these features possible and add
value to the platform, the important decisions about how Twitter functions are
not made by its users and content creators. The platform that users contribute
to and rely on is not ours. A platform that is collectively owned by the users
would be a genuine emancipatory technology. A more immediate goal is to
keep Jack Dorsey from destroying Twitter.

References

Cole, Matthew. 2017. 'Platform Capitalism and the Value Form.' *Salvage.*
    Available at: http://salvage.zone/online-exclusive/platform-capitalism-and-
    value-form (accessed 14 May 2018)
Fuchs, Christian. 2017. 'Capitalism, Patriarchy, Slavery, and Racism in the Age
    of Digital Capitalism and Digital Labour.' *Critical Sociology.* Sage. Published
    online, 9 February.
Jarrett, Kylie. 2016. *Feminism, Labour and Digital Media: The Digital Housewife.*
    New York: Routledge.
Jarrett, Kylie. 2018. 'Through the Reproductive Lens: Labour and Struggle at
    the Intersection of Culture and Economy.' *Digital Objects, Digital Subjects:
    Interdisciplinary Perspectives on Big Data Capitalism.* London: University of
    Westminster Press.
Merteuil, Morgane. 2017. 'The Digital Whore: Cyber Sexual Labour and Social
    Reproduction.' Unpublished conference paper, *Historical Materialism,* New
    York, 21–23 April.
Peterson, Tim. (@petersontee). 2017. Twitter removed its belief 'in speak-
    ing truth to power' from its rules. Twitter post, 3 November. Accessed:

14 November 2017. Available at: https://twitter.com/petersontee/ status/ 926557756131180544 (accessed 14 May 2018)

Ricketts, Joe. 2017. 'Why I'm Against Unions at Businesses I Create.' *Joe Ricketts Blog*. Available at: http://blog.joericketts.com/?p=557 (accessed 14 May 2018)

Srnicek, Nick. 2017. *Platform Capitalism*. London: Polity Press.

CHAPTER 10

E(a)ffective Precarity, Control and Resistance in the Digitalised Workplace[1]

Phoebe V. Moore

1. Introduction

'What makes you tick?'
– Claude Shannon (1961)[2]

Digitalised methods to calculate an increasing range of activities and expression at work are evidence that management aims to control what has been called affective (Hardt 1999, Dowling 2007) and emotional (Hochschild 2012 [1983]; Brook 2009, 2013) labour. Emotional and affective labour are, of course, neither new nor limited to digitalised work, and the long history of undervalued labour has been observed and critiqued by several feminist scholars over time. What is new is the trend in uses of technology to control areas of unseen labour through newly digitalised workplaces, with the use of location and sensory devices that threaten to capture and control our every movement, sentiment and thought, thereby blurring the categories between work and life themselves. The danger in granularity where the qualitative

---

work of qualified workers becomes quantified is the rise of barbarism, where there is no outside to the vulgarities of capitalism, where there is no culture nor civility or dignity, but only brutal, corporate-driven commodification and abstraction of labour. The Enlightenment held the promise of reasonable lives for all, but modern times have demonstrated that this cannot be taken for granted. Adorno warned that 'to write poetry after Auschwitz is barbaric' (Adorno 1983, 34). Adorno was not warning against writing poetry, but highlighting humanity's primary condition of barbarism; he stressed later that the most important project after such tragic brutality must be to 'restore an unbarbaric condition' (2005, 50) where the 'sole adequate praxis after Auschwitz is to put all energies toward working our way out of barbarism' (2005, 268).

The present edited collection highlights the 'hard times' we now live in. While I am not explicitly likening these 'hard times' to the Holocaust in the way Adorno notes, I argue that workplace surveillance, at its most extreme, is a form of barbarism in what are, at the very least, significantly unreasonable times. This chapter looks at workers' attempts to disrupt the new forms of the employment relationship that are being created in digitalised and potentially barbaric workplaces, where monitored and surveilled work, in gig-like conditions, has rendered people's lives almost unbearable (Akhtar and Moore 2016).

Building on Blackman and Venn's call to assess the 'capitalization or economization of affect and emotion through teletechnologies' (2010), this chapter looks at employee responses to being asked to use self-tracking and invisiblise management technologies at work to improve health and productivity through affective labour, taking note of everyday forms of resistance to this invasive level of control. New forms of work quantification that involve electronic tracking of affective and emotional labour are capital's latest methods of capturing surplus value in unstable conditions of agility, but the examples of workers' resistance in the empirical findings outlined here reveal weaknesses in these methods.

2. Precarity and Gig Work

Postmodern, radical studies of the laws of value postulate that there is an 'outside' of capital that cannot be quantified, and which thus creates possibilities for emancipation (Negri 1999, 86). Federici argues that primitive accumulation continues today, and that there is no longer a conceivable 'outside' of production relations whilst we live in a capitalist hegemony (2004) and our newest technologies are instrumental to its pursuits. However, new worker monitoring technologies quantify the qualitative, revealing previously unmeasured aspects of the labour process, like mood, fatigue, psychological wellbeing and stress. This makes workers permanently visible to management, and renders the sites of everyday resistance facilitated by worker-to-worker communication penetrable by management, meaning it is increasingly difficult to identify anything outside capital (Moore and Robinson 2016). New procedures and pursuits exceed scientific management's studies of physical movement, since concrete labour is increasingly subject to abstraction as new ways to identify and calculate previously unseen labour become apparent, and more subject to commodification in the process. This employer prescription eliminates any possibility for negativity by highlighting wellbeing (Davies 2016; Cederström and Spicer 2015). With this realisation, and

> [E]ven if the measurement of this new productive reality is impossible, because affect is not measurable, nonetheless in this very productive context, so rich in productive subjectivity, *affect must be controlled.* (Negri 1999, 87)

Quantification, as pointed out by Jarrett (2015a), recognises unseen labour as productive, not as an exchange worthy of consistent or useful reward, but to locate profit for capital.

Precarity is the purest form of alienation, where the worker loses all personal association with the labour she performs. She is dispossessed and locationless in her working life, and all value is extracted from her in every aspect of life. Because precarious digitalised workers are constantly chasing the next 'gig', spatial and temporal consistency in life is largely out of reach. Precarity is symptomatic of the fall in wage share of value added as Fordism gave way to financialised accumulation, the rise in self-employment, automation (Frey and Osborne 2013), the fall of the dotcom bubble and repeated global economic crises. In the UK, statistics in 2016 and 2017 indicate that rises in employment and economic growth are dependent on self-employment such as is seen in gig economy work. More than 900,300 people worked on zero-hour contracts in 2017, a rise of 20% from the figure for 2016.[3]

In the gig economy, also called the demand economy (AFL-CIO, 2016), a range of new online platforms have emerged where people buy and sell labour using digitalised interfaces. The sharing economy, or work in the 'human cloud', includes such platforms as Upwork, ODesk, Guru, Amazon Mechanical Turks, Uber, Deliveroo and Handy, which are called 'online platforms' in the Digital Single Market European Commission terminology. Huws (2015) and Cherry (2011) label this type of exchange and work as 'crowdsourcing', and Huws defines it as 'paid work organized through online labour exchanges' (Huws 2015, 1). Crowdsourcing has facilitated companies' outsourcing of labour and introduced new platforms for freelance and self-employed work and this trend is rising internationally. The platform economy relies on self-employed contracts, and as such its workers have no access to regular employment benefits such as health care or maternity leave. Workers have very little legal protection, and platforms are designed to reduce employer liability. Taken together, these features of gig work can put a great strain on worker's minds and bodies, leading to emotional anxiety and panic. Gig workers must be prepared for constant change and disruption to their lives, and they must consent to make personal changes, to always be on the move, and to always be trackable. So work, identity and life blur in conditions of digitalised precarity. Workers are often in a position where we cannot log out or switch off. Gig workers 'struggle to be left alone rather than to be included, a type of refusal that would have looked strange to their Fordist predecessors' (Fleming 2015, 83).

In gig work, subjectivities are required to be resilient to instability, and subjects are expected to take full responsibility for personal wellness, rather than associate stress and illness with poor working conditions. In sum, gig work is conducted as a process of social reproduction of capitalist labour relations within the context of the reproduction of accelerated capitalist subjectivities of competition (Dalla Costa and James 1972, Jarrett 2015a, 2015b, Haider and Mohandesi 2015, Kofman and Raghuram 2015, Weeks 2011). Affective work reaches below, behind and above the corporeal. Measuring unseen labour is a form of control by means of the 'modulation of affect', carried out by both recording and trying to control bodily capabilities – in our study, by providing self-tracking devices, and thus 'varying the resistance of a body' (Bogard 2010).

In digitalised and gig work, the inevitability of machinic developments takes precedence, even over clients. Pinning to the corporeal, affective gig labourers do not engage in creative production using their own affective capacities. They are engaged in a type of affective repression by which the required subordinate performances corrode their own psychosomatic and bodily wellbeing. Attempts to regulate and modulate affect, and to externalise its costs, are part of this process. Affective labour is, by definition, innumerable and outputs are potentially only seen as 'disembodied "exhaust"' (Smith 2016). Nonetheless, in gig work, every moment of our labour is captured with increasing intensity, not so that it can be remunerated, but because worker collapse could result in resistance and reduce the 'bottom line'.

Lorusso (2017) refers to precarity as a form of Derridean 'hauntology' and Fisher's *Ghost of My Life* (2014) because precarity is not 'fully part of the present' but rides on an 'anticipation shaping current behavior', and to the dream that present activities will lead to something better, a goal oriented vacuum of constant anxious striving given the failure of the present to become what we hoped. From an autonomist viewpoint, precarity is a systemic capture of the hopeful movements of exodus of the 1960s/70s, when resistance often took the form of 'refusal of work', by the 'slacker' or 'dropout' (Shukaitis 2006), with refusal to submit to Fordist work routines (Brophy and de Peuter 2007, 180–181). Capitalism has pursued this exodus into the field of life beyond work, and captured escaping flows by expanding labour into these spaces (Mitropoulos 2006, Neilson and Rossiter 2005, Federici 2008, Frassanito Network 2005). It has also appropriated radical ideas, introducing a wave of flexibilisation and selling it as liberation (Berardi 2009), blurring work-life boundaries in the process. In effect, capitalism followed the fleeing workers into the autonomous spaces of the qualitative, and restructured these spaces along quantitative lines, to bring the workers back into capitalism. Continuous appropriation manifests capitalism's continued capability to re-invent itself when faced with resistance (Berardi 2009, 77).

3. Affective Control and Resistance

Beller predicted that the development of capital was not likely to proceed without the development of technologies for the modulation of affect (Beller 1998, 91). Affect enables or disables our power to act (through the body), and its power lies in its singularity and universality (Negri 1999, 85). These ideas prefigure and inspire the Deleuzian distinction between active and reactive forms of affect or force. Affective labour is the internal work that takes place before emotions are expressed. It is linked to the biological aspects of work, whereby:

> Labour works directly on the affects; it produces subjectivity, it produces society, it produces life. Affective labour, in this sense, is ontological – it reveals living labour constituting a form of life (Hardt 1999, 99).

Corporate colonisation of unseen labour is endemic in post-Fordist management and post-bureaucratic techniques precisely because affective solidarity would lead to the most difficult form of resistance to stop, since affect already encompasses all-of-life.

Hardt and Negri (2000) depict affect and immaterial labour from a post-Fordist perspective as providing possibilities for resistance, collective subjectivities and formations of communities. The emphasis on control of affect in management strategies can be seen to be tied up with labour control and social reproduction of capitalist subjectivity and relations of masked coercion (Hartmann 1979). When workers become conscious of affect, or their power to act, they also become conscious of their ability to impact one another and to challenge abuses at work (Moore 2015). One control method that is explicitly designed to modulate and regulate affect is seen in health care worker training (Ducey 2007). Gregg (2010) outlines the blockages to any affective communication induced by email and pseudo office intimacy garnered by such activities as Secret Santas and other games that prevent affective relationships. Cognitive behavioural therapy and related psychology highlight the role of emotional and affect regulation for stress management at work, and one group has provided the tools titled 'Affect Regulation' (Psychology Tools 2017).

Firth defines affect as a 'necessary part of social and ecological assemblages, which passes through the unconscious field' (Firth 2016, 131). Negri (1999) expands on the 'unseen' aspects of affect and posits that the use value of such labour cannot be quantified in contemporary conditions in the same way that work was controlled during previous eras, because such labour exists in a 'non-place', the immaterial. But affective labour has become a 'moral' obligation imposed by corporate power.

Affective labour is not directly 'inside' capital, but neither is it a straightforward 'nonwaged reproduction of the labourer, added to labour's use value' (Clough 2007, 25). Rather, in real, affective subsumption, work happens constantly, and is both nowhere and everywhere. Work becomes all-of-life. Indeed, 'capital produces its own outside from inside the viscera of life, accumulating at the level of the preindividual bodily capacities and putting preindividual bodily capacities to work' (ibid). The absenting of management and individual responsibilisation in gig work is a method of controlling affective resistance by putting affect to work and reducing labour power, thereby reducing the possibility for consciousness of labour's exploitation.

4. Affective and Everyday Resistance

Many signs of resistance to the worst effects of digitalised affective labour are emerging, from everyday forms to trade union organising. Active resistance includes workers' hacking or appropriation of apps; sousveillance where people 'watch the watcher' by using their own methods to gain access to information they do not normally have by carrying out information and sharing jamming; using personal devices at work; situational leveraging where, for example, people may 'steal' breaks and mask them as work; or simply dragging their feet. Cases have also emerged in which workers use self-tracking for resistance and self-protection. In one case, a project worker without a fixed contract used self-tracking to protect himself from unpaid overtime. He tracked time spent on projects to prove he was being underpaid and to ensure his employer's compliance with the European Working Time Directive. Ross talks about other forms of direct action in the context of exploitative digital labour, naming 'pervasive sabotage, chronic absenteeism and wildcat strikes' (Ross 2008, 7).

From a labour process perspective, technology *itself* has not caused the conditions of precarity. Rather, the use of data from technologies, and the invisibilisation of power relations, has intensified age-old practices of scientific management and related worker control. But worker organising and resistance has begun to reveal the revived agency in labour power as a response to the latest incarnation of Ricardo's machine question. For solidarity to fully emerge amongst digitalised workers, class consciousness in the Marxist sense is necessary. Some have claimed, however, that class has fundamentally changed vis-a-vis concepts of labour. Virno (2004) wonders whether the multitude is too centrifugal to hold a class consciousness 'of its own'. Standing (2011) has asked whether a 'multi-class' configuration that identifies precarity is even necessary, since it is identifiable in other ways. Work ascribes worth to our species-being (Sayer 2005), and people find dignity and self-worth within labour. Technology and social media has been a medium for social uprising and resistance (Gerbaudo 2012), and digital activism's 'firebrand waves' have been escalating since the early 1990s (Karatzogianni 2015). Fishwick argues that critical subjective connections in the labour process are crucial for resistance, where

> [C]ontestation in and around the production process is central to the formation of the working class as a political subject. Not only does it create objective conditions of shared experience, it also allows for a collective subjective interpretation of these experiences that extends beyond the workplace and permits the articulation of coherent and salient political interests as a class (2015, 215).

Ross notes that the expectations placed upon the precariat are a 'warmed over version of Social Darwinism' (2008, 36). It is easy to see how this operates in practice, as the value of social performances is *entirely reduced* to managerial metrics.

Lordon's *Willing Slaves of Capital* looks to the work of Spinoza and Marx to ask why people continue to serve capital and have not overcome it, given its abuses. Affect and its power to act can be triggered by both the positive *and* the negative (which is often overlooked in the literature on affect). A 'last straw' can trigger the multitude, when institutional power, in the Spinozan sense of 'pouvoir', can no longer contain people's 'sadness', and our inter-affections and enlisted conatus will drive us to revolt. Lordon shares Spinoza's point of 'indignation', where political affect is brought to bear. Joy, desire and passion (and unseen labour, as I argue) are classically appropriated by capital. Lordon asks whether the social reproduction of capitalism could be appropriated to reproduce subjectivities of resistance, where 'collective human life reproduces itself', he says, and 'the passions that work to keep individuals subordinate to institutional relations can also, at times, reconfigure themselves to work against those same relations' (Lordon 2014, 138–139).

Attentive stress and disposability are intensified by unrealistic expectations fostered by a quantified, machine-like image of human productivity, and further intensified by permanent indebtedness, leading to a sense of permanent inadequacy (Gill 1995). Tracking and monitoring technologies appear to provide objective data on human capabilities, but this claim elides their social context. They measure only users, creating an illusion that the precarious worker – constructed by the affective and social field of which these technologies are a part – is identical with humanity, the defining point of human bodily capabilities, and the point from which we should start – an outer limit of 'human nature' which restricts political and social possibility. While to some degree measuring emotion, feeling, and bodily responses, dividing and distributing work with new technologies at a granular level involves the capture of affect *stricto sensu* – the very social and psycho-structural underpinnings of affective responses. Such technologies only measure variance within the range defined by precarian affect, providing an illusory, pseudo-objective view of what might be possible outside this range.

Worse still, the ideology of the quantification of all of life and work perpetuates the image that the mind controls the body, and thus, from a Spinozian perspective, serves to contain the body's power within a mental frame largely constituted by neoliberal ideology and subjectivity (the managerial self, quantified productive performance, magical voluntarism). Butler's (2004) work on *Precarious Life* looks at the body as containing mortality, vulnerability and agency (26). While this text is not about resistance as such, her recognition of the shared 'vulnerability of life' (Lorey 2010) and her call to leftist politics to aim to orient our 'normative obligations of equality and universal rights' around our corporeality and vulnerability (ibid). Perhaps now is the time for the precariat to identify itself (ourselves) and identify a real alternative, an alternative that does not prey on insecurity but builds solidarity, a constituting of the political without the requirement for a single leader, a rhizomatic formation of activation, without requiring a class identity in the orthodox sense.

Precarity is now used in academic and public discourse to reference the abandoned worker, the vulnerable, the person whose life is tied up with ongoing risk and stress. At the international level, discussions are ongoing about forming a new labour convention based on tackling violence against women and men. At the 'From Precarious Work to Decent Work'-ILO 2011 Workers' Symposium on *Policies and Regulations to Combat Precarious Employment*, trade unionists, ITUC, the Global Union Federations, workers' groups, and trade unionists met to discuss the symptoms of rising precarity noted by the Occupy Together movement, escalating unemployment and underemployment, and the crisis of democracy and collapsing economies in the West. The documents produced from these meetings outline the problem and highlight strategies for viable responses, including how to organise and enable informal forms of solidarity and resistance among workers. The Labour arm of the ILO, ACTRAV, composed the *Symposium on Precarious Work* in 2012 to look for ways to mitigate the fact that 'people everywhere, it seems, are suffering from precarity as a result of economic and financial crisis, and weak Government policy responses to these' (ACTRAV 2012, 1). What these actions didn't predict was the dramatic rise in gig work which has become ubiquitous in many cities.

In the early 2000s I talked to a range of precarious digital workers about their experiences of work at the Fab Lab centre in Manchester. The emerging picture was one of overwork and stress, which contradicts dominant images of the freedoms of creative and digital labour:

> I have dealt with unreasonable expectations and impossible management cultures in full time work... I would like less stress and more freedom to work on what I want, as this is where the real 'innovation' happens.

I deal with constant overwork and funding problems.

The main problems are the economic recession, people losing control over their lives.

Play? At the moment it is all work.

Near deadlines stress is a real problem, and whatever the ergonomics, sitting for 12+ hours a day is bad for your health and posture.

We need realistic expectations. You can work 80 hours a week for a while, but you must remember that it won't do you good in the long term.

These quotes from IT and creative industries gig workers reveal a set of persistent recurring problems, including unreasonable performance expectations, and pressure (through incentives and self-conception of capability and necessity). There is a growing acceptance that jobs require flexibility, volunteering, and the extraction of surplus value, and this means that an emerging form of self-perception keeps precarious gig workers in a 'condition of animated suspension' (Berlant 2011, 256).

5. Pushing Back in Hard Times

5.1. Everyday Forms of Resistance in Gig Work

Mags Dewhurst is a same-day medical pushbike courier for CitySprint UK Ltd, and Chair of the Independent Workers of Great Britain. I asked Ms Dewhurst about some of the changes she has witnessed over the five years she has done this work. Dewhurst replied that there has been a rise in technology such as handheld computers (XDA/PDA like Palm Pilots) and apps, both in the courier industry and food delivery. These technologies have digitised what used to happen on paper, and are used primarily for the collection of signatures to authorise pick up and collection of parcels. However, the related devices also allow companies to GPS track all couriers' movements in real time, as well as monitor the process of collection and delivery at every stage. Dewhurst stated that:

[Y]our every move and action are tracked in a digital audit trail. This is quite different from the days when couriers used to work off paper and rely solely on the use of the radio (Walkie Talkie) to receive jobs. Now everything is digital there is much less freedom and [a] much higher amount of control, thus meaning we are much less 'independent', even though our contracts say we are totally free and independent.

I asked Dewhurst what, in her view, is the biggest threat to workers' rights, in this context. She noted that bogus Independent Contractor (IC)/Subcontractor contracts are prevalent in gig economy work. She told me that the rise of digitisation, automation and algorithmic management have risen, stating that 'used in combination, they're toxic and are designed to strip millions of folks of basic rights'. I asked which rights are being stripped in her context of work. Dewhurst replied, 'All of them. The only bit of legislation that protects me would be the equality act, but that would only protect certain characteristics and would be hard to win anyway. Holiday pay, NMW [national minimum wage], sick pay, pensions, parental leave, redundancy, tax and in [national insurance] contributions… is removed via IC contracts'.

Mags and her colleagues, in response to the pressure they face in gig work,

> Built a branch of the IWGB UNION [Independent Workers Union of Great Britain] (IWGB). This is the mechanism we have found most effective for creating change – as it helps consolidate a fragmented community and gives people hope and strength in numbers and through collective fights. So far we have won three major pay rises of 20-30% at London's big three courier companies; CitySprint, Ecourier and Absolutely Couriers. We also won at Gophr a small app company but they recently backed out of the agreement. We are also in the process of challenging our IC status in the courts at four of the big courier companies. We've also had limited success with the Deliveroo strike in August. Although we didn't manage to stop the new pay structure coming in, we helped the workers escalate their strike, created loads of positive publicity and helped to shine a big light on the gig economy and exposed the contradictions inherent in it – which are all present in the courier industry as well, obviously.

I asked what more could be done to organise and reform work, and what is stopping people from doing it? Dewhurst indicated that the difficulty with unionising gig economy workers is that it is hard to get access to workers who are constantly on the move because their work is scattered across large areas. Dewhurst noted that 'if we can't get legislation to force companies to let unions in from the off, which is highly likely, then unions need to try harder'. She noted that a problem is that unions often have a very negative attitude that only serves to prevent action. Dewhurst related that she often hears big unions complaining about anti-trade union legislation and a lack of participation, and blaming the government for why they are not winning. In her mind,

> [T]his is the wrong attitude and is a recipe for inaction and is defeatist. If this is the attitude, of course nothing will happen and of course you won't convince anyone to take action. What was great about the Deliveroo strike was that it was autonomous: the drivers did it by themselves,

we merely assisted once it got going. It exposed the failings of government, business, and the unions!! Now slowly, the big guys are waking up and gearing up but I doubt much will happen. As ever we will rely on workers to have the courage themselves to take action and force change and that is where the real power lies.

One warehouse operative, Ingrid (not her real name), who has worked in one warehouse in Britain for 11 years, provided information to me about a new worn device that was rolled out in her workplace in February 2016. All warehouse work-floor operatives were unexpectedly required to use the hand-worn scanner. The current researchers asked what the workers were told the devices would be used for. Ingrid replied that management told workers that the devices would provide management with information about any mistakes made and who in the warehouse had made them, so that they can be given help not to do it again.

In practice, however, Ingrid indicated that the technology has been used, not only to track individual mistakes, but also to track individual productivity and time spent working and on breaks. Workers were told that management would hold individual consultations on the basis of the data, but this had not happened. Instead, at a specific interval in the months that followed the devices' implementation, workers were told that people would be fired within days, and it transpired that data from devices were part of the decision-making process for who to dismiss. Ingrid was not clear how the data were interpreted however, as seen in her response here:

> Recently they sacked 2 or 3 people, and they decided this based upon who did least work. Maybe it was in May, when things get a bit quieter at work. They sacked 3 people: one of them was lazy, so I understand why. But the other 2 were very good. A week before the sackings, the management said 'everyone be careful, because we are going to fire someone from the temporary staff'. So everybody speeded up.

Ingrid indicated concern that the data accumulation was in fact, being rigged. In one case she and co-workers suspected that specific people were given easier tasks during a period of amplified monitoring. While warehouse operatives are permitted to join trade unions, Ingrid indicated that she is not part of a trade union and that she is not aware of any membership in her workplace. In any case, no consultation was held with relevant trade unions nor with workers before the technology was integrated. Ingrid stated:

> We're aware that the tracking might be used to put pressure on us to work faster, and it might be used to sack people. But lots of us feel that we don't care anymore. Because physically we just can't do any more.

5.2. *The Quantified Workplace Experiment and A(e)ffective Resistance*[4]

From 2015–16, one group of professional workers in an office in the Netherlands carried out an experiment they called the 'Quantified Workplace' project (hereafter labelled as QWP). Up to 50 employees were given the option to obtain a FitBit Charge HR Activity Tracker, and in the end around 35 took them. Some employees ordered different sizes which did not arrive, and this and other problems led in the end to about 25 participants being engaged at various points throughout the year that the project ran. The company contracted a data analyst, Joost Plattel, who set up individualised dashboards and RescueTime for participants. Volunteers for the project received workday lifelog emails asking them to rate their subjective productivity, wellbeing and stress.

Findings from interviews showed variable responses to the research questions. The highest rates of increase in coded categories were in autonomy, desire for coaching and support, and concern for privacy. People's perceptions of whether the QW project had an impact on behaviour change decreased by 48% from month 3 to 8 of the project. While at the beginning of the project, participants were not sure of the need to set goals for personal involvement in the project, by the end of the project, the number of responses indicating that it would be good to set goals increased by 27%. Workers' sense of uncertainty about the project decreased by 70% by the eighth month. This result, however, is not reflected in the level of engagement with the project (see Table 1).

Importantly, the project ran during a period of change management as one multinational company absorbed a smaller company that had been a tight-knit group of real estate and work design consultants. The smaller company

Themes	Frequency Interview 1	% Responses Interview 1	Frequency Interview 2	% Responses Interview 2	% Change between 1 and 2
Perceived behaviour change	7	3.43%	12	3.96%	15%
No perceived behaviour change	5	2.45%	11%	3.63%	48%
Difficulties in using tech	13	6.37%	24	7.92%	20%
Good to set goals	9	4.41%	17	5.61%	27%
Not important to set goals	5	2.45%	3	0.99%	-60%
Goals met	0	0	17	5.61%	-
Stopped using tech	9	4.41%	20	6.60%	50%
Unsure about project	41	20.10%	18	5.94%	-70%
Continuous tech use	8	3.92%	14	4.62%	18%
Not continuous tech use	7	3.43%	18	5.94%	73%
Concerns about performance management	5	2.45%	2	0.66%	-73%
Impact on sense of autonomy	2	0.98%	9	2.97%	203%
Positive engagement w project	25	12.25%	5	1.65%	-87%
Impact on motivation	13	6.37%	5	1.65%	-74%
Desire for competitive element	2	0.98%	6	1.98%	102%
Desire for coaching	2	0.98%	15	4.95%	405%
Impact on workplace relationships	9	4.41%	34	11.22%	154%
Increased self-awareness	25	12.25%	36	11.88%	-3%
Effect on subjective productivity	14	6.86%	16	5.28%	-23%
Concern for privacy	3	1.47%	21	6.93%	371%

Table 1: Interview findings: 'Quantified Workplace' project.

suggested and led the project. The project was part of a move toward a more agile workplace, as I was informed by the manager running the project. The project manager indicated that his intentions were to help workers adapt to an agile working environment, where change was to be expected and red tape reduced, and to see to what extent employees' self-awareness, stress, wellbeing and 'wellbilling' (the amount of revenue an employee generates for the company), was impacted during the period of transition (interview October 5, 2015).

In this context, workers were expected to transform affective and physical aspects of themselves, through becoming healthier, happier and more productive with the use of intensely investigatory devices. The company was interested in comparing subjectively and objectively measured productivity, this being linked to health and activity tracking and 'billability'. I was not given access to the data gathered by the company on whether improved activity led to higher productivity and billability. However, the project did fit with the company's moves toward working anywhere, in a gig-like scenario, which was encouraged at the time that the project merger was put in place, and also led to increases in teamwork; and efficiency. Furthermore, the merger was a significant *change* for all who had worked in the smaller company since all participants in the QWP had been employed in the smaller company. So, their experience of change and affective labour were measured by the processes put into place by the QWP. Workers were expected to manage any emotional or affective impacts as the company went through a merge and acquisition process. My interviews with participants demonstrate acts of resistance that involve exit from the project because of concerns about privacy, concerns about digital devices' validity, and concerns about the corporate surveillance that a project of this type engenders.

Responses in the first interviews demonstrate scepticism about the validity of the FitBIt is readings, and desire for more device intelligence:

> A big question for me and for a few others as well, is uh, how reliable the FitBit is.
> [...] This thing [FitBit] might be more intelligent than just recording my data.

One respondent in the second interviews indicated frustration:

> I don't get any answers, I just fill in my things, but I don't get an answer if it is good or not, I just want to know if I [am] good and just start working.

One comment in the first interviews indicated that employees originally thought there would be more 'complaints about privacy'. However, in the first interviews, only three comments indicate concern about what personal data management were viewing, though this increased to 21 in the final interviews. Most participants were cautious about corporate privacy practices. In the first survey, 66% agreed that 'consumers have lost all control over how personal information is collected and used by companies'; 62% disagreed that 'most businesses handle the personal information they collect about consumers in a proper and confidential way'; 43% disagreed that 'existing laws and organizational practices provide a reasonable level of protection for consumer privacy today'.

One response to the question 'How/have your thoughts about the Quantified Workplace project changed?' stated,

> I still [have] and even [have] more doubt [about] the project. And I don't wear the Fitbit very often. And when I will wear it, it is for myself and to see how active I am.
>
> After monitoring my workplace behaviour over a couple of months I found out that it didn't change a lot. It confirmed my thoughts, which I had in the beginning. It is better to change your behaviour based on your feelings rather than a device.
>
> I learned not very much from it.

Nine interview responses indicated FitBit abandonment, either for a period or altogether in the first two months. Some used the FitBit for almost the entire project, while others engaged with it for less than one month/occasionally. FitBit use decreased significantly throughout the project, reflected by the monthly total average step count recorded from all employees. There was a 30% drop in average steps recorded within the first three months, a 50% drop within six months, and a 75% drop by the end. These results demonstrate explicit resistance to the QWP, calling into question the effectiveness of this kind of project where affective and emotional labour are managed in a period of agility.

6. Conclusion

Digitalised work unites the body and mind under the sign of mind, as techniques of managerial (mental) control, what Rose (2001) terms the 'politics of life itself'. The difficulty, however, is that this politics does not speak to 'life itself', any more than Fordism or medievalism. What it speaks to is a particular *quantitative, spatial representation* of life. Emphasising empowerment, Hardt and Negri (2000) illustrate affect and immaterial labour in the post-Fordist climate as providing possibilities for resistance and formation of communities. The emphasis on affect in management strategies can be seen to be tied up with labour control and social reproduction (Hartmann 2002, cited in Carls 2007, 46). As a tool of resistance, affect functions in this system as a structure which enables or disables our power to act (through the body). One can contrast an instrumental relationship, where the body is 'used' by the mind to pursue rational goals, with an expressive relationship, in which bodily or affective forces express themselves in the world, through the mind. Work in the digitalised contexts occurs in an intensely instrumentalised relationship between workers, clients and often invisible forms of management.

I conclude by assessing the possibilities for affective resistance in digitalised work. Affect is the 'power to act that is singular and at the same time universal' (Negri 1999, 85). This prefigures and inspires the Deleuzian distinction between active and reactive forms of affect or force. Affective labour is the internal work that takes place before emotions are expressed, and involves both the possibility for subconscious labour power that could lead to resistance, but also the potential for subconscious affective self-repression. It is linked to the biological aspects of work, whereby:

> Labour works directly on the affects; it produces subjectivity, it produces society, it produces life. Affective labour, in this sense, is ontological – it reveals living labour constituting a form of life… (Hardt 1999, 99)

For Spinoza, affect was an intensely embodied concept which refers to the active ways in which bodies affect one another and co-produce social life (not always in conscious ways). The full positive realisation of affect means that the 'power to act' is enacted, and solidarity is immaterial, becoming also conscious and corporeal. Thus affect transcends what is immediately conscious. For this reason, affective resistance is a serious threat to systems of workplace operation such as interface management in the gig work context. Simply put, affective solidarity would lead to the most difficult form of resistance to stop, since, akin to invasive management techniques of technological control that infiltrate all aspects of life, affect already infiltrates all-of-life.

Simondon (1958/1980) discusses transindividuality as a link to emancipation by describing technical objects as having an infinite number of possible uses when they are individualised, but he notes that their convergence is the point at which they are useful and become a system. He looks at the case of a 'made to measure' car, indicating that only non-essential parts are contingent and work 'against the essence of technical being, like a dead weight imposed from without'(18). Simondon defends the human as the organiser of the technical, stating that automation is never perfect nor complete and always contains a 'certain margin of indetermination' (4). He states that 'far from being the supervisor of a squad of slaves, man is the permanent organiser of technical objects which need him as much as musicians in an orchestra need a conductor' (4). In a similar way, people can recognise their individual existence without becoming atomised or hostile, and realise instead that our interrelations are what strengthen us and prevent us from abdicating and delegating our humanity to a robot (2). Marx observed during his lifetime the ways in which early industrialisation turned 'living labour into a mere living accessory of this machinery, as the means of its action, also posits the absorption of the labour process in its material character as a mere moment of the realisation process of capital' (Marx 1858/1993, 693). He adds: '[machinic] knowledge appears as alien' and 'external' to the worker where the worker is 'superfluous' (brackets added) (1858/1993, 605). In this text, Marx identifies the machine in the labour process and describes its capacity for quantifying, abstracting and dividing labour; he comments that 'the worker's activity, reduced to a mere abstraction of activity, is determined and regulated on all sides by the movements of the machinery, and not the opposite' (1858/1993, 693). In this way, Marx identifies agency, and even authority, with the machinery, where 'objectified labour confronts living labour within the labour process itself as the power which rules it; a power which, as the appropriation of living labour, is the form of capital' (1858/1993, 693). The means of labour, Marx wrote, is transformed, controlled and absorbed by machinery. It is very likely that workers are beginning to resist both traditional forms of management and machinery itself (see Moore 2017).

Digitalised work, in the contemporary context of agility and precarity, ultimately demonstrates that machines are now more than ever before the symbols for 'the ordering of life itself' (Merchant 1990, 227), accelerating the labour process to the cliff edge of what is possible to endure, and dragging workers with them. Workers' responses to the digitalised aspects of gig work, as well as their explicit disengagement with the quantified workplace company-led project outlined here, demonstrate awareness of the tensions surrounding new control mechanisms, the ongoing struggles in the contemporary labour process where agility is a key meme, and the urgent need for a review of all-of-life management strategies. This chapter explores where and how resistance emerges to this brave new world of all-of-life work, where monitoring and tracking of unseen labour may become ubiquitous. Future research must look at the risks this poses for workers, and at forms of resistance that emerge against modulation and control methods in the quantified workplace.

Notes

1 A version of this chapter has been published in Adam Fishwick and Heather Connolly (2018) *Austerity and Working Class Resistance: Survival, Disruption and Creation in Hard Times* (Rowman and Littlefield 2018).
2 Comment made while testing first wearable computer invented and designed by Claude Shannon and Edward O. Thorp at MIT, to be used for casino roulette (Thorp 1998).
3 Data source: https://www.theguardian.com/uk-news/2018/apr/23/number-of-zero-hours-contracts-in-uk-rose-by-100000-in-2017-ons
4 Lukasz Piwek provided data analysis support for this project.

References

ACTRAV. 2012. *From Precarious Work to Decent Work. Outcome Document to the Workers' Symposium on Policies and Regulations to Combat Precarious*

Employment. International Labour Organisation, Bureau for Workers' Activities. Available at: http://www.ilo.org/wcmsp5/groups/public/@ed_dialogue/@actrav/documents/meetingdocument/wcms_179787.pdf (accessed 14 May 14 2018)

Adorno, Theodor W. 1983. 'Cultural Criticism and Society.' In *Prisms*, 17–34. Cambridge, MA: MIT Press.

Adorno, Theodor W. 2005. *Minima Moralia. Reflections on a Damaged Life*. London and New York: Verso.

AFL-CIO. 2016. *Our Principles on the On-Demand Economy*. Available at: https://aflcio.org/our-principles-demand-economy (accessed 14 May 2018)

Akhtar, Pav and Phoebe Moore. 2016. 'The Psycho-Social Impacts of Technological Change in Contemporary Workplaces and Trade Union Responses.' *International Journal of Labour Research* 8 (1–2): 102–31.

Beller, Jonathan. 1998. 'Capital/Cinema.' In *Deleuze and Guattari: New Mappings in Politics, Philosophy and Culture*, eds. Eleanor Kaufman and Kevin Jon Heller. 76–95. Minnesota: University of Minnesota Press.

Berardi, Franco 'Bifo'. 2009. *Precarious Rhapsody*. New York: Minor Composition.

Berlant, Lauren. 2011. *Cruel Optimism*. USA: Duke University.

Blackman, Lisa and Couze Venn. 2010. *Affect*, special issue: *Body & Society* 16 (1).

Bogard, William. 2010. 'Digital Resisto(e)rs.' *Code Drift: Essays in Critical Digital Studies* cds012. Available at: http://ctheory.net/ctheory_wp/digital-resistoers/ (accessed 14 May 2018)

Brook, Paul. 2013. 'Emotional Labour and the Living Personality at Work: Labour Power, Materialist Subjectivity and the Dialogical Self.' *Culture and Organization* 19(4).

Brook, Paul. 2009. 'The Alienated Heart: Hochschild's Emotional Labour Thesis and the Anti-Capitalist Politics of Alienation.' *Capital and Class* 33 (2): 7–31.

Brophy, Enda and Greig de Peuter. 2007. 'Immaterial Labor, Precarity and Recomposition.' In *Knowledge Workers in the Information Society*, eds. Catherine McKercher and Vincent Mosco. Lanham, MD: Lexington.

Butler, Judith. 2004. *Precarious Life: The Powers of Mourning and Violence*. London: Verso.

Cederström, Carl and André Spicer. 2015. *The Wellness Syndrome*. Cambridge: Polity.

Cherry, Miriam A. (2011) 'A Taxonomy of Virtual Work', 45 GA. L. REV. 951, 962–69.

Clough, Patricia. 2007. 'Introduction.' In *The Affective Turn: Theorising the Social*. Durham and London: Duke University Press, pp. 1–33.

Dalla Costa, Mariarosa and Selma James. 1972. *The Power of Women and the Subversion of Community*. Brooklyn, NY: Petroleuse Press.

Davies, William. 2016. *The Happiness Industry: How the Government and Big Business Sold Us Well-Being*. London: Verso Books.

Dowling, Emma. 2016. 'Valorised but Not Valued: Affective Remuneration, Social Reproduction and Feminist Politics Beyond the Crisis.' *British Politics* 11 (4): 452–68.

Dowling, Emma. 2007. 'Producing the Dining Experience: Measure Subjectivity and the Affective Worker.' *Ephemera* 7 (1): 117–32.

Ducey, Ariel. 2007. 'More Than a Job: Meaning, Affect, and Training Health Care Workers.' In *The Affective Turn: Theorizing the Social*, eds. Patricia Clough and Jean Halley. Durham, NC: Duke University Press. 187–208.

Federici, Silvia. 2008. 'Precarious Labour: A Feminist Viewpoint.' *In the Middle of A Whirlwind*. Available at: https://inthemiddleofthewhirlwind. wordpress.com/precarious-labor-a-feminist-viewpoint/ (accessed 14 May 2018).

Federici, Silvia. 2004. *Caliban and the Witch: Women, the Body and Primitive Accumulation*. New York: Autonomedia.

Firth, Rhiannon. 2016. 'Somatic Pedagogies: Critiquing and Resisting the Affective Discourse of the Neoliberal State from an Embodied Anarchist Perspective.' *Ephemera* 16(4): 121–142.

Fisher, Mark. 2014. *Ghosts of My Life: Writings on Depression, Hauntology and Lost Futures* London: Verso Books.

Fishwick, Adam. 2015. 'Paternalism, Taylorism, Socialism: The Battle for Production in the Chilean Textile Industry, 1930–1970.' In *Handbook of the International Political Economy of Production*, ed. Kees van der Pijl, 211–28. London: Edward Elgar.

Fleming, Peter. 2015. *Resisting Work: The Corporatization of Life and is Discontents*. Temple: University Press.

Frassanito Network. 2005. 'Precarious, Precarization, Precariat?' Available at: http://www.metamute.org/editorial/articles/precarious-precarisation-precariat (accessed 14 May 2018)

Frey, C. and Osborne, M. 2013. The Future of Employment: How Susceptible Are Jobs to Computerisation? (Oxford Martin School, University of Oxford). Available at: https://www.oxfordmartin.ox.ac.uk/downloads/academic/The_Future_of_Employment.pdf

Gerbaudo, Paolo. 2012 *Tweets and the Streets: Social Media and Contemporary Activism*. London: Pluto Press.

Gill, Stephen. 1995. 'The Global Panopticon? The Neo-Liberal State, Economic Life and Democratic Surveillance.' *Alternatives: Global, Local, Political* 20 (1): 1–49.

Gregg, Melissa. 2010. 'On Friday Night Drinks: Workplace Affects in the Age of the Cubicle.' In *The Affect Theory Reader*, eds. Melissa Gregg and Gregory J. Seigworth, 250–268. Durham and London: Duke University Press.

Haider, Asad and Salar Mohandesi. eds. 2015. Social Reproduction special issue. *Viewpoint Magazine* 5.

Hardt, Michael. 1999. 'Affective Labour.' *boundary 2* 26 (2): 89–100.

Hardt, Michael and Antonio Negri. 2000. *Empire*. Cambridge, MA: Harvard University Press.

Hartmann, Heidi. 1979. 'Capitalism, Patriarchy and Job Segregation by Sex.' *Signs* 1 (3): 137–69.

Hochschild, Arlie Russell. 2012 [1983]. *The Managed Heart: Commercialization of Human Feeling*. Berkeley, CA: University of California Press.

Huws, Ursula. 2015. 'Online Labour Exchanges, or "Crowdsourcing": Implications for Occupational Safety and Health'. European Occupational Safety and Health Agency.

Jarrett, Kylie. 2015a. 'Devaluing Binaries: Marxist Feminism and the Values of Consumer Labour.' In *Reconsidering Value and Labour in the Digital Age*, eds. Christian Fuchs and Eran Fisher, 207–23. New York: Springer.

Jarrett, Kylie. 2015b. *Feminism Labour and Digital Media: The Digital Housewife*. Abingdon: Routledge.

Karatzogianni, Athina. 2015. *Firebrand Waves of Digital Activism 1994–2014: The Rise and Spread of Hacktivism and Cyberconflict*. Basingstoke: Palgrave Macmillan.

Kofman, Eleonore and Parvati Raghuram. 2015. *Gendered Migrations and Global Social Reproduction*. Basingstoke: Palgrave Macmillan.

Lordon, Frédéric. 2014. *Willing Slaves of Capital: Spinoza and Marx on Desire*. London, New York: Verso.

Lorey, Isabell. 2010. 'Becoming Common: Precarization as Political Constituting.' *e-flux*, 17 (June). Available at: http://www.e-flux.com/journal/17/67385/becoming-common-precarization-as-political-constituting/ (accessed 14 May 2018)

Lorusso, Silvio. 2017. 'A Hauntology of Precarity'. Institute of Network Cultures, *Enteprecariat*. 21 Feb. Available at: http://networkcultures.org/entreprecariat/a-hauntology-of-precarity/ (accessed 14 May 2018)

Marx, Karl. 1858/1993. 'Fragment on Machines.' In *Grundrisse: Foundations of the Critique of Political Economy*. Translated and with a foreword by Martin Nicolau. London: Penguin Books.

Merchant, Carolyn. 1990. *The Death of Nature: Women Ecology and the Scientific Revolution*. London: HarperCollins.

Moore, Phoebe. 2017. *The Quantified Self at Work, in Precarity: Work, Technology and What Counts*. London: Routledge.

Moore, Phoebe. 2015. 'Tracking Bodies, the Quantified Self and the Corporeal Turn.' In *The International Political Economy of Production*, ed. Kees van der Pijl, 394–408. Cheltenham: Edward Elgar.

Moore, Phoebe and Andrew Robinson. 2016. 'The Quantified Self: What Counts in the Neoliberal Workplace.' *New Media & Society* 18 (11): 2774–92.

Massumi, Brian. 2002. *Parables for the Virtual: Movement Affect, Sensation*. Durham: Duke University Press.

Mitropoulos, A. 2006. 'Precari-Us?' *Mute* 29: 88–92. Available at: http://www.metamute.org/editorial/articles/precari-us (accessed 14 May 2018)

Negri, Antonio. 1999. 'Value and Affect.' Translated by Michael Hardt. *boundary 2* 26 (2): 77–88.

Neilson, Brett and Ned Rossiter. 2005. 'From Precarity to Precariousness and Back Again: Labour, Life and Unstable Networks.' *The Fibreculture*

Journal FCJ-022(5): np. Available at: http://five.fibreculturejournal.org/ fcj-022-from-precarity-to-precariousness-and-back-again-labour-life-and-unstable-networks/ (accessed 14 May 2018)

Psychology Tools. 2017. *Affect Regulation/Emotion Regulation* Available at: https://psychologytools.com/technique-affect-regulation.html (accessed 14 May 2018)

Rose, Nikolas. 2001. 'The Politics of Life Itself'. *Theory, Culture and Society* 18 (6): 1–30.

Ross, Andrew. 2008. 'The New Geography of Work. Power to the Precarious?' In *The Precarious Labour in the Field of Art* 5(16/13) 25 (7–8): 31–49. Oncurating.org. Available at: www.e-flux.com/wp-content/uploads/2013/05/ Ross_Precarity.pdf (accessed 14 May 2018)

Sanchez, Luis M. and Rakesh Nagi. 2010. 'A Review of Agile Manufacturing Systems'. *International Journal of Production Research* 39 (16): 3561–600.

Sayer, Andrew. 2005. 'Class, Moral Worth and Recognition'. *Sociology* 29 (5): 957–63.

Shukaitis, Stevphen. 2006. 'Whose Precarity is it Anyway?' *Fifth Estate* 41 (3). Available at: https://www.fifthestate.org/archive/374-winter-2007/whose-precarity-is-it-anyway/ (accessed 14 May 2018)

Simondon, Gilbert. 1958/1980. *On the Mode of Existence of Technical Objects.* Translated by Ninian Mellamphy. Ontario: University of Western Ontario.

Smith, Gavin J. D. 2016. 'Surveillance Data and Embodiment: On the Work of Being Watched'. *Body and Society* 22 (2): 108–39.

Standing, Guy. 2011. *The Precariat: The New Dangerous Class.* London: Bloomsbury.

Virno, Paolo. 2004. *The Grammar of the Multitude.* New York: Semiotext(e). Available at: http://www.generation-online.org/c/fcmultitude3.htm (accessed 14 May 2018)

Weeks, Kathi. 2011. *The Problem with Work: Feminism Marxism Antiwork Politics and Postwork Imaginaries.* Durham: Duke University Press.

CHAPTER 11

Beyond Repression: Reflections on Phoebe Moore's Chapter

Elisabetta Brighi

The UK government recently commissioned a report looking into the question of wellbeing at work, in particular the impact of mental ill health on the UK economy. The 'Thriving at Work' report, authored by a former chairman of HBOS insurance and by the chief executive of the mental health charity 'Mind', estimated the annual cost of poor mental health to UK businesses at £99bn, and stated that 300,000 people lose their jobs each year due to mental health issues (*The Guardian* 2017). Although informative and well-received, the report sadly stands out for lack of critical engagement with an issue now recognised as urgent. To start with, the report relies on a conceptualisation of mental health that narrowly focuses on its economic 'costs', rather than its human, social and political implications. Secondly, the report fails to investigate the relationship between mental health issues, working environments and the wider society, including its dominant economic system. The report's recommendations boil down to well-known, short-term quick fixes: e-learning modules in resilience for employees and increased monitoring of staff's mental health and wellbeing for employers. With a discussion of the relationship between affect and

How to cite this book chapter:
Brighi, E. 2019. Beyond Repression: Reflections on Phoebe Moore's Chapter. In: Chandler, D. and Fuchs, C. (eds.) *Digital Objects, Digital Subjects: Interdisciplinary Perspectives on Capitalism, Labour and Politics in the Age of Big Data.* Pp. 145–150. London: University of Westminster Press. DOI: https://doi.org/10.16997/book29.k. License: CC-BY-NC-ND 4.0

neoliberal capitalism beyond the pale, and the effects of alienation duly concealed behind a smokescreen of 'data', the solution remains the same – shift responsibility squarely to the individual, and pathologise normality.

Phoebe Moore's chapter is a timely intervention in the increasingly important conversation about affect and platform capitalism. Taking as her point of departure Antonio Negri's assertion that in the global, postmodern modes of production affect has acquired 'fundamental productive qualifications', and thus 'must be controlled' (Negri 1999, 86, 87), Moore investigates the affective dimension of platform capitalism and charts the way in which technologies have come to exercise such control. The landscape that opens in front of our eyes is one where the injunction of productivity has entirely captured the affective, emotive sphere, rendering wellness just another dimension of performance, just as life becomes another dimension of work. The digitalised workplace of the 'gig' platform economy pits the precarity of workers whose lives are disfigured by the imperative of mobility, flexibility and resilience against a technological management of labour that relentlessly monitors, tracks, measures and sanctions it. As Moore rightly puts it, precarity thus emerges as the purest form of alienation.

The literature on affect and platform capitalism has looked extensively at the ways in which emotions are mobilised and monetised in the modes of production of contemporary capitalism (Hardt 1999, Blackman and Venn 2010, Massumi 2015, Ilouz 2017). Two converging issues are at stake here: the first is that affect seems to have become the real currency of neoliberal capitalism; the second, is that capital seems to have completely captured the emotional, psychological and personal sphere, the sphere of affect. Moore draws on an extensive literature and contributes to it by focusing on the particular form of 'all-of-life work', that is gig work in the 'demand economy'. Here affect emerges as both intensely central to work and intensely regulated through work. In gig work the most intimate aspects of workers' lives, including dispositional, emotional and psychological traits, are at once interpellated, monetised and regulated. The neoliberal imperative of resilience means that workers must constantly draw from their reservoir of mental and emotional resources to succeed in a type of environment that is not only uncertain and hyper competitive, but that often trades in affect (Neocleous 2012, 2013). On the other hand, today's technology offers employers the ability to control and regulate workers' affective sphere, incentivising moods that are functional to the reproduction of capitalist labour relations (Atkinson 2015, Ahmed 2010). Moore's chapter richly illustrates these two points theoretically and empirically.

What perhaps remains to be analysed in greater detail are the effects of the capitalist capture of affect on the lives of workers, both as individuals and as a group or class. In this respect, there is an opportunity for a greater engagement with those literatures, from social and clinical psychology to psychoanalysis, that look at the intimate correspondence between social structures and 'structures of feelings', between social and economic conditions and the individual psychic and affective plane. Understanding more clearly the affective contours of alienation, however, is crucial if any project of emancipation is to succeed.

Amongst psychoanalysts and psychotherapists there is widespread agreement regarding the psychologically nefarious nature of neoliberalism as incarnated in platform capitalism (Davies 2017, Tweedy 2016, Wilkinson and Pickett 2010). As Paul Verhaeghe recently argued, with precarity and uncertainty dominating the neoliberal workplace, with labour constantly being monitored, tracked and evaluated, workers become stripped of any sense of autonomy, control, independence and ultimately meaning (2014a). This depressive condition of extreme dependency coexists with a manic attitude of extreme objectification to create a number of lacerating self-perceptions: on the one hand, the belief that one is ultimately and independently responsible for one's own success or failure; on the other, the belief that one is disposable, insignificant and utterly dependent. The former reinforces narcissistic and punitive fantasies about dominance, control and production of the self, including its affects; the latter exacerbates alienation, abandonment and apathy. The neoliberal workplace creates therefore a social environment unable to contain our worst fears and instincts – in fact, one that exacerbates these traits and pits them one against the other, while it systematically thwarts the reparative, creative and fulfilling potential of social interaction (Verhaeghe 2014b). Deleuze and Guattari (1972/2004) believed that capitalism produced schizoid personalities, while Žižek (2009) later identified capitalism with perversion. There is now an argument to be made about neoliberalism translating into an epidemic of bipolar disorder – or, indeed, psychosis, with its related tendencies of splitting, projection, and paranoia (Bell 2006, 2016). Moore makes a passing reference to these psychoanalytic dynamics when she writes about the degree to which affect is regulated in the workplace of the 'gig economy':

> Pinning to the corporeal, affective gig labourers do not engage in creative production using their own affective capacities. They are engaged in a type of *affective repression* by which the required subordinate performances corrode their own psychosomatic and bodily wellbeing. [my italics]

Because of their complexity, however, the emotional, psychological and affective dynamics that whirl around in the neoliberal workplace exceed the relatively simple process of repression and cannot be exhausted in this category. If repression was the only psychological mechanism really at play, the current condition would not be so self-lacerating – and the possibility to transcend it would be less difficult to imagine.

This feeds into a second, important theme explored in Moore's chapter, one which also necessitates further analysis. This is the theme of affective resistance and of the construction of an emancipatory project able to move beyond platform capitalism. Here again Moore draws on Michael Hardt (1999) and

Antonio Negri, as well as Spinoza, to make the argument that 'affect and immaterial labour' provide 'possibilities for resistance, collective subjectivities and formations of communities'. In fact, Moore argues, 'affective solidarity' leads 'to the most difficult form of resistance to stop, since affect already infiltrates all-of-life', and again, 'affective resistance is a serious threat to systems of workplace operation' – which of course explains neoliberalism's determination to control it. The material presented by Moore is certainly significant – in the chapter there are a number of examples of workers exercising their power to resist the ever more intrusive reach of neoliberal technologies by exiting projects because of concerns about privacy and/or corporate surveillance, or by turning the asymmetry generated by tracking technology on its head, so as to have more, rather than less, control. Yet these examples fall somehow short of conjuring up a 'real alternative'. If the aim, as Moore claims, is 'an alternative that does not prey on insecurity but builds solidarity, a constituting of the political without the requirement for a single leader, a rhizomatic formation of activation, without requiring a class identity in the orthodox sense', the data presented only goes so far. This is not so much an issue of quantity, or critical mass, but rather a qualitative issue that points back to the question of what might be really at stake in affective resistance, beyond the issue of repression.

According to Negri (2017), in the conditions of global post-Fordist capitalism, 'the struggle will always be a combination of exodus and desertion. Desertion from command and exodus beyond command'. But what does that entail exactly from an affective perspective? What does it mean to affectively desert the neoliberal workplace and to psychologically refuse its command? What does it mean to feel and act politically in platform capitalism? I would argue that the vocabulary of alienation and repression does not cut deep enough into the affective entanglements of neoliberalism to permit the construction of emancipatory projects. 'For solidarity to fully emerge amongst digitalised workers, class consciousness in the Marxist sense is necessary', writes Moore. And yet she is aware of the centrifugal forces that today threaten to dismember any notions of 'class'.

The capitalist capture of affect is important precisely because it completes the process of the atomisation of society: it brings alienation to perfection. As such, it reduces the possibility, not only of class consciousness, but of individual consciousness, to its minimum – in fact it actively aims to pervert, manipulate, control and regulate consciousness. The possibility of deserting and refusing the capitalist command today inevitably plays out on this battlefield, at the level of this extreme individualisation, and boils down to a discernment of sorts. Against the barbaric neoliberal transformation of notions of the 'care of the self' into a purely commodified and self-interested version of depressive, hedonistic accumulation, the alternative may well unfold through the articulation of a non-servile virtuosity (Virno 1996, 200), a consciousness about ourselves that is aware of our entanglement with others; that refuses to project unwanted feelings of anxiety onto vulnerable others by preying on insecurity;

that demystifies the delusion of autonomy and independence and uncovers its sadistic, violent import; that refuses to relate to ourselves and to others as commodity; that believes in the human capacity to create, live, care and heal.

In his *Political Theory of Exodus*, Paolo Virno (1996) praises intemperance, as opposed to incontinence, as a cardinal virtue. Incontinence, according to Virno, is a vulgar unruliness and disregard for the law that bursts into the public sphere with the aim of capturing its institutions and power – the same disruptive quality with which symptoms violently burst into consciousness after years of repression. Virno argues that intemperance, on the other hand, 'is not ignorant of the law' nor does it merely oppose it – rather, it 'discredits it' on ethical and political grounds, and 'in the name of the systematic interconnection between Intellect and political Action' (Virno 1996, 199). The aim, therefore, is not to overthrow the state nor capture its institutions, but rather to safeguard positive prerogatives, forms of life and 'works of 'friendship' that have been achieved and conquered, not without struggle, en route. Given the atomisation of contemporary labour relations, I would argue that the development of a class consciousness is contingent on the development of an individual consciousness which, in turn, *is first and foremost affective* in nature. The task may still be to educate the masses, but the place to start today may be a 'sentimental education'– i.e., an education about the emancipatory and self-sabotaging affects mobilised in the neoliberal workplace.

References

Ahmed, Sara. 2010. *The Promise of Happiness*. Durham: Duke University Press.

Atkinson, Paul. 2015. 'Happiness and the Capture of Subjectivity.' *Self and Society* 44(4): 394–401.

Bell, David. 2006. 'Primitive Mind of State.' *Psychoanalytic Psychotherapy* 10 (1): 45–57.

Bell, David. 2016. 'Neo-Liberalism is Dangerous for your Mental Health.' *Frontier Psychoanalyst*. Radio broadcast. Available at: https://www. mixcloud.com/Resonance/frontier-psychoanalyst-25th-january-2016/ (accessed 14 May, 2018)

Blackman, Lisa and Couze Venn. 2010. *Affect*, special issue: *Body & Society* 16 (1).

Davies, James (ed.). 2017. *The Sedated Society*. Basingstoke: Palgrave Macmillan.

Deleuze, Gilles and Félix Guattari. 1972/2004. *Anti-Oedipus: Capitalism and Schizophrenia*. London: Continuum.

Hardt, Michael. 1999. 'Affective Labor.' *boundary 2* 26 (2): 89–100.

Illouz, Eva. 2017. *Emotions as Commodities: Capitalism, Consumption and Authenticity*. Abingdon: Routledge.

Massumi, Brian. 2015. *Parables for the Virtual*. Durham: Duke University Press.

Negri, Antonio. 1999. 'Value and Affect.' Translated by Michael Hardt. *boundary 2*, 26(2): 77–88.

Negri, Antonio. 2017. 'Post-operaismo o operaismo?' Lecture delivered at the University of Cambridge, 25 April. Available at: http://www.euronomade. info/?p=9189 (accessed 14 May 2018)

Neocleous, Mark. 2012. '"Don't Be Scared, Be Prepared": Trauma-Anxiety-Resilience.' *Alternatives: Global, Local, Political* 37(3): 188–98.

Neocleous, Mark. 2013. 'Resisting Resilience.' *Radical Philosophy* 178: 2–7.

Siddique, Haroon. 2017. 'Mental Health Problems are Forcing Thousands in UK Out of Work – Report.' *The Guardian*, 26 October. Available at: https://www.theguardian.com/society/2017/oct/26/thriving-work-report-uk-mental-health-problems-forcing-thousands-out (accessed 14 May 2018)

Tweedy, Rod, ed. 2016. *The Political Self: Understanding the Social Context for Mental Illness.* London: Karnac Books.

Verhaeghe, Paul. 2014a. *What About Me? The Struggle for Identity in a Market-Based Society.* London: Scribe Publications.

Verhaeghe, Paul. 2014b. 'Neoliberalism has Brought out the Worst in Us.' *The Guardian*, 29 September. Available at: https://www.theguardian.com/commentisfree/2014/sep/29/neoliberalism-economic-system-ethics-personality-psychopathicsthic (accessed 14 May 2018)

Virno, Paulo. 1996. 'Virtuosity and Revolution: The Political Theory of Exodus.' In *Radical Thought in Italy: A Potential Politics*, eds. Paulo Virno and Michael Hardt. Minneapolis: University of Minnesota Press.

Wilkinson, Iain. 2001. *Anxiety in a 'Risk' Society.* London: Routledge.

Wilkinson, Richard and Kate Pickett. 2010. *The Spirit Level: Why Equality is Better for Everyone.* London: Penguin Books.

Žižek, Slavoj. 2009. *The Ticklish Subject: The Absent Centre of Political Ontology.* London: Verso.

CHAPTER 12

Goodbye iSlave: Making Alternative Subjects Through Digital Objects

Jack Linchuan Qiu

1. Introduction

Since the arrival of the 'digital revolution', we have been repetitively reminded about the emancipatory power of technological objects. Apple's iconic '1984' commercial was a good example, showcasing that their new Macintosh computer could liberate human subjectivities from the tyranny of Big Brother. However, more than 30 years later, when the iPhone turns ten years old in 2017, we look back and see a very different, even opposite picture: digital objects such as smartphones have not only failed to deliver their emancipatory promise (Qiu 2016a), but have created instead new conditions of enslavement, so much so that I would contend that the abolition of digital slavery, or iSlavery, is an imperative duty we have no choice but to take on.

The keyword 'iSlave' was originally a slogan invented during a transnational campaign in 2010 by labour activists in Hong Kong and Switzerland (see Figure 4), which I picked up and fleshed out in the 2016 volume *Goodbye iSlave: A Manifesto for Digital Abolition*. The book title is thus a salute to those working on the frontlines of digital labour activism, to their bravery and creativity. The subtitle of the book contains the word 'manifesto', which was something much

How to cite this book chapter:
Qiu, J. L. 2019. Goodbye iSlave: Making Alternative Subjects Through Digital Objects. In: Chandler, D. and Fuchs, C. (eds.) *Digital Objects, Digital Subjects: Interdisciplinary Perspectives on Capitalism, Labour and Politics in the Age of Big Data*. Pp. 151–164. London: University of Westminster Press. DOI: https://doi.org/10.16997/book29.l. License: CC-BY-NC-ND 4.0

bolder than the original idea I had when I started this book. However, I think it suits my goal pretty well, because I hope to make two provocations: first, digital media has done much more damage to the world and to humanity than most of us would like to realise; second, we can and have to use the same technological objects to resist and abolish new and old modes of slavery, to regain human dignity, and to create new subjectivities of a post-capitalist era.

In this essay, I will first discuss ways to define slavery in the twenty-first century, which I will apply to conditions of digital capitalism from the assembly line to the data mine. Then I will briefly introduce two basic modes of iSlavery: one is the 'manufacturing iSlave' or production-mode iSlavery, such as Chinese migrant workers at Foxconn – the world's largest electronics producer, known for its notorious sweatshop conditions, which are comparable, arguably, to the trans-Atlantic triangular trade. The second mode is 'manufactured' or consumption-mode iSlavery, such as Facebook free labour and people who are addicted to digital gadgets. Section 2 will focus on antislavery struggles and openings for digital abolition through collective resistance, creative memes, and social media on the picket line (Qiu 2016b), which can be observed abundantly in the Chinese factory zones and online. My goal is not only to criticise the status quo but also to illuminate hope for our collective digital future.

But let me confess upfront: I have been a user of Apple's products for more than three decades. I am as complacent in what I'm about to critique as every i-gadget consumer who happens to read this essay. Frankly speaking, to arrive at the theme of slavery marks a point in a completely unexpected journey for myself. Yet I'm now presenting this unlikely idea because I see great utility in connecting slavery with things digital. To me, slavery is much more than a past condition or a provocative metaphor for contemporary reality. It is, more precisely, a comparative method that re-historicises our thinking about digital media and labour, China and the world. This is crucial because I happen to possess too many scattered empirical observations from my work on Foxconn since 2010, for which I need a larger and more coherent analytical framework, and because studies of digital media in China have suffered increasingly from methodological nationalism or Chinese exceptionalism. But with a comparative slavery framework, we can re-connect China with world history, reconstrue trans-Atlantic and trans-Pacific struggles as one continuous *longue durée* process. This conceptual enlargement can be a theoretical breakthrough. After all, slavery is about the reduction of human subjects into inhuman objects, an ultimate form of objectification and alienation, a process always accompanied by resistance, recalcitrance, and the re-making of subjectivities.

2. Conceptualising Slavery

Borrowing from the scholarship of history, sociology, anthropology and legal studies, I have constructed a conceptual framework, as shown in Figure 1, to

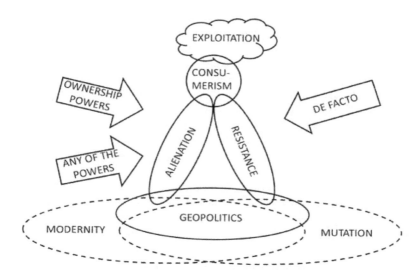

Figure 1: A conceptual framework illustrating ways to define slavery.

define slavery in the modern era. The Figure shows that there are two deep foundations for enslavement, one being capitalist modernity, the other the capacity of slave regimes to mutate over time. Slavery is surprisingly resilient. It transforms as capitalism takes on new forms (Blackburn 1997). Standing on the quicksand of capitalist modernity, the immediate and tangible foundation for slavery is geopolitics, by which I mean the politico-economic and military complex of empire, expanding over oceans and continents, and now into the New World of cyberspace, smart devices and Big Data.

Slavery has two pillars, one of which is alienation or, more precisely, 'natal alienation' as Orlando Patterson (1982, 7) calls it. The other pillar is resistance by the enslaved, whose revolutionary spirits inspire us to re-imagine a better digital economy and a more humane world. While conventional wisdom often focuses exclusively on suppressive slave regimes and alienating experiences of enslavement, it is important to stress that slave resistance has always been part and parcel of the social reality in conditions of slavery, past or present (Linebaugh and Rediker 2013; Rediker 2007).

The ultimate goal of slavery is to exploit the body or body parts of the enslaved under conditions of abnormal labour-capital relationship (Fuchs 2014). In order to reach this goal, surplus value from alienated labour has to be extracted from processes of consumption, dominated by hegemonic cultures of consumerism – which are now coded in corporate algorithms, the latest instruments of enslavement through the manipulation of social media platforms.

Finally, borrowing from legal scholarship, especially the 2012 Bellagio-Harvard Guidelines on the Legal Parameters of Slavery, I define iSlavery as *de facto*

154 Digital Objects, Digital Subjects

conditions instead of *de jure* status. If any 'powers attached to ownership' are found to exist – such as possession, transfer, or disposal – then this suffices to indicate 'institutions or practices similar to slavery' (Allen 2014, 213, 220).

The first global regime of modern slavery, as I shall submit, was the seventeenth-century trans-Atlantic system. Although there were Africans being trafficked to the Caribbean in the 1500s, it was only in the 1600s that the racial structure, the mode of production and transcontinental trade centred on sugar, became stabilised. This regime expanded tremendously in the 1700s until its demise in the 1800s, bookended, for instance, in the British Empire by the 1807 Slave Trade Act and in the USA by the conclusion of the American Civil War in 1865.

But slavery still exists in the twenty-first century. Since the year 2000, the International Criminal Court in The Hague and the High Court of Australia have both used slavery charges to successfully indict former militia and gang members. In so doing, both courts recognised that the criminal offences constituted slavery, despite this term's usual historical application, because they looked at *de facto* conditions as summarised in Figure 1. The question is: can we further extend this framework of understanding about modern slavery into the world of digital media and smartphones?

A few conceptual clarifications are in order. For one thing, the type of slavery that I'm critiquing here differs from the 'slave society' in classic Marxist theory, which Marx and Engels understood as an archaic mode of production that took place before feudalism. In its present shape, twenty-first-century slavery is a techno-social novelty. In another words, iSlavery in its current shape never existed before.

Furthermore, we know from historical studies that slaves are not just poor labourers toiling in plantations or factories, but that there is also a high-class category of what Patterson calls the 'ultimate slave' (1982, 299), such as *familia Caesaris* – pardon my Latin – the so-called 'families' of Caesar, who served as surrogates of the emperor. They could be extremely wealthy and powerful. But they could be executed without legal procedure when the emperor disliked them. These 'ultimate slaves' also sometimes rebelled, even turning themselves into kings and queens, for instance, when Turkish slaves founded Mamluk kingdoms in medieval Egypt. This was able to occur because the surrogate had become the sole means of communication for the emperor, and 'the control of communication is power. Sublation of the relationship immediately becomes a possibility' (1982, 333). In other words, in this case the slave-master intersubjectivity was subverted, first in thinking and the realm of symbolic interactions, then in the real world of society and its institutions.

The third clarification is that the notion of iSlavery is *not* racially defined: over and again, we have learned this lesson from history: interracial resurrection of the 'motley crew' often serves as arguably the most formidable form of antislavery struggle (Linebaugh and Rediker 2013, 211). Because of this I would submit that an effective movement of digital abolition – an effective global class struggle indeed – can only succeed when it transcends identity politics, when the enslaved form solidarity on the basis of their common exploitation, not the colour of their skin.

This is my main thesis based on the above conceptualisations: digital capitalism revives slavery, but it also spurs new antislavery movements that hold the premise of emancipation. Developing this thesis, we possess a conceptual lens that opens new vistas and brings in fresh thinking. It enables us to travel back and forth between the seventeenth and twenty-first centuries.

More specifically, my comparative analysis follows the three models of triangular exchange that are schematically outlined in Figure 2. On the left is the seventeenth-century trans-Atlantic triangular trade between Europe, West Africa, and the New World. This needs no belabouring because it is a classic formation based on the flow of African slaves, sugar and money.

At the bottom is twenty-first-century iSlavery. Here Apple is singled out due to its close affinity with Foxconn. However, it applies not only to Apple but other major gadgets brands as well, such as Samsung, Huawei, Sony and Amazon Kindle. Structurally speaking, the Apple-Foxconn relationship is comparable to the Europe-West Africa exchange four centuries ago. Together they expand to the New World of digital consumption and social media, where user-generated content (UGC) is the new 'sugar', so to speak.

On the right is a new model of antislavery exchange, where organised 'network labour' functions as a third pillar of network society, forming dialectical relationships with network enterprise and network state. The cultural capital and social innovations of network labour materialises through working-class information and communication technologies (ICTs) (Qiu 2009), which are

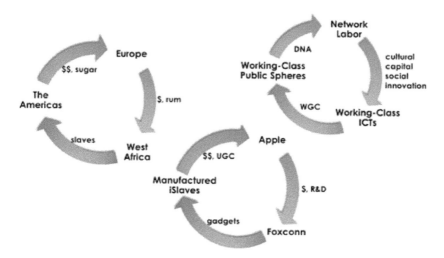

Figure 2: Three circuit models of slavery and antislavery.

used to create collective and activism-oriented worker-generated content (WGC). WGC converges in working-class public spheres, leading to digitally networked action (DNA), which produces new meanings and a new praxis for network labour, thereby contributing to an alternative circuit of antislavery, regionally and globally.

The rest of this paper compares the two circuits of objectification, commodification, and capitalist accumulation on the left and the bottom of Figure 2. We will then to zoom into the circuit of antislavery and new subject formation on the right, which is but one model of re-subjectification and re-humanisation toward genuine, sustainable, systemic change.

3. Two Modes of iSlavery: Manufacturing and Manufactured

There are two modes of iSlavery: the manufacturing or production-mode iSlave on the one hand, and manufactured iSlave or consumption-mode slavery on the other. In the manufacturing domain, the story starts in the bowels of the earth, in places like the Democratic Republic of Congo, where 'blood minerals' such as coltan are extracted by miners including child labour, who are under warlords' control, even under gunpoint (Van Reybrouck 2014). These minerals are essential to the electronic components in our smart devices. The components are assembled in massive factories such as those operated by Foxconn.

Foxconn is the world's largest electronics manufacturer. According to *Wall Street Journal*, it employs approximately 1.4 million workers in mainland China (Mozur and Luk 2013), an army more numerous in number than all the armed forces of the US military combined. What are the labour conditions in Foxconn? The company first came under media scrutiny in 2006, when reporters sneaked into Foxconn 'Peace' dormitory in Shenzhen, South China, and were astounded by what they saw: up to 300 workers sleeping on three-level bunk beds in one huge room without air conditioning. According to a worker living there: 'The odour of sweat and dirty feet was suffocating' (Zhang and Li 2006). This reminds us of the lower deck of the slave ship in the Middle Passage, with African bodies being packed together, suffocated in the packed space with extremely poor ventilation.

Another parallel is the transfer of labouring bodies, who are unfree and cannot escape. The auction of African or African-American slaves is well recorded in archives and recent films such as *Twelve Years a Slave*. In Foxconn, we encounter the so-called 'student interns' sent by vocational schools in the Chinese hinterlands to the factory. These are usually youngsters in their late teens. Without working at Foxconn for three months, they simply could not graduate. At school they majored in accounting, English, or pharmaceutics. At Foxconn, they are assigned to the most tedious of assembly line work – making iPhone back cases, for instance (Chan Pun and Seldon 2015).

As I learned from my interviews with their production line-leaders in 2012, each day these 'interns' had to stand for ten hours while making iPhone cases. In the first week, all female students would break down in tears; in the second week, all males would cry due to excruciating pain in their legs. Yet they could not leave, because otherwise they wouldn't be able to receive their graduation diploma. Both the schools and the factory benefit handsomely from this transfer of enslaved bodies.

What happens if a worker gets sick due to vocational diseases, like leukaemia? What about cases of work injury, when the employees can no longer work? Will the factory take care of them, as required by China's labour law? No. In the 2016 book, I documented several sad cases of workers being disposed of, such as the case of Zhang Tingzhen, who lost half of his brain due to a work injury sustained at Foxconn (Qiu 2016a). This is not essentially different from the discarding of African bodies when they became liabilities during the Atlantic trade.

The most horrifying tragedies took place in 2010, when 15 Foxconn workers jumped to their death from tall buildings within six months (Chan and Pun 2010). Never before had such a series of suicides been recorded in the history of industrial capitalism. However, if we go back to the trans-Atlantic trade, we find a surprisingly similar device of labour discipline and social control against the attempts of the enslaved population from taking their own lives: the anti-jumping nets (see Figure 3, below).

According to Olaudah Equiano, a slave boy who survived the Middle Passage in the 1700s, he witnessed fellow Africans jumping through that netting

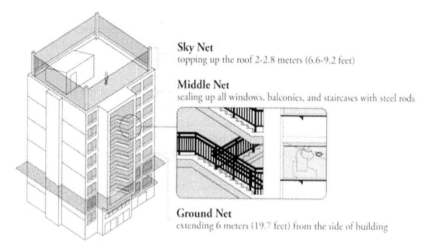

Figure 3: A typical Foxconn building being sealed off with anti-jumping nets.

because they wished to die and free themselves from the miseries of enslavement (Equiano 1789/1995). At the time, anti-jumping nets were a standard feature of slave ships. These nets became obsolete when the trans-Atlantic trade was abolished in the nineteenth century. But in 2010, they re-appeared on top of Foxconn buildings where i-products are made. There are three levels of netting: the 'Sky Net' at the top, the 'Ground Net' at the bottom, and the 'Middle Net' sealing the windows and corridors in between. Foxconn claims to have taken down the anti-jumping nets, although I still see them when I visit the factory facilities in the Pearl River Delta and the Yangtze River Delta.

Due to China's media censorship, we do not have a full account of suicides in Foxconn since 2010. But they have continued, as indicated by the suicide of Xu Lizhi, now a famous worker-poet in China's literary scene, who leaped to his death from Foxconn Shenzhen in 2014 (Tharoor 2014). In August 2016, in Foxconn Zhengzhou, where most of the latest iPhones are made, we still had reliable information about a worker leaping to their death after assembling iPhone 7s.

This is why we call it 'manufacturing iSlave': because along the assembly line and around it, there are many parallels between the electronics sweatshops of the twenty-first century and seventeenth-century slavery of the Atlantic system, seen through a global and *longue durée* perspective. The culprit is not a single company or a single country. It is rather a planetary system I term 'Appconn', i.e. a new global regime that not only produces gadgets but also fatal alienation, objectification, enslavement, the disposal of 'useless' labour, and the anti-jumping nets.

We turn next to 'manufactured' or consumption-mode iSlavery. It starts with the real case of a Chinese teenager, from a working-class family, who in 2011 sold one of his kidneys to buy an iPhone and an iPad. This was an extreme case of voluntary servitude, an extreme tragedy of a human subject being deprived of his soul. Why on earth would anyone be so fanatical as to trade his health for gizmos? He did it because of peer pressure. Why, then, are so many people devoted to their i-devices in such a fanatical way?

The historical comparison is with the addictive substances of the Atlantic system centuries ago, such as tobacco and alcohol, although the real driving force of the seventeenth-century triangular trade was sugar, including rum that was the by-product of sugar production. Today we have the functional equivalents in our digital gadgets: Facebook, WeChat, Candy Crush (even the name sounds sugary!).

The result of addiction is not just about hardware or software but about a fundamental shift in lifestyle toward what Sidney Mintz calls 'desocialized eating', when consumption is regularised and individualised in order to meet the rhythm of consumer goods production and marketing rather than the sociocultural needs of communities and families (1985, 121). This is the crucial revelation: historically, the increase of slave production in the New World had to be matched by the rise of consumption in the Old. A hegemonic culture of consumerism is key to the domination of Appconn, when system-generated consumption markets serve as a pillar of the New World System, which is as indispensable as its production apparatus. A strong addictive substance comes from the games and social media platforms – as much as it was for those who are addicted to sugar, alcohol, and tobacco. We lost our freedom when we became addicts (Schull 2012).

Another angle to assess addiction is to look at how much time the Appconn regime has been able to extract from us. Time is a key dimension for the Marxist analysis of exploitation. For Marx, capitalist accumulation of surplus value is ultimately about the acquisition of socially-necessary labour time – either by extending work hours or by the intensification of production processes (Marx 1867/1992). According to Robin Blackburn (1997, 581), all the slaves under the control of the British Empire contributed 2.5 billion hours of labour time in 1800, mostly by working in sugar fields and associated factories. If we apply the same calculation to Foxconn, by my calculation the modern factory of digital gadgets extracted 4.8 billion hours of labour time in 2014. That is, about two British Empires in 1800. How much time has Facebook extracted from us? My conservative estimation for 2014, using only the total number of daily active users is 653 billion hours, a truly mind-boggling amount equivalent to approximately 261 British Empires or 137 Foxconns.

'The "i" word is practically an intoxicant,' writes Judy Wajcman (2015, 178) in *Pressed for Time*. One way to recover our humanity, she continues, is to restore our 'temporal sovereignty' – to use the same digital tools as instruments of antislavery, to recover and re-invent human subjectivities.

4. Antislavery: Resistance Through and Beyond WGC

With the darkening of the sky, we see brighter stars of hope. iSlavery is not the end of the world. It is, rather, a fresh start for the constant struggle of the human species to regain subjectivities and reconstruct intersubjectivities, which also constitutes a broad class struggle toward liberty – liberty for all working people and their families, who now have their own digital devices.

Among historians, there are two strands of thought about antislavery. One emphasises abolition – by the elite, the educated, lawyers, religious groups and the middle class, including white saviours – from the top down (Clarkson 1839; Eltis and Walvin 1981; Drescher 2009). The other strand sees antislavery through the eyes of the oppressed – Africans and Afro-Americans, the indigenous people, the women, the illiterate, the black Jacobins, who resist the powers that be at the grassroots level and from the bottom up (James 1938/2001; Linebaugh and Rediker 2013; Reynolds 1981). While I am an abolitionist, my work leans more towards the second strand that stresses the resistance of the enslaved.

Most important are three insights from the historical literature that throw light on my analysis. First, antislavery takes many forms: singing & dancing, stealing, sabotage, hunger strikes, suicide – the list goes on (Rediker 2007).

Second, slavery and antislavery, accommodation and resistance, coexist in global and regional contexts. Third, bloody confrontations are exceptional; more common forms of resistance took place in culture, in daily work and life, and in the constant process of subject making, un-making, and remaking (Genovese 1976).

With these historical patterns in mind, one must admit that China today is also unique, especially the central part played by the Chinese state in moulding Appconn through the provision of cheap labour, land and infrastructure (Pun Lu Guo Shen 2011). Another factor, a geopolitical one, is Beijing's attempt to fold in Taiwanese capital in order to achieve its goal of re-unifying the 'Great Chinese Nation'. This makes local state agencies – in the form of city governments competing with each other in desperate endeavours to win corporate favour – stand out above and beyond the conventional power centres of Beijing, extending deep inside the country. The Chinese state, be it national or subnational, remains a key arena for social struggle and power contestation (Zhao, 2008). This means Appconn is not invincible if the authorities such as ACFTU (All China Federation of Trade Unions) can be pressurised into carrying out its basic duties. ACFTU is a strategic institutional space that is often better understood by Chinese workers than by intellectuals.

Another vital development in China today is the wide diffusion of the Internet and the rise of the information 'have-less' (Qiu 2009), a category between the so-called haves and have-nots of the digital divide, providing a crucial techno-social basis for the making of network labour – a new working class of the digital era. These are groups such as migrant workers with less income and resources, but they are also less committed to the politico-economic status quo. A crude indicator for the have-less is educational attainment. When China's official Internet statistics unit released its first survey results about user demographics in 1998, those without a Bachelor's degree (roughly, the have-less group) accounted for 41.1% of all Internet users in the country, a figure which climbed to 78.8% in 2008, and 88.4% in 2016 (CNNIC 1998; 2008; 2016). Nearly nine out of ten Chinese Internet users belong to the working class and lower classes. What would they communicate, online and off?

Western media and Chinese commercial media alike routinely portray Chinese workers as docile and obedient. When the Foxconn 'suicide express' occurred, the tragedy received sensational coverage. But when workers fought back in the immediate aftermath of the 'suicide express', the media looked the other way as if there were nothing newsworthy. The struggle continues on a daily basis though, and is often livecast online via Weibo, China's Twitter-like digital platform. Factory workers, including in Foxconn, use online videos to document their collective resistance, for instance, against violent guards. The most commonly used images, however, are stills, such as those taken at the Yuyuan shoe factory strike in 2014 (Qiu 2016b).

In retrospect, we see not only myriad ways of using 'social media on the picket line' (Qiu 2016b), but also at least three phases of working-class subject formation facilitated by digital media. Before 2004, actions centred on QQ, the instant messenger. Between 2004 and 2009, the online forum Weblog, along with podcast and video sites, attracted more attention. Since 2009, Weibo and WeChat have been the dominant players. The technological platforms accumulate on top of existing ones, as do workers' collective experiences; the most interesting developments are probably Maoist and neo-Maoist online formations, and these deserve more study in the future.

Against such a rich backdrop of worker resistance, it makes sense to consider WGC (worker-generated content) as an alternative route, apart from UGC, that leads to subjectivities other than those constrained by neoliberalism. In many ways, WGC circulated via China's working-class social media can be compared with African singing and dancing during the Middle Passage. To unacquainted observers, it may appear to be meaningless and chaotic. But to insiders, it can be immensely spiritual and poetic, gratifying and powerful, defiant and fun.

I would, however, contend that, although Chinese WGC is indeed impressive, today's acts of social media on the picket line are still less remarkable than that of revolutionary Atlantic history. (Linebaugh and Rediker 2013). The famous Wedgwood antislavery medallion on the left side of Figure 4 is but one remarkable symbol from the eighteenth-century abolition movement. Its cameo design of an African image with the Christian message – 'Am I Not a Man and a Brother?' – was reproduced in various material forms: fine porcelain, watches, gold pins. This 'meme' of abolition travelled across the social classes, beyond geographical and historical limits. It inspired and joined forces with a plethora of antislavery endeavours, from literary interventions such as *Uncle Tom's Cabin* to the 'free produce store' taking the blood out of agricultural products,

Figure 4: Wedgwood abolition medallion (1787) and the iSlave meme (2010).

especially cotton and sugar (essentially nineteenth-century Fair Trade). Comparatively speaking, the digital abolition movement of twenty-first-century China, and globally, has not yet developed such impactful memes. Nor has it been successful in building coalitions and transforming broader society. Much, therefore, remains to be learned across the historical span.

5. Concluding Remarks

The main message from this essay is about historical continuity, despite the racial specificity of African or Afro-American versus Chinese or Asian labour. Yes, the two enslaved groups are oceans apart and centuries away from each other. Yes, there was a gender shift from male to female as the most quintessential form of the enslaved body. But they are both objectified and exploited, weighed down by the capitalist world system and the colonial masters, old and new. It is this subjugation, alienation, objectification and violent suppression that constitute their strongest bond – across racial categories, across national boundaries, across history.

At this point it should be clear that digital media remain in the shadow of slavery, now cast from China and Congo to the New World of Appconn and Big Data algorithms. It is therefore imperative to conceive of an alternative system and help it materialise. To achieve this goal we need a more holistic conception of digital labour. It is imperative to see through digital capitalism, and to understand the worsening of contemporary labour conditions along the assembly line and inside the data mine, as anything but coincidental.

Chinese workers, intellectuals and activists have much to learn from the Atlantic theatre of African resistance and the lessons of American abolition. One of them is the centrality of cultural resistance, where objectified labour joins the antislavery struggle through processes of re-subjectification and where consumer advocacy can play a central role in reclaiming our intersubjectivities in the production and consumption mode, converging in the creation of new revolutionary subjects.

The other lesson is an immensely empowering revelation. That is, historical slavery, despite its formidable appearance, has been and will be defeated, if we know how it works. This paper starts with a note on the resilience of slave regimes under conditions of pre-capitalism and capitalism itself. Let us end on a different note: the forces of antislavery and efforts to recover our collective humanity are even more resilient – if we look back on how abolitionists have succeeded in the past against all odds then we can indeed imagine an alternative, post-capitalist world.

By my understanding, the global slave system of the 1780s, with its harnessing of political, cultural and religious forces, was probably the most powerful ever known. Today's Big Data capitalism, or twenty-first-century iSlavery, is not nearly as powerful as that world order of the 1780s. Yet it only took a generation after the 1780s for the trans-Atlantic trade to start to crumble; the first modern antislavery legislation in human history was passed in 1807, in the Palace of Westminster, London. Bearing this historical note in mind, we really have no reason to despair and feel hopeless. We indeed shall act together with confidence and our collective optimism of the will.

Acknowledgement

This chapter benefited from Hong Kong's General Research Fund project 'Working-Class Public Spheres: Media and Activism since the Foxconn Suicide Express' (project ID: 14612715).

References

Allain, Jean. 2012. *The Legal Understanding of Slavery: From the Historical to the Contemporary*. Oxford: Oxford University Press.

Blackburn, Robin. 1997. *The Making of New World Slavery: From the Baroque to the Modern, 1492–1800*. London: Verso.

Chan, Jenny, Pun Ngai and Mark Seldon. 2015. 'Interns or Students: China's Student Labour Regime.' *Asian Studies* 1 (1): 1–31.

Chan, Jenny, and Ngai Pun. 2010. 'Suicide as Protest for the New Generation of Chinese Migrant Workers: Foxconn, Global Capital, and the State.' *Japan Focus* 8 (37). Available at: http://apjjf.org/-Jenny-Chan/3408/article.html (accessed 14 May 2018)

Clarkson, Thomas. 1839. *The History of the Rise, Progress, and Accomplishment of the Abolition of the African Slave-Trade by the British Parliament*. London: Parker.

China Internet Network Information Centre (CNNIC) 1998, 2008, 2016. Available at http://cnnic.com.cn/IDR/ReportDownloads.

Drescher, Seymour. 2009. *Abolition: A History of Slavery and Anti-Slavery*. Cambridge: Cambridge University Press.

Eltis, David and James Walvin. 1981. *The Abolition of the Atlantic Slave Trade: Origins and Effects in Europe, Africa, and the Americas*. Madison: University of Wisconsin Press.

Equiano, Olaudah. 1789/1995. *The Interesting Narrative of the Life of Olaudah Equiano; Or, Gustavus Vassa, the African, Written by Himself*. New York: Penguin.

Fuchs, Christian. 2014. *Digital Labour and Karl Marx*. New York: Routledge.

James, C. L. R. 1938/2001. *The Black Jacobins: Toussaint L'Ouverture and the San Domingo Revolution*. New York: Penguin.

Genovese, Eugene. 1976. *Roll, Jordan, Roll: The World the Slaves Made*. New York, Vintage.

Linebaugh, Peter and Marcus Rediker. 2013. *The Many-Headed Hydra: Sailors, Slaves, Commoners, and the Hidden History of the Revolutionary Atlantic*. Boston: Beacon.

Marx, Karl. 1867/1992. *Capital, Volume 1*. London: Penguin.

Mintz, Sidney. 1985. *Sweetness and Power: The Place of Sugar in Modern History*. New York: Penguin.

Mozur, Paul and Lorraine Luk. 2013. 'Gadget Maker Foxconn Freezes Overall China Hiring.' *Wall Street Journal*, February 20. Available at: http://ow.ly/MEiLa (accessed 14 May 2018).

Patterson, Orlando. 1982. *Slavery and Social Death: A Comparative Study*. Cambridge: Harvard University Press.

Rediker, Marcus. 2007. *The Slave Ship: A Human History*. New York: Viking Penguin.

Reynolds, Henry. 1981. *The Other Side of the Frontier*. Kensington: University of New South Wales Press.

Pun, Ngai, Huilin Lu, Yuhua Guo and Yuan Shen. 2011. *Suicide Express behind the Glory of Foxconn*. Hong Kong: Commercial Press.

Qiu, Jack L. 2009. *Working-Class Network Society: Communication Technology and the Information Have-Less in Urban China*. Cambridge: MIT Press.

Qiu, Jack L. 2016a. *Goodbye iSlave: A Manifesto for Digital Abolition*. Urbana: University of Illinois Press.

Qiu, Jack L. 2016b. Social Media on the Picket Line. *Media, Culture & Society* 38 (4): 619–33.

Schull, Natasha D. 2012. *Addiction by Design: Machine Gambling in Las Vegas*. Princeton: Princeton University Press.

Tharoor, Ishaan. 2014. 'The Haunting Poetry of a Chinese Factory Worker Who Committed Suicide.' *Washington Post*, 12 November. Available at: http://ow.ly/MDaWh (accessed 16 May 2018)

Van Reybrouck, David. 2014. *Congo: The Epic History of a People*. London: HarperCollins Publishers.

Wajcman, Judy. 2014. *Pressed for Time: The Acceleration of Life in Digital Capitalism*. Chicago: University of Chicago Press.

Zhang, Juan and Qiang Li. 2006. 'Foxconn Workers: Lowest Salary 340 Yuan per Month, 700-Plus People Sharing One Room.' *Neteast Commercial Channel*, 17 June. Available at: http://ow.ly/MG8m1 (accessed 14 May 2018)

Zhao, Yuezhi. 2008. *Communication in China: Political Economy, Power, and Conflict*. Lanham: Rowman and Littlefield.

CHAPTER 13

Wage-Workers, Not Slaves: Reflections on Jack Qiu's Chapter

Peter Goodwin

Jack Qiu's chapter, like his book *Goodbye iSlave: A Manifesto for Digital Abolition* (Qiu 2016), is a powerful exposé of some of the appalling labour conditions which lie behind the glitz of the 'digital revolution', and of the resistance to these conditions by those who suffer them. Equally powerful is his comparison of the position which Foxconn and Apple occupy in the globalised capitalism of the early twenty-first century, with that occupied by the Atlantic slave trade in the international capitalism of the seventeenth and eighteenth century. Given the huge social, political and, indeed, moral importance of the issues he so effectively raises, it seems almost indecent to quibble.

But for all its power – and truth – I think we have to question the notion of iSlavery in this context. Is Qiu perhaps sacrificing some important analytical rigour for undoubted – and welcome – polemical effect?

As Qiu outlines in this chapter, and at far greater length in Chapter 2 of his 2016 book, slavery has taken various forms at various times. It has historically been an important part of the development of capitalism, rather than a hangover from pre-modernity. And it has always generated various forms of

How to cite this book chapter:
Goodwin, P. 2019. Wage-Workers, Not Slaves: Reflections on Jack Qiu's Chapter. In: Chandler, D. and Fuchs, C. (eds.) *Digital Objects, Digital Subjects: Interdisciplinary Perspectives on Capitalism, Labour and Politics in the Age of Big Data*. Pp. 165–167. London: University of Westminster Press. DOI: https://doi.org/10.16997/book29.m. License: CC-BY-NC-ND 4.0

resistance among the enslaved. But if slavery can be part of capitalism, what distinguishes a slave from a wage-worker or proletarian? Surely it is that a slave is owned by a capitalist and can be bought and sold (along with the totality of her or his labour power), while a wage worker retains possession of her or his labour power which s/he sells to one capitalist or another. The distinction is an important one, socially, politically, economically and historically. If it were not important, then neither would be Lincoln's 1863 Emancipation Proclamation in the American Civil War, or the 1865 thirteenth Amendment to the US Constitution.

Karl Marx, in the manuscript 'Results of the Immediate Process of Production' (written when the abolition of capitalist slavery in the US was very much a current event) was clear on the economic difference:

> The slave is the property of a particular master; the worker must indeed sell himself to capital, but not to a particular capitalist, and so within certain limitations he may choose to sell himself to whomever he wishes; and he may also change his master. The effect of all these differences is to make the free worker's work more intensive, more continuous, more flexible and skilled than that of the slave, quite apart from the fact that they fit him for a quite different historical role.' (Marx 1976/1864, 1032-1033).

I doubt whether Qiu would disagree with any of this. But the distinction between worker and slave has always been unclear, both in reality and in discourse. One grey area is that much wage labour has involved extra-market elements of coercion, from gang-masters to company police, to tied housing or company dormitories, to the truck system, and so on. It is this real – and horrible – grey area that Qiu describes. The discursive grey area is that, from the very arrival of the modern working class on the scene, labour organisers and socialists – including Marx and Engels – have frequently referred, generally rhetorically, to 'wage-slavery' or 'wage slaves'. And in the period when capitalist slavery in its purest form in the United States fed the textile mills of Europe, socialists sometimes chided factory-owning abolitionists for ignoring 'their own' wage slaves, while supporters of real slavery sometimes made the same accusation of hypocrisy in support of their own reactionary cause. It is in exploring both these real and rhetorical grey areas that the strength of Qiu's argument lies. But one cannot avoid the fact that the workers Qiu is talking about are wage workers, not slaves in the pure sense, and will remain exploited wage workers even when the battles are won to remove the grotesque abuses which Qiu documents.

Qiu stresses one side of the history of anti-slavery – the history of slave resistance and slave rebellion – as against the other, and still better known history, of morally motivated white abolitionists. So alongside exposing the abuses, he focusses on the acts of resistance and rebellion by the Foxconn workers.

The other side of Qiu's picture of iSlavery is altogether less plausible, at both an analytical and a rhetorical level. Qiu distinguishes between two modes of iSlavery: 'the manufacturing or production-mode iSlave on the one hand, and manufactured iSlave or consumption-mode slavery on the other'. What we have just been talking about (the workers of the giant Foxconn factories) are Qiu's 'manufacturing or production mode iSlaves', and although I have criticised Qiu's technical conflation of worker and slave, on this 'production-mode iSlavery', I have absolutely no quarrel with the thrust of his argument. But Qiu's second 'consumption-mode iSlave' seems to me to be both analytically thin and to have exactly the opposite of rhetorical power.

Qiu gives the example of a 'Chinese teenager, from a working-class family, who sold one of his kidneys to buy an iPhone and an iPad in 2011'. He notes that this was an 'extreme case' of what he calls 'voluntary servitude', by which he seems to mean addiction. 'The historical comparison is with the addictive substances of the Atlantic system centuries ago, such as tobacco and alcohol, although the real driving force for the seventeenth-century triangular trade was sugar, including rum that was the by-product of sugar. Today we have the functional equivalents in our digital gadgets: Facebook, WeChat, Candy Crush'. He concludes, 'we lost our freedom when we become addicts'.

I would question whether the term 'addiction' is a helpful characterisation of the general use of social media or of digital devices (and Qiu himself, remember, states that his example of selling a kidney to buy an iPhone is an *extreme* one). But even if one accepts that it is helpful, then that does not make those of us who today need our iPhones or Facebook accounts 'slaves', any more than it made into 'slaves' the eighteenth-century white Europeans of all classes who needed their regular fix of sugar.

References

Marx, Karl. 1976/1864. *Capital Volume 1*. Translated by Ben Fowkes. Harmondsworth and London: Penguin Books in Association with New Left Review.

Qiu, Jack. 2016. *Goodbye iSlave: A Manifesto for Digital Abolition*. Urbana, Chicago and Springfield: University of Illinois Press.

SECTION III

Digital Politics

CHAPTER 14

Critique or Collectivity? Communicative Capitalism and the Subject of Politics

Jodi Dean

1. Introduction

The questions posed for the symposium 'Digital Objects, Digital Subjects: Activism, Research & Critique in the Age of Big Data Capitalism' take up possibilities of digital activism and of critique in a digital age. What does digital mean as a qualifier of activism and condition of critique? On the one hand, this is obvious: we are talking about our current conditions of networked media, personalised mass communication and the production of the devices that support it; we are talking about Big Data, about the general setting of communicative capitalism. On the other hand, there is something that is rather less clear in qualifying activism and critique with 'digital', namely the underlying theory of the subject. What notion of the political subject is posited or assumed in inquiries into digital activism and critique, and how is this subject impacted by a digital age? Is this impact, if there is one, best understood in terms of 'digitality', or might 'digital' in fact mark or periodise a certain understanding of capitalism and the ways it determines our setting? (I should add here that

How to cite this book chapter:
Dean, J. 2019. Critique or Collectivity? Communicative Capitalism and the Subject of Politics. In: Chandler, D. and Fuchs, C. (eds.) *Digital Objects, Digital Subjects: Interdisciplinary Perspectives on Capitalism, Labour and Politics in the Age of Big Data.* Pp. 171–182. London: University of Westminster Press. DOI: https://doi.org/10.16997/book29.n. License: CC-BY-NC-ND 4.0

in critical media studies it is of course Christian Fuchs who has insisted on the necessity of analysing digital media in terms of capitalism and its categories of labour, production, and value rather than, say, bourgeois categories of information.) In my view, 'digital' directs us to our setting in communicative capitalism. It tells us less about the subject of politics than it does about the processes aligned to block this subject's appearance, processes that nevertheless contribute to the concentrations and aggregations that are opportunities for the subject's appearing.

I take it as uncontroversial that a theory of the political subject is important for any approach to activism and critique (digital or otherwise). Do we think, for example, that the subject of politics is necessarily an activist subject? Or do we assume that it is acted upon, subjected, conditioned or determined? Likewise, do we imagine the political subject as engaging in or impacted by critique? Are online practices of sharing and opining, Twitter storms and Facebook updates, the practices of a political subject? What about hacking or blogging? Perhaps most important, do we proceed as if this subject were individual, or collective; is it present in the actions and events carried out in its name and, if so, how?

In this essay, I first briefly sketch a theory of the political subject (anchored in Lacan), that brings together the Slovenian view of subject as gap in the structure (Žižek and Dolar; see my discussion in Dean, 2016) with the early Badiou's (2009) emphasis on subjectivation and the subjective process as responses to the intervention of the subject. Second, I illustrate the theory by turning to crowds. Crowds are not the political subject, but their 'egalitarian discharge' (a term I take from Canetti 1984) can exert effects that are retroactively attributed to the divided people (people as the rest of us [Dean, 2012], a revolutionary alliance of the oppressed) as their subject. The emphasis on crowds enables, third, a way to find 'grave-diggers' in communicative capitalism's mobilisation of and reliance on complex networks and their power law distributions of links. The politics of digital networks then takes shape as a dual problem of the one versus the many and maintaining the gap of the subject – a politics of collectivity rather than critique. Finally, I put my thesis up against Hardt and Negri's approach to networked biopolitics to demonstrate the relevance of the party form for us today as that perspective, that instrument and organisational means, necessary for revolutionary politics.

Rather than jumping right in to the theoretical discussion, I want to set out descriptively the general problem I aim to solve in terms of survivors and systems. Two dominant themes in contemporary theory and activism constellate around either survivors or systems. So some activists and theorists, not to mention many students and others active on social media, are deeply invested in identity politics and intersectionality. They take identity to be a crucial site of politics, one that must be defended and asserted against multiple violations and harms. Lacking either solidary social and political associations or an economically reliable future, they raise the multiple intersecting challenges obstructing access to success and happiness. They imagine these challenges as, like them, specific rather than general. Betrayed by institutions, they have little faith in organised collectivity. So they repeat, spontaneously, the dominant injunction to rely on themselves and go it alone, despite the fact that they are already outraged by the obstructions that block them from being able to 'go it alone.' In this vein, some advocates hold up livability, survivability, as a crucial achievement. 'Survivor' thus becomes, in this strand of theory and activism, a key figure for the contemporary subject of politics.

Yet even as social media and left political culture more broadly valorise survivors, a concurrent strand of contemporary theory distances itself from people, from anything like a subject, indeed from the human. For these theorists, understanding the present requires a posthumanist focus on systems – geologic, galactic, algorithmic, chaotic and so forth. We see this general move in emphases on extinction, exhaustion, objects and things.

These two theoretical currents correspond to neoliberalism's dismantling of social institutions and to communicative capitalism's intensification of capitalism via networked media/informatisation. University, schools, family and unions are less stable and more in flux. Social welfare protections have been dismantled in the name of people taking responsibility for themselves. The breakdown of social groups and institutions renders individuals ever more vulnerable to exploitation, violence and coercion; they are ever more likely to experience others as competitors or threats, and view them with suspicion. Taking care of oneself now appears as a politically significant act, rather than as a symptom of the dismantled social welfare net and obscenely competitive labour market wherein we have no choice but to care for ourselves if we are going to keep up. The spontaneous response is individual: outrage, a demand that something be done, a call for change. Communicative capitalism supplies the infrastructure for this spontaneous politics of the individual: mobile phones and social media. These media reward immediate reactions such as the tweet, the status update, signing of a petition, emailing a representative – individual activities all ancillary to the singular act said really to matter: voting. What passes for politics enslaves individuals ideologically to bourgeois individualism and its individualised political practices. Jobs are less reliable, and people feel like everything is more competitive, more precarious. More and more choices in a more and more complex and uncertain informational field are downloaded onto the individual, even as these individuated choices have little to no impact on the real determinations of our lives in a setting where satellites, fibre-optic cables, server farms, Big Data, and complex algorithms power high-speed trading, enable just-in-time production, intensify labour markets and concentrate wealth in ever fewer hands.

The Nazi jurist Carl Schmitt characterised liberalism as replacing politics with ethics and economics. I would say that when combined with communicative capitalism, neoliberalism is characterised by ideological investment in survivors and systems (intensifications, respectively, of ethics and economics).

Neoliberalism compels (and social media encourages and encloses) individualised self-cultivation, self-management, self-reliance, and self-absorption, at the same time as communicative capitalism installs and accelerates impersonal determining processes, circuits and systems. Singularised, rendered-unique, hyper-individuated persons find themselves confronting a setting that is utterly determining and outside their control. Survivors struggle to persist in conditions of unliveability rather than to seize and transform these conditions. Systems are presented as the processes and objects determining us, something to view and diagram, perhaps even to predict or mourn, but never to affect. And for good reason – no individual can make a difference. Individuals can have political feelings – and social media encourage the expression and circulation of these feelings, the generation of affective intensities via the outrage of the day. Individuals can document and report – here's a photo of this event, here's how I felt about that bit of news. Individuals can even speak – social media (like anarchist politics) tells us that no one can speak for us and lets us each speak for ourselves, even as the cacophony of voices means that it is ever harder to feel heard, and so we are then all enjoined to listen. But how can we listen to everyone, even to many, without trying to get each other to be ever briefer, and even at 140 characters it is impossible to hear very many at all, and at this point haven't we become an audience again, the cost of being a free provider of content that of also becoming a permanent member of an audience for a performance that never ends? An audience not of mass media but of personalised media, a media of and by many, that we curate for ourselves?

At any rate, our present ideological configuration of survivors and systems makes it hard to see the political subject. We can see fragile individuals and powerful algorithms and geologic forces, but we omit entirely the subject capable of political action – the divided people, historically figured as working class, peasantry, reserve army of the unemployed, the colonised, those who have fought back against slavery, against patriarchy, against oppression. Communicative capitalism operates as a system of desubjectivation – and those who place their political focus on algorithms, objects, geology, and extinction provide ideological expression of this desubjectivation.

But there is another way, a way that begins from the divided people as the subject of politics.

2. Subject: The People as Subject

As we learn from Marx, we don't make our own history. Politics is not a matter of our own choosing, something we make as we please under self-selected circumstances. What these circumstances are and how they are circumscribed is neither fixed nor infinitely malleable. History's repetitions are not repetitions of the same; what was once a tragedy is later a farce. Expressed in more Žižekian terms, repetition can work as negation, negativity or death drive, producing not just impasses but also ruptures.

For Žižek (along with Mladen Dolar), these ruptures are the subject: the subject is the gap in the structure. My claim is that the political subject is a gap in the social structure because the people are the subject of politics (by people, I mean the divided people; the proletarianised and oppressed, not the people as populist totality).

In their self-relating, people always come up against themselves. They encounter the practical, material limits of their association, the psychic and affective pressures of their commonality. The excess of their reflective relation to themselves as 'the people' is the torsion of politics. Politics takes place in the non-identity, gap, or torsion between people and their self-organisation. Political subjectivation forces this non-identity, making it felt as an effect of a subject. The 'subject of politics' is not just any gap or absence. The political subject appears through the active occupation of the constitutive lack in the people.

There is politics because the political subject is collective and it is split. This split is practical and material, the condition of our physical being. The people can never *be* politically (or, differently put, the 'people' is not an ontological category). They are only present as parts, as subsets, as claims. This is the case with crowds occupying public squares, elected assemblies, armies in battle and opinion polls. All are necessarily parts. Their partiality – the gap between parts and (imaginary) whole – is the exciting cause of political subjectivation. Even as parts, the people are only present temporarily. They may try to inscribe their presence, their having been, in documents, practices and organisations which will take their place and operate in their stead, a taking and operating which is also and unavoidably partial. Some degree of alienation is unavoidable because creating new institutions cannot eliminate the minimal difference between the collectivity and the people. The condition of politics, then, is simply this practical material split between the people and the collective that actually comes together.

The split in the people goes all the way down. It can't be limited to the idea that some are excluded from the people (and hence that including them would solve the problem of the gap). Nor can it be rendered as the problem of representation (and hence addressed via ontology, as if our alienated condition would be remedied through a rebirth into ontological fullness if only we could do away with representation). And it is surely not resolved via platforms that seek to replace political forms like unions and parties with forms of preference aggregation. Such technological fixes reproduce communicative capitalism's ideology of survivors versus systems, that is, individuals with their individual needs confronting a large infrastructure outside their control. I am thinking here of Alex Williams's positioning of 'parties and unions structured around outdated principles of structural unity' as something to be overcome in favour of platforms 'capable of hosting an unknowable range of contingent political actions' (Williams 2015, 227). Not only does the expression 'structural unity' misrepresent the political need for unity of action in the face of an enemy, but the party (especially in Lenin's version) names 'the flexible organization of a fidelity to events in the midst of unforeseeable circumstances' (Bosteels 2011,

243). Williams omits the element of fidelity, of consistency, indeed, the political dimension of 'platform' where a party's platform announces its commitments, values, plans, and intentions. 'Array of contingent political actions' doesn't name a politics at all; really, it is no more than an embrace of Facebook and Twitter.

The people do not know what they want. They are not fully present to themselves. Conflicting and contradictory desires and drives render the people a split subject perpetually pushing to express, encounter and address its own non-knowledge. As the collective subject of politics the people is nothing but this gap, the force or push of many through and against claims, representations and institutions offered in their name.

The economy (over-)determines the *setting* of subjectivation. It configures the terrain on which we organise the consequences of a subjectivation. To come back to my argument, politics cannot have just any point of departure because it does not take place in an open, unconditioned manifold. Rather, it pushes forth in a setting ruptured and structured by a fundamental antagonism. So the economy, the mode of production that characterises a society – digital or otherwise – doesn't *determine* the political subject. It is the setting for the subjectivation of the rupture or gap that attests to the force of the subject. Further, the economy is the setting of the *struggle over* this attestation – what, if anything, a rupture means, the terms and images available for this meaning, and the constellation of forces lined up for or against a given attestation that an event was an effect of the subject of politics.

Crowds – collectivities, provisional heterogeneous unities – help illustrate how the people as the political subject appear in and as a gap.

3. Crowds – Force of Collectivity

Over the last decade, crowds and protests have shown us the people sensing their collective power, the capacity of many to inscribe a gap in the expected. This 'inscription of a gap in the expected' was manifest during the Occupy movement – finally people were protesting, rising up. We've seen crowds pushing against the separations of democracy in Tunisia, Egypt, Spain and Greece; in a wide array of anti-austerity protests; in protests for reproductive freedom in Poland and Ireland; in the massive outpouring of women in the US on 21 January 2017, and so on.

The very powers that let crowds force a gap in the expected, however, also introduce a set of political challenges. Crowds are destructive, creative, unpredictable, contagious and temporary. They don't endure. People go home. Crowds are politically indeterminate – people amass for all sorts of conflicting reasons, feelings and compulsions (which is why interviewing single participants misses the point; you can't interview a crowd – and here I have in mind Paolo Gerbardo's [2017] in many ways very interesting and essential book, *The Mask and the Flag*. Gerbardo breaks up the crowd into individual recollections.

By doing so he is able to reduce an international chain of disruptive crowd events into citizen participation, 'citizenism,' thereby effacing the challenge of the various occupations and demonstrations of 2010-2011 to the status quo. The strength that comes with the indeterminacy of the crowd's message is a weakness when the crowd disperses. The crowd doesn't have a politics; it is the opportunity for a politics – which is another way of saying that the crowd inscribes a gap; it breaks up the expected, the everyday, but it doesn't tell us how or in what direction.

How the crowd gets a politics depends on the response to the crowd event and whether this response is faithful to the egalitarian substance of the crowd. In *Crowds and Power*, Elias Canetti (1984) describes the moment of the crowd's emergence as the 'discharge.' This is the point when 'all who belong to the crowd get rid of their differences and feel equal'. Up until that point, there may be a lot of people, but they are not yet that concentration of bodies and affects that is a crowd. As the crowd's density increases, libidinal effects are unleashed: 'In that density, where there is scarcely any space between, and body presses against body, each man is as near the other as he is to himself, and an immense feeling of relief ensues. It is for the sake of this blessed moment, when no-one is greater or better than another, that people become a crowd.' Canetti gives us the crowd as a strange attractor of *jouissance*, a figure of collective enjoyment. The libidinal energy of the crowd binds it together for a joyous moment, a moment Canetti renders as a 'feeling of equality' and that we might also figure as the shared intensity of belonging. The feeling won't last; inequality will return with the dissipation of the crowd. But in the orgasmic discharge, 'a state of absolute equality' supplants individuating distinctions.

What we get from Canetti, then, is the substance or essence of the crowd form as an absolute equality. This equality is only temporary, but it is essential to the crowd discharge, the feeling for which the crowd amasses. Canetti argues that the crowd's equality infuses all demands for justice. Equality as belonging – not separation, weighing and measure – is what gives 'energy' (Canetti's term) to the longing for justice. The crowd concentrates equality and a longing for justice (and so carries out a function Marx associates with the factory).

The crowd event may register as the movement of the people. Some other will view the crowd as having been the people because she apprehends the *jouissance* of the egalitarian discharge. She responds to the courage and justice intertwined in the crowd, perhaps with some anxiety in the wake of its *jouissance*. Her response indicates that the rupture of the crowd event was a subjectivation (my analysis here is guided by Badiou [2009] in *Theory of the Subject*). The other sees the people in the crowd, their collective force, as the universal struggle of the oppressed. She responds to the rupture as a moment in the subjective process of the emancipatory egalitarian movement of the people. The crowd was not just these particular people here right now. They were *the people* fighting for justice. Fidelity to the egalitarian discharge is an effect of the crowd event; the people as subject is thus understood as its cause.

Neither capital nor its state want the people to appear. So they try to mend the rupture, close the gap as quickly as possible. They deny something happened, relying on the repetitive novelty of relentless media to deflect and disperse attention. They claim it wasn't the people; it was thugs, a mob, outsiders. They make it business as usual, the citizens participating like citizens are supposed to do. Spontaneous responses on the Left challenge claims for the divided people as the collective subject of the crowd event by emphasising specific groups, issues, and identities, by highlighting who wasn't there, by prioritising their own unique spin on the event just for the sake of being different. Social media encourages such responses, the more and more varied the better. Communicative capitalism feeds on multiplicity, confusion, indeterminacy, anything that can disperse the force of the crowd.

4. Central Feature of Digital Networks – Power Law Distributions

And yet, communicative capitalism nevertheless produces crowds. We can quickly point to several different kinds: crowds of 'friends', followers, and users in social media; crowds of workers in factories (see Jack Qiu's book, *Goodbye iSlave* [2017]), as well as Christian Fuchs's detailed case studies of digital labour); crowds of commodities and disposable things; crowds of Big Data (in fact Big Data might be one of the most powerful crowd symbols in our current digital era); and crowds of those dispossessed from their work, homes, lives, and futures by the intensified inequality of the networked economy. These crowds need to be understood in terms of the 'long tail' of a power law distribution – the many to the one.

Communicative capitalism stimulates the production of networks that generate power law distributions. It relies on the creation and enclosure of general fields or commons characterised by free choice, growth and preferential attachment. Out of the common a 'one' emerges, the one at the top, the one with the most hits or links, the blockbuster or superstar. Here exploitation consists in stimulating the production of a field in the interest of finding, and then monetising, the one. Many contribute, many work. One is rewarded. The bigger the field, the more powerful, valuable, or elite the one.

Inequality is a necessary and unavoidable feature of complex networks, that is, networks characterised by free choice, growth, and preferential attachment. As Albert-Laszlo Barabasi demonstrates, complex networks follow a power law distribution of links. The item in first place or at the top of a given network has twice as many links as the item in second place, which has more than the one in third and so on, such that there is very little difference among those at the bottom but massive differences between top and bottom. Many novels are written. Few are published. Fewer are sold. A very few become best sellers. Twitter is another example: it has over a billion registered users; one pop singer, Katy

Perry, has over 94 million followers. Most people have 200. Popular media expresses the power law structure of complex networks with terms like the '80/20 rule,' the winner-takes-all or winner-takes-most character of the new economy, and the 'long tail.'

Notice that it doesn't matter what kind of network or field we are talking about – novels, Twitter, Amazon, Google, movies – the content is unimportant. Capitalist productivity depends on the expropriation and exploitation of communication. Any communicative action is equivalent to any other; their meaning or use value matters less than their exchange value, the fact that they can be shared. A repercussion is that capitalism has subsumed communication such that communication does not provide a critical outside. Volume, number and the crowd overpower critique. And in complex networks this volume, this number, is organised hierarchically in power law distributions: the one versus the many.

The challenge of politics in communicative capitalism is to make effective the power of the many – how the crowd can be in and for itself, that is, how crowds can produce effects that can be attributed to the divided people as their subject. Social media functions to dissipate efforts to hold open the gap produced by the crowd rupture, so that what for a moment was the people is later forgotten, diminished, reinterpreted. Yet its very processes produce new crowd forms through which collectivity tries to exert its force – hashtags, memes, selfies and other common images. My point is not that hashtags are revolutionary. Rather they point to political openings that arise as critique loses efficacy.

5. Hardt and Negri

I've emphasised the fact that complex networks produce hierarchy. In contrast, Hardt and Negri highlight the democratic dimension of biopolitical labour. They claim that the same networked, cooperative structures that produce the common generate new democratic capacities, and even 'make possible in the political sphere the development of democratic organizations' (Hardt and Negri 2009, 354). Given the ways that the exchange value of communicative contributions displaces their meaning or use value, and given the ways that communicative capitalism drives processes that individuate and singularise, on the one hand, and concentrate resources and power in the one, on the other, it is hard to see how their claim for new democratic capacities is anything different from the techno-utopianism of the nineties. The same holds for newly possible democratic organisations, especially in light of Hardt and Negri's rejection of 'vanguard organizations.' They tell us that the vanguard party corresponds to a different, earlier, structure of labour (a different technical composition of the proletariat). According to their periodisation, the vanguard party corresponds to the early twentieth century's professional factory workers. The deskilled workers of the mid-twentieth century fit with that period's mass party. But today, they argue, the political form appropriate to biopolitical labour must be democratic, cooperative, autonomous, and horizontally networked. The vanguard party is inadequate, 'anachronistic,' because it doesn't look like the networks of contemporary biopolitical production.

This argument is not convincing. Complex networks are not the horizontal, cooperative and autonomous forms that Hardt and Negri imagine. As Albert-Laszlo Barabasi's work (2003) on complex networks demonstrates, free choice, growth and preferential attachment produce hierarchies and inevitable dramatic differences between the one that is most chosen and preferred and the many that are not (see my discussion in Dean 2016, 12–13). The ostensibly creative, cooperative and democratic character of networked communication doesn't eliminate hierarchy. It entrenches hierarchy by using our own choices against us. And, as Barabasi's work on complex networks makes clear, this hierarchy isn't imposed from above. It is an immanent effect of free choice, growth, and preferential attachment.

A political form mirroring biopolitical production would not be horizontal and democratic. Its democracy would produce power law distributions, unequal nodes or outcomes, winners and losers, few and many. We see this phenomenon on Twitter as people fight through trending hashtags. Hashtags provide common names that serve as loci of struggle; when they trend, they rise above the long tail of the millions of unread, unloved Tweets coursing through the nets. The democratic element – people's choice to use and forward – produces the inequality that lets some hashtags appear as and even be, for a moment, significant. The fact of emergent hierarchies suggests that an emergent vanguard may well be the political form necessary for struggles under biopolitical conditions, that is to say, communicative capitalism.

The structure of the complex networks of biopolitical production indicates that, *contra* Hardt and Negri, a vanguard party is not anachronistic at all. It is instead a form that corresponds to the dynamics of networked communication. This structure indicates an additional problem with Hardt and Negri's rejection of the vanguard party. They characterise Lenin's party as involving an organisational process that comes from 'above' the movements of the multitude. Historically, this insinuation is clearly false. The Bolsheviks were but one group among multiple parties, tendencies and factions acting in the tumultuous context of the Russian Revolution. They were active within the movements of the oppressed workers and peasants. The movements themselves, through victories and defeats, short and long-term alliances, new forms of cooperation, and advances in political organisation gave rise to the party, even as the party furthered the movements.

For Hardt and Negri, the goal of revolution is 'the generation of new forms of social life' (Hardt and Negri 2009, 354). They describe revolutionary struggle as a process of liberation that establishes a common. Such a process, they argue, consolidates insurrection as it institutionalises new collective habits and practices. Institutions are then sites for the management of encounters, extension of social rupture, and transformation of those who compose them.

The resemblance between these institutions and the vanguard party is striking. The party involves a common name, language, and set of tactics. It has practices that establish ways of being together. Its purpose is to occupy and extend the gap within society that class struggle denotes. As Georg Lukács insists, Lenin's concept of party organisation prioritises flexibility and consistency: the party has and must have a capacity for self-transformation. What Hardt and Negri describe as the extension of insurrection in an institutional process is another way of theorising the party.

Hardt and Negri outline instead a platform of demands without a carrier, without a body to fight for them. Their model of institutions suggests that a party or parties could be such a carrier, but rather than present their platform as a party platform, Hardt and Negri present it as a series of demands to be made to existing governments and institutions of global governance (but who makes these demands?). The demands are for the provision of the basic means of life, global citizenship, and access to the commons. Hardt and Negri acknowledge that 'today's ruling powers unfortunately have no intention of granting even these basic demands' (Hardt and Negri 2009, 382). And Hardt and Negri's response is laughter, 'a laugh of creation and joy, anchored solidly in the present' (Hardt and Negri 2009, 383). No wonder they don't present their demands as the platform of a party. The demands are not to be fought for. They mark potentials already present in the biopolitical production of the common, limits to capitalist control.

Hardt and Negri imply that the party form is outmoded. I've argued that not only do contemporary networks produce power law distributions of few and many, but that emergent hierarchies – particularly when understood in terms of the vanguards and practices that already emerge out of political movement – point to the ways that party organisations emerge. Current examples of this tendency include the adoption of common tactics, names and symbols that bring together previously separate, disparate, and even competing struggles. When local and issue politics are connected via a common name, successes in one area advance the struggle as a whole. Separate actions become themselves plus all the others. They instil enthusiasm and inspire imitation.

Many of us are convinced that capitalist crises have reached a decisive point. We know that the system is fragile, that it produces its own grave-diggers, and that it is held in place by a repressive international state structure. Yet we act as if we did not know this. The party provides a form that can let us believe what we know. As we learn from Lenin, revolutionary political consciousness is the collective perspective organised in the party, oriented by its theory and far-reaching historical tasks. Without the party the people can be hard to see. Their acts become co-opted and displaced, channelled and packaged so as to buttress the system they oppose. In communicative capitalism, multiple resistances blur into a menu of opinions and choices, options disjoined from truth. The legacy of peoples' struggle and their crowd event are conveyed by university, culture, and momentary organisations, subjected to the demands of capitalism and deactivated as living resource. The power of systems re-emerges as the locus of the power that matters – communication, circulation, accumulation. If we want to defeat these systems, we can't repeat or reinforce them. We have to seize them. And that requires political organisation.

To return, then, to the thematics of survivor and system: these tendencies in contemporary theory occlude the space of the subject, preventing us from acknowledging contradictions in communicative capitalism – but the long tail is a crowd, and the crowd can be organised, concentrated, politicised. Further, some emergent hierarchies – hashtags, common images, common political forms like occupations and even parties – become important means of contestation, of political struggle. Beyond critique is collectivity.

References

Badiou, Alain. 2009. *Theory of the Subject*. New York: Continuum.

Barabasi, Albert-Laszlo. 2003. *Linked*. New York: Penguin.

Bosteels, Bruno. 2011. *The Actuality of Communism*. London: Verso.

Canetti, Elias. 1984. *Crowds and Power*. New York: Farrar, Straus and Giroux.

Dean, Jodi. 2012. *The Communist Horizon*. London: Verso.

Dean, Jodi. 2016. *Crowds and Party*. London: Verso.

Gerbaudo, Paolo. 2017. *The Mask and the Flag: Populism, Citizenism and Global Protest*. London: Hurst.

Hardt, Michael and Antonio Negri. 2009. *Commonwealth*. Cambridge, MA: Harvard University Press.

Qui, Jack Linchaun. 2017. *Goodbye iSlave: A Manifesto for Digital Abolition*. Urbana, IL: University of Illinois Press.

Williams, Alex. 2015. 'Control Societies and Platform Logic.' *New Formations* 84/85: 209–227.

CHAPTER 15

Subjects, Contexts and Modes of Critique: Reflections on Jodi Dean's Chapter

Paulina Tambakaki

In *Philosophy and Real Politics* Raymond Geuss takes issue with ideal theories of politics. Ideal theories, he argues, start from a 'few general principles' that they posit as historically invariant (2008, 7). They explain and justify these principles and they then draw conclusions about how people ought to live and act. Missing from these theories is a reflection on what Geuss refers to as 'contexts of action', that is, historically situated conjunctures that affect human motivations and shape political actions (Geuss 2008, 9–11). Any responsible (and realist) theory, insists Geuss, must take these contexts of action into account. For they frame and augment our grasp of politics and the ways it might be refigured. Jodi Dean's study of the conditions of communicative capitalism exemplifies this framing.

Communicative capitalism, explains Dean, desubjectifies. It makes it hard to see the political subject that is capable of political action because the collectivity that carries out this action is, in this context, blocked. Dissolved into the individual who registers her outrage on social media, collectivity is treated with suspicion and rendered obsolete. At the same time, according to Dean, neo-liberal mantras of self-management, self-reliance and self-care further

How to cite this book chapter:
Tambakaki, P. 2019. Subjects, Contexts and Modes of Critique: Reflections on Jodi Dean's Chapter. In: Chandler, D. and Fuchs, C. (eds.) *Digital Objects, Digital Subjects: Interdisciplinary Perspectives on Capitalism, Labour and Politics in the Age of Big Data*. Pp. 183–186. London: University of Westminster Press. DOI: https://doi.org/10.16997/book29.o. License: CC-BY-NC-ND 4.0

singularise. They reinforce themes of individual survival and, in so doing, they erode the prospects for a collectivisation that aims to transform – and not simply critique – individuating trends.

For Dean, collective subjects have the capacity to transform politics, and these subjects find proto-expression in the egalitarian discharges of the crowd. While these discharges are temporary, they show that it is possible to transgress the individuating and, ultimately, depoliticising conditions of communicative capitalism. More to the point, the crowds (of users, followers, hashtags and so on), with their power law distributions that communicative capitalism paradoxically produces, serve, according to Dean, as openings for the emergence of a politicised subject that is more forceful (because it is divided and collective); more permanent (because it persists after the event); and more radical (because it aims to displace and seize the system). *This* subject demands work, argues Dean. Political organisation, in the form of a vanguard, carries this work forward, undoing the normalisations of communicative capitalism. Or to put it in Dean's words: 'beyond critique is collectivity'. This argument without doubt provokes refreshing questions about the limits of critique.

Political theories have long been obsessed with the central role that critique plays in a transformative politics. From Boltanski and Chiapello's call to revive the social and artistic critiques of capitalism in order to resist it (2007), to agonistic theories that stress the excesses that arise to contest and disrupt politics, it is difficult to overlook the intimate connection established between change and critique. On the back of the assumption that dispute, resistance and dissent expose exclusions, a consensus has formed about the benefits of critique, in terms of the openings it makes possible for alternative politics. Dean unsettles this consensus when she tells us that it is collectivity, rather than critique, that is needed in order to transform socio-political configurations. Critique is not enough in the context of communicative capitalism, argues Dean, and she is right. While there are manifold disputes over the meanings and practices of contemporary politics, such disputes leave few traces; the crowd events of, say, the *Aganaktismenoi* or the Occupy movements tend to dissolve once the events have ended. There is also more opportunity for individuation and little opportunity for collectivisation understood as processes. And there are vulnerabilities, exploitations, outrage and conformity – in other words, desubjectification, much like Dean explains. But is collectivisation the answer to these developments? Or to put the same question in somewhat more exaggerated terms, is more politics the answer to the lack of transformative politics?

No doubt, the response one gives to this question largely depends on the diagnosis of the problem that collectivity claims to solve – in this case, the individuating and singularising trends that animate much of contemporary activism and certain strands of digital critique. But what if there is no disagreement in diagnosis? As I have already noted, I find Dean's account of the political challenges that arise in the wake of a communicative capitalism convincing. This agreement is exactly what, however, leads me, in a second step, to ponder whether Dean's diagnosis ends up undermining the argument that a collectivity *can* arise in and out of power law distributional openings. The emphasis on the verb 'can' draws in many ways on a familiar if not commonplace argument in the literature. When it comes to envisioning the rise of the exploited or even of the conformists, questions hover about their ability to rise, given that they are significantly incapacitated by the systems and discourses that have dominated them. If this is the case, then it becomes difficult to see how the desubjectivations of communicative capitalism can be overcome, individuating tendencies transgressed, and collectivities formed.

Of course, it is noteworthy that communicative capitalism does produce crowds and that such crowds gesture toward collectivity – especially as they can offer glimmers of division, subjectivation and egalitarian demands. But what if these crowds do not deliver any politics, because they do not manage to elicit a response to the crowd event? The issue here is not so much that collectivities are unable to form because they have become incapacitated, but that vanguards have failed to make the appearance of the crowd persist. When we think of the divisions that inhere in discussions about political organisation, then it is not unreasonable to consider the possibility that vanguards might not be immediately available to counter the hierarchies that complex networks of communication establish. And if vanguards are not available, then the crowd might be all we have left to do politics *and* critique. For example, when I think of the Occupy movements I cannot deny the effectiveness of their critique of the institutional establishment grounded on the slogan 'we are the 99%'. What I want to contest, however, is whether this critique brought any rupture to the political establishment – and if it did what kind of rupture this was. In other words, the claim I want to advance with this example is that the critiques that crowds develop might be durable after the event without immediately leading to any transformative politics. This widening split between transformation and critique calls forth a serious rethinking not just of the aims (and perhaps even limits) of critique, but also of the relation between democracy and critique, for we are accustomed to think that democracies are sites of openness and, inevitably, of transformation and critique.

Dean takes issue with democracy, and particularly with Hardt and Negri's faith in democratic practices as vehicles for change. Democratic practices, she argues, harness unequal outcomes and one-versus-many distributions. Understood as the 'people's' choice to use and forward', democracy produces 'significant' hashtags that nurture inequalities and entrench hierarchies. For these reasons, democracy, and Hardt and Negri's preferred modes of horizontal and autonomous organisation, are too limited as platforms for change, not because change is difficult to achieve, but because such institutions are easily displaced as vehicles that support the exploitative system they seek to resist. This thought-provoking argument presses us to consider anew *how* change occurs within and through democratic institutions (if at all). Indeed, if the democratic lexicon is, as Dean intimates, supportive of communicative capitalism, then perhaps there is little value in expecting that change might come through democratic institutions. There would also be little value in investing in democratic institutions.

Dean thus suggests that the time has come to disinvest from democratic institutions and to anticipate the emergence of another, more political and more equal, world around the common of communism. The common she tells us, *pace* Hardt and Negri, is hierarchical. Its hierarchies call for an oppositional politics that inspires fidelity and change. But what if this common (digitalised or not) is analogous to what Jacques Rancière (1999) understands by the order of the police, and therefore as something immune to anything other than collective, if momentary, subjectivations? This grim possibility that confronts most attempts to envision another politics taps into existing anxieties generated by communicative capitalism. From my perspective, it serves as an opportunity to bolster our energies to rework politics, democracy and the limits of critiques. It is in this direction that Dean's 'Collectivity or Critique' takes an inspiring and thought-provoking lead.

References

Boltanski, Luc and Eve Chiapello. 2007. *The New Spirit of Capitalism*. London and New York: Verso.

Geuss, Raymond. 2008. *Philosophy and Real Politics*. Princeton and Oxford: Princeton University Press.

Rancière, Jacques. 1999. *Disagreement: Politics and Philosophy*. Translated by Julie Rose. Minneapolis, MN: University of Minnesota Press.

CHAPTER 16

The Platform Party: The Transformation of Political Organisation in the Era of Big Data

Paolo Gerbaudo

1. Introduction

To each generation its constitution, famously proposed Condorcet, arguing that the institutional system necessarily had to adapt to historical changes. To each generation its form of organisation, one could quip in response, witnessing the constant historical change that has invested the political party in the course of history. When one utters the word 'party', i.e. political party, the mind flies, at least for most people on the Left, to a very specific form of party, to what the French political sociologist Maurice Duverger (1959) called the 'mass party', the type of party that emerged at the height of the industrial era. But many other forms of party have existed in history such as the party of notables that was prevalent in the 19th century. And after the decline of the mass party new types of parties have emerged such as the so-called catch-all party and the cartel party described respectively by Otto Kircheimer (1966) and by Richard Katz and Peter Mair (1994). We are now at a time when a new party type is

How to cite this book chapter:
Gerbaudo, P. 2019. The Digital Party: The Transformation of Political Organisation in the Era of Big Data. In: Chandler, D. and Fuchs, C. (eds.) *Digital Objects, Digital Subjects: Interdisciplinary Perspectives on Capitalism, Labour and Politics in the Age of Big Data.* Pp. 187–198. London: University of Westminster Press. DOI: https://doi.org/10.16997/book29.p. License: CC-BY-NC-ND 4.0

emerging, its birth-pangs being visible in a number of new political formations that have arisen in different political countries around the time of the financial crisis of 2008. This is what in this chapter I discuss as the 'platform party' or 'digital party' namely the 'party type' that corresponds to the digital society, in the same way in which the mass party reflected the nature of the industrial society.

The platform party may also be described as 'digital' because of its adoption of digital technology as a key means of communication and organisation. This emerging template incarnates the new forms of organisation, the new values and social relationship that are dominant in a digital society. Examples of platform parties are manifold, and available in very different national contexts. Among the most representative are Podemos in Spain, the Five Star Movement in Italy, the Pirate Party in Northern European countries, La France Insoumise in France or organisations such as Momentum in the UK. These formations have been described, as 'digital parties', 'Internet parties' or 'network parties' because of the the way they have presented themselves as the champions of the new forms of organisation and of new values of the digital society.

Such digital character is visible at different levels of depth in both their external communication and in their internal organisation. Externally, these formations have harnessed the power of social networks such as Facebook and Twitter or dedicated YouTube channels to build a vast base of supporters and sympathisers. Internally, they have developed a number of online decision-making platforms to invite all registered members to discuss and vote on policies, candidates and leadership. Yet these features do not seem sufficient to classify these parties as belonging to the same set. There is more to their commonality than meets the eye, something that makes it justifiable to associate them with one another, even while other parties that also make use of digital technology are excluded from this association. Why can we claim, for example, that Momentum is a digital organisation while the (British) Conservative party is not? Or on what grounds can we argue that the 5 Star Movement better corresponds to the ideal type of the platform party than does its adversary, the centre-left Partito Democratico? What do the formations cited above, that straddle the Left/Right divide, often claiming to transcend it altogether, have in common? What form of organisation is typical to the digital party? And how do platform parties reflect the nature of digital culture, and of the new forms of subjectivity and power that emerge in the era of social media and Big Data?

Platform parties are not simply parties which use digital technology in a purely instrumental sense, as a way to achieve specific ends, while otherwise maintaining the organisational forms and dynamics of the past; instead the change is far more profound and systemic. These parties pursue a far-reaching restructuring of their organisational forms and their philosophy in ways that are coherent with the nature of a digital society and its drive towards directness, disintermediation, interactivity, adaptability and instantaneous responsiveness (Van Dijck 2013). These formations betoken an attempt to mend and simplify politics, thus responding to the perception of a yawning gap between the citizenry and the political process. They strive for customisation, adaptability and interactivity, in a way that makes them resemble social media and app platforms such as Facebook, Airbnb or Uber.

This organisational restructuring is informed by a strong 'participationism', i.e. by the belief that the unrestrained participation of ordinary people in discussions, decisions, and actions is a force for good. Yet this attempt does not lead to a condition of pure horizontality, and to a wholesale end of representation and hierarchy, as some of the most fervent evangelists of digital disintermediation would lead us to believe. In fact, while eliminating some of the forms of intermediation existing in bureaucratic mass parties, and in particular the so-called intermediary levels, of the apparatchiks, the bureaucrats, and the local cadres, platform parties do not go as far as eliminating leadership at the top. On the contrary, many of these parties are characterised by strong leadership. They are as much 'participationist' as they are 'presidentialist'. Within them the drive towards disintermediation takes the form of an organisational polarisation, in which the hyperleader – a charismatic, mediatised and celebrity-culture informed leader – mirrors himself in and allies himself with the superbase – a highly activated and responsive digital assembly of all party members or 'users', that finds new opportunities of day-to-day participation in social media conversations and in discussions and decision-making conducted on the online 'participatory platforms' set up by all these formations.

2. From the Industrial Party to the Platform Party

In each historical era there tends to be an analogy between the mode of production, and what we could call the 'mode of organisation', namely the set of organisational mechanisms, practices and structures that are prevalent at the time. In other words, political parties are historically specific: they are not organisational structures imposed on society from above, but phenomena that in order to be effective necessarily contain and reflect the social tendencies which are specific to any given society in different historical periods.

As argued by Italian political scientist Marco Revelli the mass party incarnated the logic of production of the industrial society, the organisational structures and forms of social experience proper to that period. The party came to resemble the Fordist factory, by establishing a solid and heavy organisational structure marked by a strong closure towards the outside, and hierarchy and vertical integration on the inside. The mass party was thus a perfect mirror of industrial society, with its tendency to 'gigantism to incorporate large masses of men in a stable way, by arranging them in solid and permanent structures'. (Ravelli 2013). 'The party was conceived as a factory where politics had to be produced through collective "political work", as if it were a sort of manufacture, inspired by the Taylorist criteria of efficiency and rationalisation. In this structure the militants were the equivalent of workers on the assembly line, the local cadres the production technicians, and the central committee the corporate management body' (ibid). Here we encounter the party as a 'Modern Prince', to use the expression of Antonio Gramsci in *The Prison Notebooks*: a neuralgic centre through which to coordinate political action, to conquer the state and at the same time to control society, following the logic of the vertical integration of the great Fordist factory (1971).

This organisational model came into crisis due to a series of profound economic and cultural transformations that began to develop from the sixties, largely due to the crisis accumulation model of Fordist capitalism that weakened the working class and the old bourgeoisie. The rise of new protest movements, the student protests of 1968, ecological movements, feminism and urban protests were the sign of the growing complexity of a society that was becoming more and more difficult to integrate vertically. The rampant individualism and consumerism of the neoliberal era superseded the political militancy of the industrial era.

The mass party crisis opened the way for a new party form that was discussed in political science through a series of concepts: 'professional-electoral party' (Panebianco, 1988) 'catch-all party' (Kirchheimer, 1990) and the 'cartel party' (Katz and Mair, 1995). It seems fit for the purpose of our analysis to note that these terms ultimately point to the same trend: the emergence of a new 'light' post-Fordist party as an alternative to the mass party. The 'television party' is the term I prefer to adopt in this analysis because this is a party for which television, rather than the press or the party newspaper, becomes the main channel of communication with the electorate, and a substitute for a committed militancy. This turn involves a profound transformation in the organising structure of political parties. First, the platform party is a party that loses the support of an active base of militants and experiences a severe decline in the number of registered members. Secondly, it is a party that no longer has the heavy bureaucratic structure of the mass party, but adopts a light structure that looks more like an electoral committee, as expressed by the concept of 'professional-electoral' party. Thirdly, it is a party that, unlike the mass party, no longer has clearly defined social bases, and seeks opportunistically to draw its support from different socio-demographics according to circumstances, so it is also described as a 'catch-all party', or even as an 'opinion party', a party no longer based on predefined economic interests but chasing fleeting wishes and opinions.

The television party is a type of political party that Italians know well because it is the one that has been manifested in the political venture of Silvio Berlusconi and his 'party-company' Forza Italia. For this party a central role is played by the media process on account of its access to television and its power of influence on the population, which, in Berlusconi's case, was guaranteed by his ownership of half of the national television frequencies. It is also a party that introduces a strong personalisation of politics, in which the face of the leader, adopting the role of an actor giving a political performance, becomes the central source of recognisability, and the means of building a sentimental connection – to use the term of Antonio Gramsci – between the citizens and the party (1971). It is also precisely because of its almost complete reliance on television appearances as a means of connection between the leader and the people, that the television party thus loses the support of an active militancy.

Following the analysis of Revelli, the television party manifests the transformation of the production mode into a post-Fordist society. This party no longer resembles the Fordist factory, but rather service companies, particularly those in the field of communication and advertising, which are the vanguard of the post-industrial service economy. It is significant that Silvio Berlusconi founded Forza Italia on the territorial network of his Publitalia advertising company and on the media firepower of his television channels. The television party internalises marketing and advertising techniques used to understand and manipulate the people's desires. It is a party populated by a small army of communications consultants, pollsters and spin doctors. It sees politics as an extension of the sphere of consumption, and looks at the citizenry as an 'electoral market', which can be treated just like any other market of goods and services, and where the strategic area is represented by centrist voters, more likely to swing between parties. It is also a party that generates a passive attitude in the electorate, which recalls the 'couch-potato' habit of TV viewers. A party that, transforming politics into a variety show, forces citizens into apathy and disillusionment.

Building on this model, we can argue that we now stand at a new stage in the evolution of the party-form. The profound shifts in the mode of production signalled by the diffusion of social media and of apps, and by the rise of Web 2.0 companies such as Facebook, Twitter, Uber, Airbnb and many others, is engendering the rise of a new party type. The digital party, reflects in its *eidos* the new tendencies that are emerging in a 'network society' (Castells 2011), much in the same way in which the mass party reflected the nature and tendencies of the industrial society and the television party the emerging trends of the post-industrial era. Thirdly, the platform party is not a class party. Rather it is a party marked by strong inclusivity and an interclassist tendency. While relying for electoral support on the lower and younger sector of an impoverished middle class, these parties for the most part do not appeal to classes, but to individuals as part of those classes. Fourthly, it is not an ideological party, or at least it is not ideological in the narrow, twentieth-century sense of the term. The platform party does not have a long-term messianic vision to change society, but rather has a preference for issues that are felt to be concrete and immediate.

To summarise, using an expression of startup and software jargon, the platform party is a 'light' and 'agile' yet powerful party structure. It is light in its organisational skeleton, but powerful in the depth and intensity of the participation of its members; it is agile at the top and highly reactive at the base. It thus conjoins two features that seemed irreconcilable in past parties: a lean directive structure and an active, though mostly in the limited sense of 'reactive', militant support base.

3. The Party as a Platform

The platform party is the form the political party adopts in the era of social media and apps, at a time when new forms of communicating, working, and purchasing online are revolutionising all sorts of social patterns. How does this change in technology lead to a modification in the nature of the party? What difference do social media and online platforms, heavily used by formations such as Podemos, the Five Star Movement and Pirate Parties, make for the digital party? Following our foregoing discussion on the analogy between the mode of production and the mode of organisation, it can be said that the platform party internalises the new forms of social experience of the digital age, and the forms of production, consumption and interpersonal relationships that are prevalent in it. Central to these trends, is the role played by digital platforms, which is at the origin of the platform party alternate name: 'digital party'.

In political science, the term 'platform' is normally used to refer to political parties' political platforms, namely the set of policies they pursue and propose to the electorate. Yet in the context of the digital party we have a rather different kind of platform in mind. The platform hinted at here is the digital 'platform', a term used to describe the logic inherent in a set of online services, from Facebook and Twitter to consumer apps such as Uber and Airbnb, that have come to define the era of social media and Big Data. Digital platforms, such as those used by these and other companies, are mini operating systems, execution environments of various programmes and applications, enabling users to accomplish a diverse set of activities: socialising with friends and acquaintances (Facebook); publishing personal thoughts or news (Twitter); finding sentimental and sexual partners (Match.com, Tinder); ordering a taxi (Uber, Grab etc.); or reserving accommodation (Airbnb, Booking.com etc.).

Over the last few years a lot has been said about the nature of such platforms and their social, political and economic consequences. Media theorist Joss Hands (2013, 1) has defined platforms as '"Cloud"-based software modules that act as a portal to different types of information, with nested applications that aggregate content, often generated by the "users" themselves'. In his recent book *Platform Capitalism*, Nick Srnicek (2016, 43) has approached them as 'digital infrastructures that allow two or more groups to interact'. They are therefore positioned as '*intermediaries* that connect multiple users: customers, advertisers, service providers, manufacturers [...] and even physical objects.' The key aspect of online platforms is the way in which they disintermediate social and economic relationships. However, this process of disintermediation carries a more complex reality. By disintermediating, in fact, platforms create new digital intermediaries which go hand in hand with new power relationships.

The disintermediation/re-intermediation introduced by digital platforms revolves around a series of key elements: their dependence on data and information generated by users as expressed in the term 'user-generated content'; their high degree of personalisation; their aggregative logic which allows, for example, people with similar interests to know each other, or producers and consumers in a certain location to connect, or advertisers to target a niche market; the partially closed or 'enclosed' character of such systems, as a means of harnessing 'network effects'. Online platforms seek to respond to the extreme mutability of contemporary society and economy by building systems able to intercept consumer demand instantaneously; by developing complex forms of intelligence on the behaviour and consumer choices of individuals; by creating new services to quickly respond to new needs (or creating new needs); and by 'perturbing' pre-existing markets through new forms of brokering, as expressed in the discourse of 'digital disruption' used to describe companies such as Uber and Airbnb.

Platform parties reflect different elements of this new platform logic that underpins the world of social media and apps. First the platform party integrates in its operations a series of online platforms, ranging from social media such as Facebook and Twitter for external communication, to various instant messaging services such as WhatsApp and Telegram for internal communication. Secondly, platform parties have developed their own dedicated discussion and voting platforms: the so-called 'participatory platforms' that have become a symbol of their attempt to build forms of direct and participatory democracy. These formations adopt digital companies' logic of data mining, aggregation and analysis adapting it for the purpose of creating consensus and political mobilisation. Similarly to what happens with companies such as Facebook, Twitter and Airbnb, platform parties unite in the same 'database' citizens who, despite their individual idiosyncrasies, are united by common interests, demands and wishes. See for example, the way in which France Insoumise has used the NationBuilder software to enlist half a million supporters to the campaign of Jean-Luc Melenchon, by simply having them hit the button 'je soutien' (I support). Or witness how other parties have used participatory platforms and social media accounts to gather thousands of supporters, often in a very short time-span. Online platforms thus become not just a participatory architecture for these parties, but effectively also an organisational 'scaffolding' that serves to compensate for their lack of a dependable bureaucratic structure, found in twentieth-century parties and trade unions.

4. Cloud/Start-up/Forum

Adopting the platform logic of digital companies, the platform party comes to reflect some of the typical functions and characteristics associated with digital culture. This tendency of of the platform party is visible in various 'faces' of the platform party that correspond to different aspects of its operation: the cloud party, the start-up party and the forum party.

First, the platform party is a a *cloud party*, an agile party which alike online software platforms is accessible by every device and every place. In this context, digital communication becomes a substitute for physical infrastructure such as the offices, circles and sections that constituted the organisational structure of traditional parties. The platform party is also a *start-up party*. It shares the rapid growth rate of start-ups, their ability to quickly scale up to respond to growing consumer demand for their products and services. This dynamic is paralleled by the similarity of these parties to social movements – which is why they are often described as 'movement-parties' – but also in the 'gaseous' and extremely flexible nature of such formations that results from their lack of of a dependable and stable organisational infrastructure. However, start-ups are also characterised by a high degree of 'child mortality'. And indeed while many platform parties are formed few mature from a start-up to an established company.

Decisive for the success of these formations is the launch phase and the creation of an enthusiastic supportive atmosphere. Platform parties try to excite the enthusiasm of the base, using highly emotional communication on their social media channels, and staging symbolic events demonstrating the support they enjoy, occasions in which their phantom online crowd of supporters is temporarily manifested as a physical crowd.

The platform party is ultimately a party whose success depends heavily on the degree of participation of its supporters, and on the discussions they develop on its organisational and communicative platforms. Therefore it can be described as a *forum party*, to refer to the online discussion forums that sustain its everyday existence and which constitute the site of a permanent digital assembly of all members where the most diverse topics are debated from current news, to policies, even to candidates and leadership. This participatory feature of the platform party is inscribed precisely in its platform nature, which makes the party akin to a sort of 'container', whose content is process-oriented and largely dependent on the ongoing interactions of members.

Participation in the life of platform parties can take different forms, with a higher or lower degree of formalisation. On the one hand, participation takes place on social media and with ongoing discussions on such channels as Facebook and Twitter that end informing the positioning of these formations. On the other hand, it is pursued in a more formalised way on the decision-making platforms that constitute the true heart of digital parties, and where dilemma decisions with important consequences for the life of these political organisations are taken.

Podemos, Five Star and Pirate Parties have established their own participatory platforms, which constitute the most important organisational innovation such platform parties bring to the fore. These platforms have gained great importance in marking the difference between these parties and traditional parties accused of being deaf to the will of the base. These participatory platforms appear to cater not merely for the desire to participate but also for the extreme fragmentation and dispersion of post-industrial society.

The digital forum, like the forum of antiquity, is a gathering space, a meeting place where individuals otherwise prey to atomisation can participate in collective discussions and adopt common identities. This aggregative operation has similarities to the logic of applications such as Uber and Airbnb and the way they profile users and gather them in micro-niches. If in the case of commercial platforms the purpose is to connect consumers with producers of a given service, in the case of platform parties it is to aggregate all those who are interested in a certain policy and in a related public good (such as clean air or public education). The platform party is an aggregation system that responds to a social condition in which the mass – the key metaphor which informed the mass party of the industrial era – is not a starting point, but rather the result of a lengthy political process sustained in discussions and deliberations conducted on the Internet, and achieved by means of identification with a charismatic the leader, who acts as a spokesman for the 'general will' emerging from such interactions.

5. Superbase and Hyperleader

The promise that is at the heart of all the platform parties is a new democracy beyond the deep crisis of existing democracy. These parties are animated by the diagnosis that the growing inequality, insecurity and injustice of contemporary society is the result of the disconnect between voters and those they elect, and the betrayal of a political class increasingly detached from the needs of ordinary people. In response to this condition, platform parties have used digital technologies as a means of building new forms of democratic participation appropriate to the social experience in the digital age. The promise of radical democracy made by platform parties revolves around the lofty project of direct and participatory democracy, in which citizens entirely bypass their representatives. However, this techno-utopian narrative does not coincide with reality. The adoption of more or less radical forms of digital democracy does not lead to the total elimination of organisational hierarchies and of the asymmetry between the base and the vertex which is is inherent in the party form, but to a radical redefinition of such relationships.

To understand this restructuring we have to return to one of the classic debates on the nature of the party-form and on the problematic relationship that exists between democracy, organisation and representation, raised in the early twentieth century by Robert Michels (1915). Michels argued that parties were characterised by an iron law of the oligarchy that could be summed up as follows: democracy requires organisations; organisations are characterised by an oligarchic tendency, and are inevitably dominated by a small ruling class;

therefore democracy is impossible. These contradictions between democracy and organisation resurface in the context of the digital party.

Platform parties are presented as radically democratic parties that want to give citizens a direct say on collective decisions, thus eliminating forms of mediation suspected of distorting the democratic process. However, and here is the paradox, they are often characterised by the presence of highly centralised and unifying charismatic leadership. How can these two trends coexist?

To solve this puzzle, we need to understand precisely what kind of disintermediation is offered by these parties. Hereby, disintermediation involves a strengthening of organisational extremes – the base and the vertex – at the expense of the intermediate structures, the party bureaucracy and the party cadres. The platform party refer to the base as a synonym of the membership, but also to the emergence of a 'superbase' – to use a term used in chemistry to describe an extremely basic and reactive compound – that is, a situation in which the members acquire strong negotiating power thanks to their ongoing participation in online discussions and voting. This is however accompanied at the other extreme by the emergence of a 'hyperleader' who enjoys great power and freedom of action. The superbase derives its power from its participation in decision-making platforms which, as previously discussed, host consultations on various proposals and political issues.

These democratic processes offer new possibilities for the involvement of ordinary members in decisions that were previously controlled by delegates. Furthermore, they have facilitated interesting experimentations with new forms of participatory policy development. However, a number of issues point to the limited democratic quality of these forms of online participation. First, doubts have been raised over the level of influence possessed by the staff of these platforms in the timing of consultations and in the formulation of questions. Second, the low frequency with which such consultations are convened has been criticised. Third, in some cases, there have been allegations of manipulation of such consultation, which may well be the case when voting is conducted on proprietary systems with no external validation, as has often happened in the case of the Five Star Movement. Finally, most of the times these consultations have returned highly expected results, with super-majorities supporting the options favoured by the party leadership. Rank-and-file rebellions have been very rare. One of the most notable ones happened in January 2014 in the Five Star Movement, when the base voted for the repeal of the illegal immigration offense in spite of contrary recommendations made by Grillo and Casaleggio.

Strengthening the power of the base does not mean, however, that these parties create a horizontal decision-making space, as libertarians advocating direct democracy would want. The superbase mirrors itself in a hyperleader, a highly centralised and personalised leadership that materialises itself in the body of the charismatic leader. This is a phenomenon that does not only affect platform parties. In the era of Trump, Sanders, Mélenchon, Salvini and Marine le Pen, this tendency is manifested in the most diverse contexts, and in particular in anti-establishment and populist formations, whether of the right or of the left.

The term 'hyperleader' was used in Podemos's internal debate to describe Pablo Iglesias' role. The hyperleader was understood in this context as a charismatic leader who has the task of representing the party and its members in the media sphere. Similar, has been the role of Beppe Grillo, in the early phase of the Five Star Movement, when he lent his symbolic capital, accrued through a long career as comedian, to the movement.

The hyperleader is often also the founder, the one individual without whom the party would not exist, much in the same way as it happens with founders of digital companies such as Jack Dorsey for Twitter or Mark Zuckerberg in the case of Facebook. It is indicative that in the European elections of May 2014, the symbol that the voters found on the ballot next to the word 'Podemos', was not the circle logo of the party, but the photo of Pablo Iglesias with his determined and angry face. There are obvious similarities between the hyperleader and the figure of the 'benevolent dictator' seen in a number of digital culture phenomena from Jimmy Wales, the founder of Wikipedia, to Linus Torvalds, the founder of Linux. As is the case with these figures, the hyperleader presents himself as the ultimate guarantor of the party and its founding principles.

The superbase intervention is mostly reactive rather than active, requiring constant retroalimentation from the hyperleader, and the conflicting alliance between the two serves to crush intermediate levels – the official, heavy bureaucratic structures of traditional parties – which many suspect to be distorting popular will. However, this does not mean that platform parties do without such intermediate structures altogether. They rely on the presence of a tiny but strategically important 'political' staff responsible for managing their resources, communication channels and platforms. In some cases, this structure recalls social movements, heavily depending on the free labour made available by volunteers. In other cases, however, it may come to assume the features of a 'political enterprise', a party-company, to revive a concept used to describe Forza Italia from the 1990s.

This type of distortion – and it could not be called otherwise – is clearly visible in the case of the Five Star Movement, whose logo is registered as a trademark and in which management of the decision-making platform is assigned to a private company, Casaleggio Associati, whose role goes far beyond mere communication consultancy but is closer to an outsourced political management firm. Undoubtedly, this is an organisational model that ensures a high level of efficiency compared to most traditional political parties, but it is efficiency gained at the price of democracy and transparency.

The new forms of authority and organisation that are emerging within platform parties will be a matter of debate for many years. What can however already be said at this stage is that emerging formations as the Pirate Parties, the Five Star Movement and Podemos have managed to subvert a tired political system, and have demonstrated a remarkable ability to experiment with new forms of organisation which display great potential and have facilitated the mobilisation of hundreds of thousands of people who were previously distant from the political process. Yet, digital parties also display major contradictions between the claims of direct participation and disintermediation they put forward, and their reliance on a charismatic and highly and centralised leadership. It remains to be seen whether these contradictions may be successfully resolved, or whether the platform party may end up substituting the iron law of oligarchy, with another iron law centering on the benevolent, and sometimes not too-benevolent, dictatorship of the hyperleader.

References

Castells, Manuel. 2011. *The Rise of the Network Society: The Information Age: Economy, Society, and Culture* (Vol. 1). London: John Wiley & Sons.

Duverger, Maurice. 1959. *Political Parties: Their Organization and Activity in the Modern State*. London: Methuen & Co.

Gramsci, Antonio. 1971. *Selections from the Prison Notebooks of Antonio Gramsci*. Edited and translated by Quintin Hoare and Geoffrey Nowell Smith. New York: International Publishers.

Hands, Joss. 'Introduction: Politics, Power, and "Platformativity"'. *Culture Machine* 14.

Katz, Richard S. and Peter Mair. 1995. 'Changing Models of Party Organization and Party Democracy: The Emergence of the Cartel Party.' *Party Politics* 1 (1): 5–28.

Kirchheimer, O. (1966). The Transformation of the Western European Party Systems. in J. LaPalombara and M. Weiner (eds.), *Political Parties and Political Development* (Princeton, NJ: Princeton University Press).

Kirchheimer, Otto. 1990. 'The Catch-All Party.' In *The West European Party System*, ed. Peter Mair, 50–60. New York: Oxford University Press.

Mancini, Paolo. 2013. 'The Italian Public Sphere: A Case of Dramatized Polarization.' *Journal of Modern Italian Studies* 18(3): 335–47.

Michels, R. (1915). *Political Parties: A Sociological Study of the Oligarchical Tendencies of Modern Democracy*. New York: Hearst's International Library Company.

Panebianco, Angelo. 1988. *Political Parties: Organization and Power*. Cambridge UK: Cambridge University Press.

Revelli, Marco. 2013. *Finale di partito*. Turin: Giulio Einaudi.

Srnicek, Nick. 2016. *Platform Capitalism*. Cambridge: Polity Press.

Van Dijck, José. 2013. *The Culture of Connectivity: A Critical History of Social Media*. New York: Oxford University Press.

CHAPTER 17

The Movement Party – Winning Elections and Transforming Democracy in a Digital Era: Reflections on Paolo Gerbaudo's Chapter

Anastasia Kavada

Are political parties changing fundamentally in the digital age? In his contribution to this edited volume, Paolo Gerbaudo advances a compelling case that they are, focusing on parties across the Left-Right spectrum, like the Five Star Movement in Italy or Podemos in Spain. As a response to Gerbaudo's argument, I would like to focus on two interrelated points: first, that the evolution of the political party form may be better explained by changes in communication technologies rather than by the influence of models of economic organisation; second, that the platform (or 'digital') parties described by Gerbaudo are also *movement parties* that are constituted around contradictory objectives – to win the electoral game and to transform the system of representative democracy – a contradiction which may explain their organisational structure.

How to cite this book chapter:
Kavada, A. 2019. The Movement Party – Winning Elections and Transforming Democracy in a Digital Era: Reflections on Paolo Gerbaudo's Chapter. In: Chandler, D. and Fuchs, C. (eds.) *Digital Objects, Digital Subjects: Interdisciplinary Perspectives on Capitalism, Labour and Politics in the Age of Big Data.* Pp. 199–204. London: University of Westminster Press. DOI: https://doi.org/10.16997/book29.q. License: CC-BY-NC-ND 4.0

Gerbaudo convincingly suggests that what he terms the 'digital party' has three key characteristics: it is based on an infrastructure of digital assets located on the Cloud, it serves as a forum of interaction for the grassroots, and it resembles a start-up company in its agility and 'high mortality rate'. However, the strengthening of the party grassroots does not lead to a less hierarchical party structure, according to Gerbaudo. It simply thins the middle layer of party cadres and creates a 'hyperleader' who acts as the embodiment of the party.

In tracing these changes, Gerbaudo argues that 'In each historical era there tends to be an analogy between the mode of production and what we could call the "mode of organisation", namely the set of organisational mechanisms, practices and structures that are prevalent at the time.'

Following Revelli, Gerbaudo argues that in the industrial era the party was conceived as a Fordist factory, adopting a hierarchical and bureaucratic structure to coordinate a mass of participants. After the end of the 1960s, party organisation developed along a post-Fordist model with an emphasis on nimbleness, while power was concentrated in the hands of a few technocrats. Often dubbed 'the television party', this new formation aimed to appeal to a broader electorate, rather than simply represent the interests of a specific political class. In this historical trajectory, the platform/digital party constitutes the latest form that corresponds to new types of economic organisation as represented by start-up and digital companies like Facebook and Google.

While Gerbaudo's analogy between economic and political organisation is evocative, his essay does not provide a detailed explanation as to why these forms are related. Gerbaudo also implies that the prevalent organisational models in a given era emerge from the economic rather than the political sphere. Thus, the political parties of the industrial age followed the organisational model of the factory and not vice-versa. But why would this be the case? The reasons are not immediately apparent, particularly when we consider that the organisation of companies and political parties is constituted around different objectives. The former aim at the production and selling of goods and services at a profit, while the latter are oriented towards winning elections and seizing control of the state.

An alternative and perhaps more fitting explanation could be that the parallels between models of economic and political organisation partly stem from developments in communication technologies, rather than from the direct influence of economic forms on political ones. Thus, economic organisation was transformed by new technologies of production and distribution that affected the coordination of the factory in line with capitalist demands around flexibility and cost reduction. At the same time, the evolution of the political party form resulted from concerted efforts to appeal to the electorate within an increasingly 'mediatized' political system (Blumler and Kavanagh 1999) and in a changing media environment.

The organisation of the party up until the Second World War centred on the coordination of local volunteers who would disseminate leaflets, knock on doors, recruit new party members and mobilise potential voters to attend political rallies. In this pre-modern age of electoral campaigning, as Norris (2000) calls it, the party machinery was based on the partisan press and on direct interactions between party volunteers and the electorate. The rise of the mass media, with the emergence of radio in the 1930s and particularly with the advent of television, ushered electoral campaigning into a 'modern' phase. As Gerbaudo also alludes in his analysis of the 'television party', the political party form during the modern period centred on the use of television for electioneering. The strategic appearance of the party in broadcast media was controlled from behind the scenes by a small group of party technocrats and 'spin doctors' in a 'war room' model of campaigning. The party thus became increasingly centralised, while the influence of the grassroots was weakened. The organisation of political parties was infused with the news values of television with regards to 'the scheduling of political events ([…], the language of politics […], and the personalisation of its presentation (with a sharper focus on top leaders)' (Blumler and Kavanagh 1999, 212). From the 1980s onwards, electioneering entered a 'third age' (ibid) of postmodern campaigning in response to the rise of 24-hour rolling news, the proliferation of television channels and the fragmentation of media audiences. Political marketing and the micro-targeting of voters, together with sophisticated polling techniques, became crucial aspects of electoral campaigning (Norris 2000).

Within this context, the advent of the Internet and social media is associated with two countervailing dynamics. On the one hand, it has heightened individual micro-targeting through the collection and analysis of personal data and the growth of political advertising on digital media platforms. On the other hand, the Internet has facilitated the coordination of grassroots volunteers which has brought door-to-door campaigning back to the fore. This became evident in the first presidential campaign of Barack Obama in 2008, which used digital media to mobilise party volunteers on the ground, and also launched MyBarackObama.com, a campaign-owned social network site (Chadwick 2013). The explosion of discussion forums and email lists, as well as the ease of online referenda and consultations, have allowed the political party base to have greater input into the formulation of party policy.

What this brief historical sketch demonstrates is that the evolution of the political party form is better explained by the parties' response to a changing media and political environment than by the influence of dominant forms of economic organisation. Where economics seems to play a greater role is in shaping the political conditions that underlie this drive for organisational change – namely, the interrelated crises of capitalism and representative democracy. As Gerbaudo suggests, platform parties have emerged at a time when trust in political institutions is low, while citizens feel alienated and disempowered from politics. This is accentuated by the economic crisis of the last decade, which has resulted in cuts to the welfare state and a slew of austerity measures. Governments seem both unable and unwilling to address the growing gap between rich and poor, and to ensure that economic activity benefits the many rather than the few. The rise of anti-establishment feeling has fuelled a wave of protest against political corruption and the undue influence of economic interests on the political system. It has also led to demands for more direct control of and participation in politics, a demand that has manifested in different ways, from the assertion of national sovereignty, to fears over the control of borders and unchecked immigration, to calls for more direct and participatory democracy, for a more decentralised system that challenges the concentration of power in the hands of the few.

The organisational form of platform parties has emerged in response to these political conditions and in some cases as a direct result of protest movements. The Five Star Movement arose out of protest against political corruption, while Podemos is linked to the Indignados movement of 2011, which attempted to prefigure a different kind of democracy based on direct participation, transparency and the rejection of central leadership.

The platform parties analysed by Gerbaudo are thus *movement parties*, which points to a fundamental change to the objectives that these parties form around. Social movements revolve around a conflict that challenges the limits of the political system in which they arise (Melucci 1996). Therefore, the movement component of contemporary platform parties means that they aim not only at getting elected but also at radically changing the system of representative democracy of which they are part. The latter objective means that the political party is not simply a machine of electoral campaigning, but also a space for experimenting with new forms of party (and national) governance. These experiments allow the party to channel more authentically the demands of ordinary citizens, and provide it with ideas about innovating governance if it ever finds itself in power.

Yet, as experiments in governance, digital parties do have differences among themselves in the ways they design grassroots participation, which may reflect their different positions across the political spectrum. If these parties are platforms, as Gerbaudo suggests, then their platform design can be revealing of their broader desires around democracy, political participation and the power of the party base. A focus on this architecture of participation can also help us to distinguish parties that are truly committed to a vision of radical democracy from those that simply adopt the discourse – but not the actual practice – of grassroots participation as a cynical ploy to win more votes. For example, online referenda can be more authoritarian than democratic when the party base does not have input in the formulation of questions. The political economy of the party's digital platforms can also provide clues as to its experimentation with new forms of governance. For instance, Rousseau, the digital platform of the Five Star Movement, belongs to the private company of one of its founders, Gianroberto Casaleggio, a company now run by his son Davide after Gianroberto's death. This allows the owner of the company to profit from the party platform and to become a gatekeeper without holding an official position within the party (Politi and Roberts 2017). By contrast, Podemos believes in making the software code of its platform freely available, arguing on its website that open source equals open democracy (Podemos n.d.).

However, the two objectives around which movement parties are organised are not always commensurable. Movement parties aim at both winning the electoral game by following the rules of the existing system *and* at moulding their organisation around a model of democracy that does not yet exist. This may explain the contradictory presence of the hyperleader and the superbase in current platform parties. Hyperleaders help the party to win elections in a communication environment that is still characterised by the personalisation of politics. At the same time, and as Gerbaudo suggests, the rise of the super-base constitutes a key aspect of these parties' radical democratic politics.

But is it perhaps too early to identify with certainty the new type of party that is emerging? Are we still in a phase of transition? If this is the case, then the movement party may still shed some of its characteristics, particularly those that are carry-overs from a previous era, as it completes its tranformation. In this scenario, the figure of the hyperleader can be considered a remnant of the past or of a dated and no longer desirable present: of a system of representative democracy based on media spectacle, personalisation and empty rhetoric. The fact that many of these leaders are white, male, middle or upper class adds to this sense of déjà vu. One hopes that the hyperleadership will be cast aside once the superbase finds better ways to win elections and govern itself.

I am not suggesting this as a possible development but as one that we may wish and strive for. In an age of interregnum, when 'the old is dying and the new cannot be born' (Gramsci 1971, 276), Michels' iron laws are thrown in disarray and the hegemony is challenged. In such times, identifying the new system that may emerge from the turmoil is not only a matter of political analysis. It is also a matter of envisioning and experimentation, of prefigurative practices and self-fulfilling prophecies that require political will, courage and imagination.

References

Blumler, Jay G. and Dennis Kavanagh. 1999. 'The Third Age of Political Communication: Influences and Features.' *Political Communication* 16, 209–30.

Chadwick, Andrew. 2013. *The Hybrid Media System: Politics and Power*. Oxford and New York: Oxford University Press.

Gramsci, Antonio. 1971. *Selections from the Prison Notebooks*. Edited and translated by Quintin Hoare and Geoffrey Nowell-Smith. London: Lawrence & Wishart.

Melucci, Alberto. 1996. *Challenging Codes: Collective Action in the Information Age*. Cambridge, MA: Cambridge University Press.

Norris, Pippa. 2000. *A Virtuous Circle: Political Communications in Post-Industrial Societies*. Cambridge, MA: Cambridge University Press.

Podemos. *Releasing the Code of Podemos' Digital Heart*. Available at: https://podemos.info/releasing-the-code-of-podemos-digital-heart/ (accessed 14 May, 2018)

Politi, James and Hannah Roberts. 2017. 'Five Star Movement: The Unanswered Questions About Italy's Populist Party.' *Financial Times,* 17 September. Available at: https://www.ft.com/content/546be098-989f-11e7-a652-cde3f882dd7b (accessed 14 May 2018)

CHAPTER 18

The Appropriation of Fixed Capital: A Metaphor?

Antonio Negri
Translated from Italian by Michele Ledda with editorial support by David Chandler, Christian Fuchs and Sara Raimondi.

1. Labour in the Age of the Digital Machine

In the debate over the impact of the digital on society, we are presented with the serious hypothesis that the worker, the producer, is transformed by the use of the digital machine, since we have recognised that digital technologies have profoundly modified the mode of production, as well as ways of knowing and communicating. The discussion of the psycho-political consequences of digital machines is so broad that it is just worth remembering it even though the results obtained by this research are highly problematic.

They normally propose the passive subjection of the worker to the machine, a generalised alienation, the epidemic character of depressive illnesses, the definition of algorithmic Taylorism and so on and so forth. Among these catastrophic novelties rings the old Nazi adage: 'The earth on which we live is revealed to us as a dead mining district which slices the very essence of man'.

How to cite this book chapter:
Negri, A. 2019. The Appropriation of Fixed Capital: A Metaphor? In: Chandler, D. and Fuchs, C. (eds.) *Digital Objects, Digital Subjects: Interdisciplinary Perspectives on Capitalism, Labour and Politics in the Age of Big Data.* Pp. 205–214. London: University of Westminster Press. DOI: https://doi.org/10.16997/book29.r. License: CC-BY-NC-ND 4.0

It seems more sophisticated to think about the impact of the digital by asking if, and perhaps how, the minds and bodies of workers appropriate the digital machine.

Let us quietly remember that if the new impact of the digital machine on the producer happens under the command of capital, not only does the producer yield value to constant capital during the production process, but also, insofar as he is a cognitive work force both in his individual contribution to the productive effort and in his cooperative use of the digital machine, he connects to the machine and can be merged with it, when the connection is effected through the immaterial flow of cognitive labour. In cognitive labour, living labour can invest fixed capital, being both its substance and its active engine at the same time, even though it is subjected to it when it develops its productive capacity.

Therefore, in Marxist circles people have started to talk about 'appropriation of fixed capital' on the part of the digital worker (or the cognitive producer). When the increase in productivity of the digital workers or even the productive capacities of 'digital natives' are analysed, these themes and problems spontaneously present themselves. Are they simply metaphors?

2. The Appropriation of Fixed Capital

And in particular, are they simply political metaphors? By saying 'the appropriation of fixed capital' on the part of the producers (by contrast with the enterprise, which acts for profit) one conjures up themes that have had great resonance in the political and philosophical domains in the past 50 years. The theme of the hybrid human/machine has been developed widely in German anthropology (of Helmuth Plessner, Arnold Gehlen, Heinrich Popitz) as well as in French materialism (Simondon), and in materialist feminism (Donna Haraway and Rosi Braidotti) (cf. Braidotti 2013, Gehlen 1980, Haraway 1991, Plessner 1924, Popitz 1995, Simondon 2017). Suffice to recall here Guattari's theory of the machinic assemblages that runs throughout his work and greatly influences the philosophical design of *A Thousand Plateaus* (Deleuze and Guattari 1987). Probably the most important thing that has happened within these philosophical theories is that their structure – which is homogeneously materialist, despite the many differences between them – has shown new characteristics which are not reducible to any variant of the past. Of course, materialism has long abandoned the epic form elaborated by Enlightenment authors from d'Holbach to Helvétius, and has acquired from twentieth-century physics clearly dynamic features. However, in the theories mentioned above, it now shows a 'humanistic' imprint which, far from renewing idealistic apologies of 'man', is characterised by an interest in the body, in its singularity and density both in thought and in action.

Materialism presents itself today as a theory of production that is widely unbalanced towards the cognitive aspects and the effects of the cooperative hybridisation of production itself. Is it the change in the mode of production, from the predominance of the physical to the hegemony of the non-physical, which has produced these effects on philosophical thought? Since I am not a follower of reflection theories, I do not believe so. However, I am convinced that this marked change in the materialist tradition has been simultaneous with the growth of the digital mode of production. We can now attempt to answer the question of whether 'appropriation of fixed capital' is a political metaphor? It certainly is, if from this assumption we draw a definition of *power* (constituent power, if need be) in political terms, and the appropriation of fixed capital becomes the analogical basis for the construction of an ethical and/or political subject that is appropriate to a materialist ontology of the present and a communist teleology of the yet-to-come.

3. Karl Marx on Fixed Capital

However, the development of the theme 'appropriation of fixed capital' is not always metaphoric. It was Marx who, in *Capital* (Marx 1867/1976; 1885/1978; 1894/1981), showed how the very placing of the worker before (the command of) the means of production modified, besides his productive capacity, his persona, his nature, his ontology. In this respect, the Marxian narrative of the shift from manufacture to modern industry is a classic. In manufacture, there is still a subjective principle in the division of labour – and this means the worker appropriated the production process after the production process had been adapted to the worker. This is in contrast to modern industry, where the division of labour is only 'objective', as the subjective, artisanal use of the machine is eliminated and machinery is constituted against the human being. Here the machine becomes a competitor, an antagonist of the worker, or even reduces the worker to a working animal. And yet there is in Marx also another aspect: he recognises that the worker and the working tool also acquire a hybrid configuration, and that the conditions of the production process constitute in great part the conditions of the life of the worker, his 'conditions of his active life process itself, his conditions of life' (Marx 1894/1981, 180). The concept of labour productivity itself implies a tight dynamic connection between variable and fixed capital, and theoretical discoveries – Marx adds – are relayed in the production process through the experience of the worker. We will see later how Marx himself foresees, in *Capital*, the appropriation of fixed capital on the part of the producer.

Now, let us keep in mind that in *Capital*, Marx's analysis is in any case informed by the arguments of *Grundrisse*, that is, by the theorisation of 'general intellect' as substance and subject of the production process (Marx 1857/1858/1973, 706; 831): This discovery showed how central cognitive matter was to production, and how the concept of fixed capital itself was transformed by it. When Marx asserts that fixed capital – which in *Capital* is normally understood as the network of machines – has become 'man himself' (Marx 1857/1858/1973, 712), he anticipates the development of capital in our own time. Although fixed capital is the product of labour and nothing else than labour appropriated by capital; although the accumulation of scientific activity and the productivity of what Marx calls 'general intellect' are incorporated in the machines under the control of capital; finally, although capital appropriates all this for free – at some point of capitalist development living labour begins to exert the power to reverse this relationship. Living labour starts to show its priority with respect to capital and to the capitalist management of social production, even though this cannot necessarily be taken out of the process. In other words, as living labour becomes a larger and larger societal power, it operates as an increasingly independent activity, outside the disciplinary structures commanded by capital – not only as labour force but also, more generally, as vital activity. On the one hand, past human activity and its intelligence are accumulated, crystallised as fixed capital; on the other, reversing the tide, living humans are capable of reabsorbing capital in themselves and their own social life.

Fixed capital is 'man himself' (Marx 1857/1858/1973, 712), in both senses. Here the appropriation of fixed capital is not a metaphor any more but becomes an apparatus that the class struggle can take on, and that imposes itself as political programme. In this case, capital is no longer a relationship that objectively includes the producer, imposing its dominion by force. On the contrary, the capitalist relationship now includes an ultimate contradiction: that of a producer, of a class of producers, that has dispossessed capital, either in part or in whole, but in any case effectively, of the means of production, thereby imposing itself as hegemonic subject. The analogy with the emergence of the Third Estate within the structures of the *Ancien Régime* is conducted by Marx in the historicisation of the relationship of capital, and clearly presents itself in an explosive, revolutionary way.

4. Labour's Social Networks and Autonomy

At this point, we must bring into focus the new figures of labour, especially those that have been created by workers themselves in social networks. These are the workers whose productive capacities have been dramatically enlarged by their ever more intense cooperation. Now, let's examine what happens here. With cooperation, work becomes more and more abstracted from capital, meaning that it has a greater capacity to organise production itself, autonomously, and particularly in relation to the machines, even though it remains subordinate to the mechanisms of extraction of labour on the part of capital. Is this the same autonomy as the one we have recognised in the forms of autonomous work at the beginnings of capitalist production? Certainly not, it seems to us. Our hypothesis is that there is now a degree of autonomy that does not concern the production process only, but also imposes itself at an ontological level – that in these circumstances work acquires an ontological texture even when it is completely subjected to capitalist control. How can we understand a situation in which both productive enterprises, extended in space and continuous in time, and collective, cooperative inventions on the part of the workers are in the end fixed as extracted value by capital? This is difficult unless we shake off linear and deterministic methodologies and adopt a method that is articulated through apparatuses. By doing this we can recognise that, in the current situation, the production processes in the hands of the workers and the capitalist means of valorisation and control are increasingly pulled apart. Work has reached such a high level of dignity and power that it can potentially refuse the form of valorisation that is imposed on it and therefore, even under command, it can develop its own autonomy.

The growing powers of labour can be recognised not only in the expansion and increasing autonomy of cooperation, but also in the greater importance that is given to the social and cognitive powers of labour within the structures of production. The first feature, an expanded cooperation, is certainly due to the increased physical contact between digital workers in the information society, but even more so to the formation of 'mass intellectuality' that is animated by linguistic and cultural skills, by affective capacities and digital powers, as Paolo Virno has always suggested. There is also a second feature: it is not a coincidence that these abilities and creativity increase the productivity of work. Let us therefore reflect on how much the role of knowledge has changed in the history of the relationship between capital and labour. As we have already seen, during the phase of manufacture, the craftsman's knowledge was employed and absorbed in production as a separate, isolated force that was subordinated to a hierarchical organisational structure. In the phase of modern industry, by contrast, workers were considered to be incapable of the knowledge that was necessary for production, which was therefore centralised by management. In the contemporary phase of 'general intellect', knowledge has a multitudinous form in the production process, even though, from the owner's point of view, it can be isolated just as the craftsman's knowledge was in manufacture. In fact, from the point of view of capital, the way in which work self-organises remains a mystery, even when this becomes the basis of production.

In order to move forward, let us take an example: a powerful figure of associative labour is today made invisible in the functioning of algorithms. Together with the ceaseless propaganda about the necessity of capitalist control and the sermons on the impossibility of an alternative to this system of power, we often hear praise of the role played by the algorithm. But what is an algorithm? Firstly, it is fixed capital, being a machine born of cooperative social intelligence, a product of the 'general intellect'. Although the value of productive activity is fixed in the social process of extraction of surplus labour by capital, we should not forget that the force of living labour is at the root of this process. Without living labour, there is no algorithm.

Secondly, however, algorithms also present many new features. Let us consider Google's Page Rank, perhaps the best-known algorithm as well as the largest generator of profit. Now, the rank of a web page is determined by the number and quality of its links, and high quality means a link to a page that itself has a high rank. Page Rank is therefore a mechanism to incorporate the judgment and the value given by users to Internet objects. Matteo Pasquinelli (2009, 152) writes that 'while every link on the Web contains a little bit of human intelligence, all the links combined contain a great deal of intelligence'. However, a marked difference of algorithms such as Google's Page Rank is that, whereas industrial machines crystallise past intelligence in a relatively fixed and static form, these algorithms continually add social intelligence to past results in such a way as to create an open and expansive process. It seems that the algorithmic machine is itself intelligent – but this is not true. It is instead open to continuous modifications by human intelligence. When we say 'intelligent machines', we must understand that machines are capable of continually absorbing human intelligence. Another distinctive feature is that the process of extracting value established by these algorithms is itself open in an incremental way, and socialised in such a way as to eliminate the border between work and life. Google users know this very well. Finally, another difference between the production processes studied by Marx and this kind of value formation consists in the fact that today's cooperation is no longer imposed by the owner of the means of production but is generated by the relationship between producers. Today we can really speak of the re-appropriation of fixed capital by the workers, and the integration of intelligent machines under autonomous social control, which, for instance, takes place in the process of construction of algorithms that are connected to the self-valorisation of both social cooperation and the reproduction of life.

We can add that even when cybernetic and digital instruments are put into the service of capitalist valorisation, even when social intelligence is put to work in order to produce obedient subjectivities, fixed capital is integrated into the bodies and brains of workers and becomes their second nature. Ever since industrial civilisation was born, workers have always had a more intimate, insider knowledge of the machines and their systems than have capitalists and their managers. Today, these processes of workers' appropriation of knowledge can become decisive. They are not actualised in the production processes only, but they are also intensified and put into effect through productive cooperation in the vital processes of circulation and socialisation. Workers can appropriate fixed capital while they work, and they can develop this appropriation in their social, cooperative and biopolitical relations with other workers. All this determines a new productive nature, that is, a new life form that is the basis of the new 'mode of production'.

5. The Changing Relationship of Fixed and Variable Capital

In order to go even deeper into this subject, and to eliminate that semblance of utopianism which, if it doesn't damage our argument, might sometimes seem to add confusion, let us consider how some of those who have studied cognitive capitalism structure the hypothesis of the appropriation of fixed capital. David Harvey (2012) studies this appropriation through the analysis of the spaces of settlement and crossing of the metropolis by the bodies that are put to work – movements of variable capital that produce radical effects on the conditions and practices of the subjected bodies, which are nevertheless capable of autonomous movements and of autonomy in the organisation of labour. This analysis remains, however, superficial. Much more incisive is the one proposed some time ago by André Gorz (2010), who overturned the complex web of exploitation and alienation by emphasising that the intellectual powers of production are formed in the social body. Liberation from social alienation restores the capacity to act subjectively/intellectually in production. Proceeding step by step in this vein, one is not surprised to discover that today '*intangible capital*' (R&D, software but above all education, training and health) has exceeded the portion of physical capital in the global capital stock' (Lucarelli and Vercellone 2011, 87). Fixed capital appears now within bodies, imprinted into them and at the same time subordinated to them – this is even more the case when we consider activities such as research and software development, where work is not crystallised in a physical product that is separate from the worker, but remains incorporated in the brain and inseparable from the person. Laurent Baronian (2013), finally, stresses, by returning to *Capital* and its analysis of the relations of production, that the power of bodies and minds is generalised in the figure associated with the qualifying element of fixed capital. Fixed capital is here social cooperation. Here the line between dead and living labour (that is, between fixed and variable capital) is blurred once and for all.

Indeed, as Marx (1894) concludes in *Capital* on this matter, if from the standpoint of the capitalist, constant and variable capital become identical under the heading of circulating capital, and if for the capitalist the only essential difference is the one between fixed and circulating capital, it follows that, from the point of view of the producer, constant and circulating capital become identical under the heading of fixed capital, and the only essential difference is the one between variable and fixed capital. Therefore, variable capital's interest in re-appropriation needs to focus on fixed capital.

The emancipatory conditions of living labour's cooperation therefore invest and occupy more and more the spaces and the functions of fixed capital.

Still on this point, let us proceed with Carlo Vercellone and Christian Marazzi. What is called immaterial or intellectual capital is in fact essentially embodied in humans, and it therefore corresponds in a fundamental way to the intellectual and creative faculties of the labour force. We find ourselves before the overturning of the concepts of constant capital and the organic composition of capital that we inherited from industrial capitalism. In the relationship of constant and variable capital c/v, which indicates mathematically the organic social composition of capital, it is precisely v, the labour force, that appears as main, fixed capital and, to repeat an expression by Christian Marazzi (2006), presents itself as 'body-machine'. Marazzi (2006) clarifies that this is because, besides containing the labour force, the labour force also plays the role of the container of the typical functions of fixed capital, of the means of production insofar as they are sediments of codified knowledge, historically acquired knowledge, productive grammars and experiences – in short, past labour.

6. Machinic Subjectivities

One can, for instance, characterise the youth who spontaneously enters the digital world as having a machinic subjectivity. We conceive the machinic, not only in contrast to the mechanical, but also as a technological reality that is separate from and even opposed to human society. Félix Guattari explains that whereas traditionally the problem of machines has been seen as secondary, compared to the question of *techne* and technology, we must recognise that the problem of machines is primary and the problem of technology comes later. We can see, he maintains, the social nature of the machine: 'Since the "machine" is opened out towards its machinic environment and maintains all sorts of relationships with social constituents and individual subjectivities, the concept of technological machine should therefore be broadened to that of *machinic agencements* [machinic assemblages]' (Guattari 1995, 9).

The machinic, then, never refers to an individual, isolated machine, but always to an assemblage. To understand this, we can start by thinking of mechanical systems, that is, machines that are connected to and integrated with other machines. Let us then add human subjectivities and imagine humans as integrated into machinic relationships, and machines as integrated within human bodies and human society. Finally, Guattari, together with Deleuze, conceives machinic assemblages as progressive, incorporating all sorts of human elements and both human and non-human singularities. The concept of the machinic in Deleuze and Guattari (1987), and in a different form the concept of production in Foucault, highlights the need to develop, outside spiritualist identities, subjectivities of knowledge and action, and to show how these emerge from productions that are materially connected.

In economic terms, the machinic clearly appears in the subjectivities that emerge when fixed capital is re-appropriated by the labour force, that is, when material and immaterial machines and the various kinds of knowledge that crystallise past social production are re-integrated into the social subjectivities that cooperate and produce in the present. Machinic assemblages are thus partly grafted onto the notion of anthropogenic production. Some of the more intelligent Marxist economists, from Robert Boyer (2002) to Christian Marazzi (2005), characterise the novelty of contemporary economic production – as well as the shift from Fordism to post-Fordism – by focusing on '*la production de l'homme par l'homme*' (the production of man by man, Boyer 2002, 192), in contradistinction to the traditional notion of 'production of commodities by means of commodities' (Sraffa 1960). The production of subjectivities and life forms becomes more and more central in capitalist valorisation. And this logic leads directly to the notions of cognitive and biopolitical production. The machinic extends further this anthropogenic model in order to incorporate various non-human singularities in the assemblages that it produces. To be more precise, when we say that fixed capital is re-appropriated by the working subjects, we do not mean that it simply becomes their possession, but rather that it is integrated into machinic assemblages that constitute subjectivities.

The machinic is always an assemblage, a dynamic composition of the human and other beings, but the potency of these new subjectivities is only a virtual one until they are actualised and articulated within the commons and in social cooperation. Indeed, if the re-appropriation of fixed capital took place on an individual basis, by transferring private property from an individual to another, it would only be robbing Peter to pay Paul and would have no real meaning. When, on the other hand, the wealth and productive power of fixed capital is socially appropriated and therefore transferred from private property to the commons, then the power of machinic subjectivities and their cooperative networks can be fully actualised. The machinic dynamic of the assemblage, the productive forms of cooperation and the ontological basis of the commons are intertwined in the closest way.

When we see today's young people absorbed in the commons, determined by their machinic engagements in cooperation, we must recognise that their very existence is resistance. Whether we are aware of it or not, they produce resistance. Capital is forced to recognise this hard truth. Capital can economically consolidate the development of those commons that are produced by the subjectivities from which capital extracts value, but the commons is only constructed through the forms of resistance and the processes that re-appropriate fixed capital. The contradiction becomes increasingly clear. 'Exploit your self,' says capital to productive subjectivities. And they reply: 'We wish to valorise ourselves, to govern the commons that we produce'. No obstacle in this process, not even virtual obstacles, can prevent the arrival of conflict. If capital can only expropriate value from the cooperation of subjectivities and these resist exploitation, capital is then forced to increase the level of command and put in place ever more arbitrary and violent operations for the extraction of value from the commons. And the theme of the re-appropriation of fixed capital will lead us to this passage.

References

Baronian, Laurent. 2013. *Marx and Living Labour*. Abingdon: Routledge.

Boyer, Robert. 2002. *La croissance, début de siècle*. Paris: Albin Michel.

Braidotti, Rosi. 2013. *The Posthuman*. Cambridge: Polity.

Deleuze, Gilles and Félix Guttari. 1987. *A Thousand Plateaus: Capitalism and Schizophrenia*. Minneapolis, MN: University of Minnesota Press.

Gehlen, Arnold. 1980. *Man in the Age of Technology*. New York: Columbia University Press.

Gorz, André. 2010. *The Immaterial*. Chicago, IL: University of Chicago Press.

Guattari, Félix. 1995. 'On Machines.' *Journal of Philosophy and the Visual Arts* 6(8): 8–12.

Haraway, Donna. 1991. 'A Cyborg Manifesto: Science, Technology, and Socialist-Feminism in the Late Twentieth Century.' In *Simians, Cyborgs and Women: The Reinvention of Nature*, 149-181. Abingdon: Routledge.

Harvey, David. 2012. *Rebel Cities: From the Right to the City to the Urban Revolution*. London: Verso.

Lucarelli, Stefano and Carlo Vercellone. 2011. 'Welfare Systems and Social Services During the Systematic Crisis of Cognitive Capitalism.' *European Journal of Economic and Social Systems* 27(1–2): 77–97.

Marazzi, Christian. 2006. L'amortissement du corps-machine. *Multitudes* 27: 27–36.

Marazzi, Christian. 2005. Capitalismo digitale e modello antropogenetico di produzione. In *Reinventare il lavoro*, ed. Jean-Louis Laville, Michele La Rosa, Christian Marazzi and Federico Chicci et al., 107–126. Rome: Sapere.

Marx, Karl. 1857/1858/1973 *The Grundrisse*. London: Penguin.

Marx, Karl. 1867/1976. *Capital Volume I*. London: Penguin.

Marx, Karl. 1885/1978. *Capital Volume II*. London: Penguin.

Marx, Karl. 1894/1981. *Capital Volume III*. London: Penguin.

Pasquinelli, Matteo. 2009. 'Google's Page Rank Algorithm: A Diagram of Cognitive Capitalism and the Rentier of the Common Intellect.' In *Deep Search: The Politics of Search Beyond Google*, ed. Konrad Becker and Felix Stalder, 152-62. London: Transaction Publishers.

Plessner, Helmuth. 1924. Die Utopie in der Maschine. In *Gesammelte Schriften, Band 10*, 31–40. Frankfurt am Main: Suhrkamp.

Popitz, Heinrich. 1995. *Der Aufbruch zur artifiziellen Gesellschaft. Zur Anthropologie der Technik*. Tübingen: Mohr Siebeck.

Simondon, Gilbert. 2017. *On the Mode of Existence of Technical Objects*. Minneapolis, MN: University of Minnesota Press.

Sraffa, Piero. 1960. *Production of Commodities by Means of Commodities: Prelude to a Critique of Economic Theory*. Cambridge: Cambridge University Press.

CHAPTER 19

Appropriation of Digital Machines and Appropriation of Fixed Capital as the Real Appropriation of Social Being: Reflections on Toni Negri's Chapter

Christian Fuchs

1. Marx

In his essay 'The Appropriation of Fixed Capital', Toni Negri makes an argument for thinking about the role of technology in social struggles and in relation to alternatives to capitalism. He rejects technological determinism and technological pessimism. He engages with Marx's concept of technology in the *Grundrisse* and *Capital* and applies a similar view to digital technologies.

Autonomism has traditionally preferred readings of the *Grundrisse* over *Capital* because of the heavy focus on the latter in Stalinist readings of Marx. In this context, Negri stresses that the 'objectification of categories in *Capital* blocks action by revolutionary subjectivity' (Negri 1991, 8). 'I am not launching an abstract polemic against *Capital* – in fact all of us have been formed

---

How to cite this book chapter:
Fuchs, C. 2018. Appropriation of Digital Machines and Appropriation of Fixed Capital as the Real Appropriation of Social Being: Reflections on Toni Negri's Chapter. In: Chandler, D. and Fuchs, C. (eds.) *Digital Objects, Digital Subjects: Interdisciplinary Perspectives on Capitalism, Labour and Politics in the Age of Big Data*. Pp. 215–221. London: University of Westminster Press. DOI: https://doi.org/10.16997/book29.s. License: CC-BY-NC-ND 4.0

intellectually and brought to theoretical understanding by the class hatred that reading *Capital* nourished within us. But *Capital* is also the text which has been used in order to reduce criticism to economic theory, to the elimination of subjectivity into objectivity, and to the subjugation of the subversive proletariat by the repressive recomposing of knowledge in the form of a science of domination' (Negri 1988, 175). Negri argues that the *Grundrisse* is 'a political text that conjugates an appreciation of the revolutionary possibilities created by the "imminent crisis"' (Negri 1991, 8). Negri has pointed out the importance of technology in capitalism and beyond capitalism. He has in this context stressed the role of the *Grundrisse*'s *Fragment on Machines* (Marx 1857/1858/1973, 690–714; see Fuchs 2016, 360–375).

In *Fragment*, Marx anticipates the emergence of an information economy due to the development of capitalism's productive forces. He foresees a stage where 'general social knowledge', or what he terms the 'general intellect', has become 'a *direct force of production*' (Marx 1857/1858/1973, 706). Marx stresses the importance of knowledge in the development of fixed capital. His notion of the general intellect has a huge influence on Negri's work and is at the heart of the latter's concepts of the social worker, the multitude, immaterial labour, and the commons (see Hardt and Negri 1994, 10, 21; Hardt and Negri 2000, 29–30, 364–369; Negri 1991, 139–150).

The notion of the general intellect can also be found in *Capital* as the concept of general work (Marx 1867/1976, 667; Marx 1894/1981, 199). It is therefore certainly feasible to extend the analysis of knowledge in and beyond capitalism to a broad range of Marx's works, including *Capital*. In more recent works, Toni Negri has increasingly embraced *Capital*. In his latest book *Marx and Foucault*, Negri (2017) stresses for example that the analysis of relative surplus value and large-scale industry in *Capital Volume I* constitutes a '*political point of view in Marx*'. Negri (2017, 55) writes that in the *Grundrisse*, 'Marx had advanced theses that would only achieve their full and material consistency in Book I of *Capital*'. Machines are fixed capital that labour uses as a means for creating surplus value. They are also a means of relative surplus-value production. When Negri says that large-scale industry and relative surplus value are political, he means that class struggle in capitalism is a struggle over the control of human activity and time. Given that technology is a means for organising labour and labour-time, it is embedded in social struggles.

With around 150 pages, Chapter 15 (*Machinery and Large-Scale Industry*) of *Capital Volume I* is the book's longest chapter. It is also *Capital*'s technology chapter (see Fuchs 2016, Chapter 15, for a detailed discussion of this chapter). Technology in capitalism is 'converting the worker into a living appendage of the machine' (Marx 1867/1976, 614), but at the same time it develops potentials for the 'totally developed individual' (ibid, 618) and fosters the 'struggle between the capitalist and the wage-labourer' (ibid, 553) that extends to 'the instrument of labour itself, capital's material mode of existence' (ibid, 554). Modern technology is at the heart of the capitalist contradiction between productive forces and relations of production. This antagonism does not result in an automatic collapse of capitalism, as is incorrectly assumed by breakdown theories, but simultaneously fosters repeated crises and the emergence of communist potentials. The dialectical transcendence and *Aufhebung* of capitalism is not caused by technology, but is a potential that can only be realised in and through social struggle. We can learn from Marx's Chapter 15 that technology in capitalism always has an antagonistic character; it is a means of domination just as it is a potential means of liberation, and, in a post-capitalist world, a means of commoning and communism.

Also in the essay printed in this book, Negri stresses the continuity of Marx's analysis of technology in the *Grundrisse* and *Capital*. Machinery is a tool both of domination and potential liberation. It opens up spaces of exploitation and potential spaces of autonomy and self-valorisation. Negri says in his chapter in this context: 'On the one hand, past human activity and its intelligence are accumulated, crystallised as fixed capital; on the other, reversing the tide, living humans are capable of reabsorbing capital in themselves and their own social life'.

2. The Appropriation of Technology

By speaking of the need for the political appropriation of technology, Toni Negri rejects both the optimistic and the pessimistic versions of technological determinism. Techno-optimism assumes that technology is itself a form of human appropriation and automatically has positive effects on society. In the realm of the study of communication technologies, we can look to Marshall McLuhan's example that electronic media create a global village: 'The new electronic interdependence recreates the world in the image of a global village' (McLuhan 1995, 121). 'The overhauling of our traditional political system is only one manifestation of the retribalizing process wrought by the electric media, which is turning the planet into a global village' (ibid, 238).

Techno-pessimism assumes that technology as such is an autonomous realm that inherently has negative effects on society. An example is Martin Heidegger's analysis of modern technology. In *Being and Time*, Heidegger (1996, 119) characterises the newspaper and means of public transport as inauthentic and 'true dictatorship'. For Heidegger, the left-wing blog and the socialist newspaper are, just like the right-wing extremist tabloid, a form of inauthenticity. In *The Question Concerning Technology*, Heidegger (1977) introduces the notion of the *Gestell* for modern technology that he sees as inherently alienating. Heidegger detaches the analysis of technology from the analysis of capitalism and therefore leaves a dangerous void in his theory (Fuchs 2015c, 2015d). Negri (2017, 7) speaks in this context of 'Heideggerian fascism'.

In contrast to techno-optimism and techno-pessimism, Negri stresses that the appropriation of technology is a political struggle. Technology does not automatically have a liberating or dominative character, but its character is shaped by the process and outcomes of social struggles. To appropriate technology means attempting to turn it from a means of domination and exploitation into a means of struggle and commoning. The appropriation of technology is the *Aufhebung* of technology, that is, neither its elimination nor its new creation, but a dialectical transformation that preserves the best qualities of existing technologies, eliminates their destructive, dominative and exploitative character, and creates new qualities that support the common development of humans, society and nature. Appropriation as political struggle means the transformation of society from a class society into a commonist society. The transformation of technologies from technologies of capital into technologies of commoning is part of this appropriation process.

The commonist expropriation of the expropriators entails the transformation of capitalist technologies into common technologies of commoning, commonly owned and controlled technologies that foster the common good. Whereas exploitation is the 'capitalist mode of appropriation' (Marx 1867/1978, 929), commoning is the commonist mode of appropriation. In capitalism, '[a]ppropriation appears as *estrangement*, as *alienation*' (Marx 1844/2010, 83), whereas commonism is the '*real appropriation*' of the '*social* (i.e., human) being' (ibid, 102), and the 'appropriation of *human* life' (ibid, 103). Real appropriation requires socially developed productive forces as one of its preconditions in order to transform surplus labour-time into the realm of freedom. In the age of the social worker and the digital machine, the preconditions and germs of real appropriation exist and develop, but are simultaneously constrained by capitalism.

3. The Appropriation of Digital Machines

In the age of algorithms, social media, Big Data and digital machines, the relationship between fixed constant capital and variable capital has become more dynamic. Traditionally, engineers created machines that were used in the production process over a longer time period until they became physically or morally depreciated and had to be replaced. Digital machines operate on binary data. Digital capitalism has datafied our lives. Our online activities are to a significant degree digital labour that creates data that is both a commodity and part of fixed capital (Fuchs 2014; 2015a, Chapter 5). Data storage is an inherent element of the digital machine. Once created, data in digital capitalism becomes fixed constant capital (Fuchs 2015a, 183–185). It is stored on servers as part of the digital machine that enables digital capital accumulation. But data is also the building block, the circulating constant capital, on which basis digital labour creates new content and data. In the realm of Big Data, 'circulating constant capital and fixed constant capital tend to converge' (Fuchs 2015a, 184). Data is the objectification of digital labour, of human subjectivity that goes online. Data as constant capital is therefore an objectification of the general intellect. Datafication generalises human knowledge and fixes it in databases stored on servers.

Toni Negri in his chapter says that young people in particular have the potential to answer to digital exploitation and digital capital: 'We wish to valorise ourselves, to govern the commons that we produce'. When human subjects become political subjects, then commonist digital appropriation can become a form of resistance to digital capitalism. Negri reminds us in his chapter that algorithms and digital machines are not intelligent. Only humans possess intelligence. And it is the political intelligence of humans that gives them the capacity to turn digital capital into digital commons, and the capitalist digital machine into one of commoning and social cooperation.

Is Big Data commonism the alternative to Big Data capitalism? On the one hand, amassing, leaking and publishing Big Data about capitalist power and state power has become a strategy of resistance. On the other hand, one must see that Big Data generation and Big Data storage serves the interests of capitalism and the state. Big Data has emerged from capitalist control (Big Data-based capital accumulation) and state control (state surveillance of citizens because of the false surveillance ideology that not socialism, but surveillance and a police state, are the best means against political and social problems). In addition, Big Data capitalism requires massive amounts of energy that are predominantly based on non-renewable sources, advancing climate change. Big Data commonism therefore aims to limit the amount of data stored to the minimum necessary, and to get rid of surplus data that today becomes surplus value and surplus power. We need small data instead of Big Data.

But how do we appropriate an algorithm? There are two main strategies, the first of which is capital taxation. Global Internet giants constantly avoid paying taxes, an evasion that is enabled by the contradiction between the global Internet and regulation at the level of the nation state. Taxing global corporations and online advertising can create state income that can be distributed to citizens via participatory budgeting. The participatory media fee would tax global corporations and give everyone a citizens' communication income that could then be donated to non-profit media projects (Fuchs 2015b). Alternative media often lack resources. Via participatory budgeting and capital taxation, the alternative media sector could be strengthened in order to weaken the corporate character of the Internet and the media in general. Paying a salary for using Facebook is in general not a feasible strategy because it does not question the dominant character of digital monopoly capital. A universal basic income for universal labour, which includes unpaid digital labour and other unpaid reproductive labour, would be a better political strategy.

Platform co-ops and peer-to-peer production are a second strategy. These are civil society projects that organise online platforms and digital machines as user-controlled and digital worker-controlled organisations that do not operate for profit and for the interests of the few, but for the benefit of all and the common good. Resource precarity is one of the main problems alternative economy projects tend to face. Combining both strategies would generate a resource base for platform co-ops and peer-to-peer projects. If they can expand, then they can create an economic realm that poses an alternative to digital capital and is in itself a form of digital class struggle against digital capitalism.

The Left has traditionally been afraid of conquering state power. To a certain degree, the Stalinist experience justifies such scepticism. But the anarchist rejection of appropriating the state in order to transform and transcend it often leaves alternative projects powerless, marginalised and confronted with a political economy of precarity (of voluntary labour and resources) that fosters sectarianism and anarchist versions of Stalinist orthodoxy and hierarchy. In the realm of communications, we should not forget that besides citizens' media, there is the realm of public service media (PSM). Especially in Europe, there is a strong PSM tradition that, to a significant degree, operates outside the logic of capital. The problem it often faces is political clientelism. But just like there can be struggles for more autonomous realms from capital in the economy, so there can be struggles for more autonomous realms from the state in the public sphere. Today, legal frameworks keep PSM from becoming public digital services and public service Internet platform providers. Monopoly media capital sees PSM as competitors and has influenced legislation that in the end helps the economic interests of digital monopoly capital (Google, Facebook, Amazon, Microsoft, Apple, etc.). I am not arguing in favour of a state-controlled Internet, as we already can find it where secret services implement a surveillance-industrial Internet complex (as revealed by Edward Snowden), but for independent, critical public service media that offer specific online services, such as Club 2.0 (see Fuchs 2017, Section 3.3) or a public service YouTube that offers all archived public service television and radio content to the public as a common good that can be appropriated and remixed (using certain Creative Commons licences).

What does the appropriation of the capitalist digital machine mean? It means the struggle for alternatives to digital capitalism, the de-commodification, de-capitalisation and de-commercialisation of the digital and the Internet. Today, we often find private-public partnerships that foster commodification. Digital appropriation promises to be an effective form of digital struggle when organised as commons–public partnerships that negate the logic of digital capital and help the digital commons to transcend and abolish digital capitalism. The broader context of such digital struggles is the renewal of the Left as a dialectic of movement and party (Dean 2016).

References

Dean, Jodi. 2016. *Crowds and Party*. London: Verso.

Fuchs, Christian. 2017. 'Günther Anders' Undiscovered Critical Theory of Technology in the Age of Big Data Capitalism.' *tripleC: Communication, Capitalism and Critique* 15(2): 584–615.

Fuchs, Christian. 2016. *Reading Marx in the Information Age. A Media and Communication Studies Perspective on 'Capital Volume I'*. New York: Routledge.

Fuchs, Christian. 2015a. *Culture and Economy in the Age of Social Media*. New York: Routledge.

Fuchs, Christian. 2015b. 'Left-Wing Media Politics and the Advertising Tax. Reflections on Astra Taylor's Book "The People's Platform: Taking Back Power and Culture in the Digital Age"'. *tripleC: Communication, Capitalism & Critique* 13(1): 1–4.

Fuchs, Christian. 2015c. 'Martin-Heidegger's Anti-Semitism: Philosophy of Technology and the Media in the Light of the "Black Notebooks". Implications for the Reception of Heidegger in Media and Communication Studies.' *tripleC: Communication, Capitalism & Critique* 13(1): 55–78.

Fuchs, Christian. 2015d. 'Anti-Semitism, Anti-Marxism, and Technophobia: The Fourth Volume of Martin Heidegger's *Black Notebooks* (1942–1948).' *tripleC: Communication, Capitalism & Critique* 13(1): 93–100.

Fuchs, Christian. 2014. *Digital Labour and Karl Marx*. New York: Routledge.

Hardt, Michael and Antonio Negri. 2000. *Empire*. Cambridge, MA: Harvard University Press.

Hardt, Michael and Antonio Negri. 1994. *Labor of Dionysus: A Critique of the State Form*. Minneapolis, MN: University of Minnesota Press.

Heidegger, Martin. 1996. *Being and Time*. Albany, NY: State University of New York Press.

Heidegger, Martin. 1977. *The Question Concerning Technology and Other Essays*. New York: Harper.

Marx, Karl. 1894/1981. *Capital Volume III*. London: Penguin.

Marx, Karl. 1867/1976. *Capital Volume I*. London: Penguin.

Marx, Karl. 1857/1858/1973. *The Grundrisse*. London: Penguin.

Marx, Karl. 1844/2010. 'Economic and Philosophic Manuscripts of 1844.' In *Economic and Philosophic Manuscripts of 1844 and the Communist Manifesto*, 13–168. Amherst, NY: Prometheus.

McLuhan, Marshall. 1995. *Essential McLuhan*, ed. Eric McLuhan and Frank Zingrone. London: Routledge.

Negri, Antonio. 2017. *Marx and Foucault*. Cambridge: Polity.

Negri, Antonio. 1991. *Marx Beyond Marx: Lessons on the Grundrisse*. London: Pluto.

Negri, Antonio. 1988. *Revolution Retrieved: Selected Writings on Marx, Keynes, Capitalist Crisis, & New Social Subjects 1967–83*. London: Red Notes.

The Editors and the Contributors

The Editors

David Chandler is Professor of International Relations at the University of Westminster, and edits the journal *Resilience: International Policies, Practices and Discourses*. His most recent monographs are: *Ontopolitics in the Anthropocene: An Introduction to Mapping, Sensing and Hacking* (Routledge, 2018); *Peacebuilding: The Twenty Years' Crisis, 1997–2017* (Palgrave, 2017); *The Neoliberal Subject: Resilience, Adaptation and Vulnerability* (with Julian Reid) (Rowman & Littlefield, 2016) and *Resilience: The Governance of Complexity* (Routledge, 2014).

Christian Fuchs is a Professor at the University of Westminster, where he is Director of the Westminster Institute for Advanced Studies (WIAS) and the Communication and Media Research Institute (CAMRI). He has published widely on critical and Marxist theory; on digital media & society; and on media, culture and society. Christian is co-editor of the open access journal *tripleC: Communication, Capitalism & Critique* (http://www.triple-c.at). Among his books are *Digital Demagogue: Authoritarian Capitalism in the Age of Trump and Twitter* (2018); *Critical Theory of Communication: New Readings of Lukács, Adorno, Marcuse, Honneth and Habermas in the Age of the Internet* (2016); *Reading Marx in the Information Age* (2016); *Digital Labour and Karl Marx* (2014); *Culture and Economy in the Age of Social Media* (2015); *Social Media: A Critical Introduction* (2014, 2nd edition, 2017); *OccupyMedia! The Occupy Movement and Social Media in Crisis Capitalism* (2014). http://fuchs.uti.at, @fuchschristian.

The Contributors

Dr Joanna Boehnert is a Lecturer in Design at the University of Loughborough, UK. Her first book, titled *Design/Ecology/Politics: Towards the Ecocene*, links

224 Digital Objects, Digital Subjects

social and ecological theory to design theory and practice. She is the founding director of EcoLabs and has worked as a communication design researcher on issues of the environment and the visual communication of complexity at the Center for Science and Technology Policy Research (CSTPR) University of Colorado Boulder; the Centre for Research and Education in Arts and Media (CREAM) University of Westminster; and the Centre for the Evaluation of Complexity Across the Nexus (CECAN) University of Surrey. She tweets @ecolabs (high traffic) and @ecocene (academic).

Elisabetta Brighi is a Senior Lecturer in International Relations in the Department of Politics and IR, University of Westminster. Her current research interests lie at the intersection of International Security, Violence and Political Theory. They include terrorism, urban security, affect and mimesis. She has edited, most recently, the volume *The Sacred and the Political* (Bloomsbury Academic, 2016) and written the article 'The Globalisation of Resentment' (*Millennium Journal of International Studies*, 2016).

Robert Cowley is Lecturer in Sustainable Cities at King's College London. He is currently coordinating an ESRC-funded multi-centre research project comparing experimental 'smart-eco' urban initiatives in Europe and China, led by the University of Exeter. He was previously Network Coordinator for the Leverhulme Trust-funded international research consortium Tomorrow's City Today – An International Comparison of Eco-City Frameworks. His PhD, completed in the Department of Politics & International Relations at the University of Westminster, explored the public dimensions of urban sustainability schemes, with a particular focus on Portland, Oregon (USA) and the new city of Sejong (South Korea). He has lectured internationally and written a variety of publications on urban sustainability and the smart city.

Professor Jodi Dean is the Donald R. Harter '39 Professor of Humanities and Social Sciences at Hobart and William Smith Colleges in Geneva, NY. She is the author of twelve books, including *Blog Theory* (Polity 2010), *The Communist Horizon* (Verso 2012), and *Crowds and Party* (Verso 2016).

Dr Paolo Gerbaudo is a Senior Lecturer and the Director of the Centre for Digital Culture at King's College London.

Dr Peter Goodwin is a research fellow in CAMRI at the University of Westminster. He has published on communications policy, public service media and the political economy of communication.

Dr Kylie Jarrett is Senior Lecturer and Head of the Department of Media Studies at Maynooth University, Ireland. She has extensively researched the political economy of the commercial Web and is author of *Feminism, Labour and*

Digital Media: The Digital Housewife (Routledge) and *Google and the Culture of Search* (Routledge – with Ken Hillis and Michael Petit). She has a forthcoming book, *Not Safe For Work: Sex, Humor, and Risk in Social Media* (MIT Press), co-authored with Susanna Paasonen and Ben Light.

Dr Anastasia Kavada is a Reader in the Westminster School of Media and Communication at the University of Westminster. She is a Co-Leader of the MA in Media, Campaigning and Social Change and Co-Director of the Communication and Media Research Institute (CAMRI).

Dr Phoebe Moore is an internationally respected researcher and thinker on technology, work and global governance, working at the University of Leicester. Moore has published three single-authored books that look at these issues, including her more recent one, *The Quantified Self in Precarity: Work, Technology and What Counts* (2017). Moore works with trade unions and international organisations to develop worker standards.

Toni Negri is one of the world's most prominent political philosophers. Now based in France, Negri grew up in Padua in Italy, the son of an active communist. He founded the *Potere Operaio* (Worker Power) group in 1969 and was a leading member of *Autonomia Operaia*. As one of the most prominent theorists of Autonomism, Negri has published influential books such as *Marx Beyond Marx: Lessons on the Grundrisse* and, together with Félix Guattari, *Communists Like Us*. In France, he taught at Paris 8 and the Collège International de Philosophie, alongside Jacques Derrida, Michel Foucault and Gilles Deleuze. Of his many publications, Negri is perhaps most known for the trilogy of *Empire*, *Multitude* and *Commonwealth* that he co-authored with Michael Hardt. In 2017, the fourth volume in this series of books was published under the title *Assembly*. Also in 2017, Toni Negri's essay collection *Marx and Foucault* was published. His theorisation of the commons and the social worker are key critical tools for understanding contemporary society's and digital media's reality and potentials.

Jack Linchuan Qiu is Professor at the School of Journalism and Communication, the Chinese University of Hong Kong, where he serves as Director of the C-Centre (Centre for Chinese Media and Comparative Communication Research). His publications include *Goodbye iSlave* (University of Illinois Press, 2016), *World's Factory in the Information Age* (Guangxi Normal University Press, 2013), *Working-Class Network Society* (MIT Press, 2009), *Mobile Communication and Society* (co-authored, MIT Press, 2006), some of which have been translated into German, French, Spanish, Portuguese, Chinese, and Korean. He is on the editorial boards of 12 international academic journals, including six indexed in the SSCI, and is Associate Editor for *Journal of Communication*. Co-founder and steering committee member of the annual

Chinese Internet Research Conference (CIRC), Jack Qiu serves as Vice President of the Chinese Communication Association (CCA) and is on the executive board of the Association for Internet Researchers (AoIR). In addition to his academic positions, he also works with grassroots labour NGOs in Hong Kong and in mainland China, while providing consultancy services for international organisations.

Dr Paul Rekret teaches political theory at Richmond American International University in London. He is the author of *Down With Childhood* (Repeater 2017) and *Derrida and Foucault: Philosophy, Politics, Polemics* (Rowman and Littlefield 2018) and is currently writing a book on work, songs, and capitalist crisis.

Dr Paulina Tambakaki is a Senior Lecturer in Political Theory at the Centre for the Study of Democracy, University of Westminster. She is co-editor of the Routledge book series 'Advances in Democratic Theory' and she works in the areas of agonism, radical democracy, representation and citizenship. Her publications include a monograph entitled *Human Rights, Or Citizenship?* published with Birkbeck Law Press in 2011, and articles in various academic journals. Paulina is currently working on her second monograph that focuses on processes of political change, with a particular focus on the relation between democracy, idealisation and memory.

Index